SCHOOL DEVELOPMENT
Theories and Strategies
An International Handbook

Per Dalin

with the assistance of Katherine Kitson

CASSELL

imtec
The International Learning Cooperative

Cassell

Wellington House
125 Strand
London WC2R 0BB

370 Lexington Avenue
New York
NY 10017-6550

www.cassell.co.uk

First published 1998

Earlier versions of these chapters originally appeared in Per Dalin, *Skoleutvikling: Teorier for Forandring* (1994) and *Skoleutvikling: Strategier og Praksis* (1995), published in Oslo by Universitetsforlaget AS.

British Library Cataloguing-in-Publication Data
A catalogue record for this book is available from the British Library.

ISBN 0–304–33599–1 (hardback)
       0–304–33600–9 (paperback)

Typeset by Kenneth Burnley, Wirral, Cheshire
Printed and bound in Great Britain by Redwood Books, Trowbridge, Wiltshire

Contents

Series Editors' Foreword

We are about to witness yet another sea-change in the development of Western educational systems. The last two decades have been unprecedented in terms of the amount of change expected and the shift in locus of responsibility for implementation. At one and the same time the centre has assumed enormous authority *vis-à-vis* policy direction, yet the schools and their local support systems have, in the spirit of decentralization, become increasingly responsible for the quality of implementation and the standards of student performance. The tension between centralization and decentralization has been highlighted by numerous research studies that claim that 'policy does not mandate what matters', and that it is 'local implementation that determines outcomes'. This presents educational reformers with a crucial challenge – how to reconcile the conflict between centralization and decentralization.

This conundrum provides the focus for this book, and there is no-one better suited to solving and exploring it than Per Dalin. For over three decades Per Dalin has been one of a handful of world-class educational researchers and activists who have mapped out the territory of school development, researched it, and in a variety of cultural contexts made successful attempts at enhancing it. From his work with the OECD in the early 1970s, through the transformation of IMTEC into a cutting-edge international educational agency in the 1980s, and as a result of a series of high-profile educational projects in the 1990s funded by among others the World Bank, Per Dalin has firmly established himself as an authoritative figure in the reform of the world's educational systems. One of the defining features of Per Dalin and his work is that he is in the Lewisian sense a true action researcher. He is someone who intervenes in problematic educational situations with the purpose of improving them. Consequently Per Dalin's contribution to the knowledge base of educational reform has been a continual stream of publications that not only document three decades of innovation efforts, but also constitute a major effort to conceptualize the theory and practice of educational change.

It is far too soon to say that *School Development: Theories and Strategies* is the culmination of this effort. Per is still as energetic, incisive, optimistic and charismatic as he was when we first had the privilege of working with him some twenty years ago. *School Development* is, however, a major statement by a leading scholar on the most pressing challenge facing educational systems today. In it Dalin undertakes a comprehensive review of the centralization/decentralization paradox, of the theories that inform resolution, and of the strategies that will lead to eventual success.

School Development is not only a major contribution to the field, but it is also the name of this series of books. It is entirely appropriate that this book, that so eloquently charts the evolution of school development as a field of enquiry and action, is being published almost exactly a decade after the series that bears its name was originally conceived.

DAVID HOPKINS
DAVID REYNOLDS
July 1998

Preface

This book draws on the extensive work of IMTEC with school development projects in many parts of the world. An early version of this book was published in Norway in 1982, and translated into German and Dutch. A second version, in Norwegian, came out in 1986, and the last version, also in Norwegian, was published in three volumes in 1994–95, and was also translated into Swedish and German. The first of these volumes was published in English by Cassell (Dalin and Rust 1995), and this book is an edited version of the second and third volumes.

I have made an attempt the capture major theoretical and practical work in school development over the past 40 years. I have also tried to reflect major work outside the Anglo-American traditions, but this is far from complete. In fact, the major task still remains to gather and summarize school development work from non-English speaking countries. This volume, together with the first volume (Dalin and Rust 1995), begins to make the field of school development truly international.

It is also an attempt to write a textbook on school improvement where the historical traditions in theory and practice are dealt with. Although much contemporary work is dealt with and referred to, it has been equally important to include earlier work in order to appreciate the contributions to the field. In an *international* book on school improvement, one cannot assume that only recent work is relevant and applicable. Since effective school improvement strategies are dependent on several contextual factors, one should see this contribution as providing ideas for the further development of theory and practice. This affords wide options, both historically and geographically.

After more than 30 years in the field, many individuals come to my mind as having been important in my own development and my learning about school development. They range from teachers to policy makers, from researchers to practitioners, and they come from so-called developed countries as well as the former Eastern European and Western industrialized countries. It would be unfair to mention anyone by name, with the exception of one, my mentor and friend Matthew B. Miles, who died so suddenly last year. He was a great conceptualizer, a creative teacher, a brilliant consultant and trainer and a critical friend in his role as mentor.

I also thank my translator John Timmons and the editorial assistance given by Katherine Kitson. It has been a complicated book to put together.

Oslo, June 1998

Introduction

The first part of this book describes and analyses the changing context of school reform. The focus is on worldwide examples of the 'new balance' between the centre and the periphery, and how various countries have faced the challenge of decentralization. The purpose of this section is to 'set the stage' for a thorough discussion of how schools can improve as we face the new realities of the twenty-first century (Dalin and Rust 1996).

The second part gives an overview of the theoretical basis for school improvement. In addition, an attempt is made to present an historical perspective, examining how theories have evolved over the last 50 years.

It begins with theories of organizations (Chapter 2), because most significant school improvement projects involve changes in the school organization or even the school system. Our assumptions on how organizations behave are therefore significant for understanding the process of change.

From the more general theories of organizations, we move into a discussion of the school as an organization (Chapter 3). Do schools behave differently from other types of organizations? If so, what are the differences, and how would these influence successful strategies for educational change?

Closely related to organizational theories are management theories, including institutional leadership and management as well as system management. These are included in Chapter 4, with particular focus on the role of the head teacher in school improvement.

Finally, this part concludes with a description and analysis of what we know about theories of educational change (Chapter 5). Our theories and assumptions about change provide us with a basis for discussing change strategies in the third part of the book.

What do we know about educational reform, in practice? The last part of this book looks at different approaches to school reform, incorporating specific case studies with the contextual and theoretical frameworks discussed in Parts I and II.

In Chapter 6 we focus on change strategies where the *individual* is the target; for example, the in-service training of teachers. What do we know about the role of individuals in reform efforts? What constitutes successful strategies in this area?

In Chapter 7 we focus on strategies for change, in which the school viewed as an *organization* is the primary target. The main discussion is about organizational development and efforts to combine management training with organizational development.

Finally, in Chapter 8 we look at change strategies that have the entire *system* as the target for change, often managed by central authorities. We discuss the move from rule-based management to management by objectives, the role of the external authority and the new role of the inspectorate, as well as more general quality control processes. Finally, we discuss what constitute successful strategies at the central level.

We believe that these three sections constitute a *gestalt*. However, readers with an essentially theoretical interest may readily study Part II independently. On the other hand, readers whose interests are mainly practical are advised to read Parts I and III.

PER DALIN

Part I

The Changing Context of
School Reform

Chapter 1

The New Balance: Centralization and Decentralization

HISTORY OF SCHOOL IMPROVEMENT: FROM VISION TO REALIZATION

Knowing where you are heading is one thing; knowing how to get there is another matter altogether. It isn't all that easy to know where you're heading in a rapidly changing world. Educators wish desperately to know the direction that education will take, but defining what constitutes 'good schooling' for the pupil of tomorrow is no easy task.

There are those who believe that the question of 'How to' is easier to answer. It is thought to be strictly a practical question of resources. However, the history of school improvement is rife with examples of grandiose plans that never materialize, of politicians who are good at setting goals but vague when it comes to strategic planning; moreover, the politicians never seem to be around when you need them. There are examples of various experts in their respective fields whose 'reformed' lesson plans and curricula have never made it as far as the classroom. And there are untold numbers of 'improvement-oriented' teachers brimming with bright ideas for their own subjects or for the cause of school improvement in general, but who have yet to make any lasting impact beyond their own classrooms.

There have been repeated attempts to 'improve the school system'. Ever since the 1930s, European Social Democrats have been working tirelessly for greater social justice; and one of their primary tools has been the schools. Professionals and educators joined forces, and research centres undertook ambitious projects designed to bring about major changes in the way policy was conceived and implemented. In England, teachers created a national forum for school improvement through 'teachers' centres'. We could cite examples from schools of all kinds, from all parts of the world. There has been no lack of effort.

Nor has there been a lack of hypotheses and theories. I have felt the need to take a critical look at both the theoretical and the practical issues involved. How much do we really know about school improvement? Do we know as much as we should? Do we have a tenable theory, and do we make use of it? Are today's schools qualitatively a better place in which to be, and better places of learning than they were twenty years ago? For that matter, do we have any criteria for defining 'quality' in this context? These questions highlight a need to define a new vision of the school system. We are living in a transition between paradigms. The so-called modern age is over and we are moving into a post-modern era. We don't know what Britain, continental Europe, or the world as a whole will look like 50 years from now; what we do know is that the world will be subject to enormous forces that will inevitably change society in crucial ways. And for this reason, school improvement will never become a mere hobby for oddball improvement-oriented teachers and administrators. On the contrary, it is destined to remain an issue that affects everyone.

Mastering the school improvement process has never been more important. But as our past experience in school reform shows, this is not a simple process.

TOWARDS A MARKET ADJUSTMENT OF PUBLIC SERVICES

There has been intense debate about public services throughout the entire Western world during the past fifteen years. The budget deficits in many countries, particularly in the United States and several European countries, have grown so large that they threaten the economic development of the entire Western world. The response in nearly every OECD country has been to rationalize the public sector. The largest expenses are related to public services, and thus a reform of these services has become an urgent task in all of the OECD countries. Programmes are being introduced that seek to decentralize services, simplify regulations, and develop expertise and new management. Such development is taking place in a number of countries.

Although this reform movement has also made its presence felt in the field of education, it is much weaker here than in other public sectors. However, the following developments can be noted:

1. An increasing privatization of schools, with a greater number of private schools (these are often pedagogical alternatives, such as the Steiner schools). This trend is especially strong in Eastern Europe and the former Soviet Union, very distinct in the United Kingdom and Sweden, but less marked in other OECD countries.
2. A democratization of the school system, with stronger participation on the part of parents or with freedom of choice (i.e. the freedom to choose schools within a municipality) – such as in the Netherlands.
3. Administrative reforms, with particular emphasis on simplification and debureaucratization (e.g. Sweden and the Netherlands).
4. Financial reforms, particularly outcome-based financing (e.g. the Netherlands), increased dependency on private sponsors, block transfers for municipalities (or schools), as in Norway.

However, these are relatively modest reforms in the way schools are run (with the exception of the Netherlands, which currently has the world's most liberal system). In many ways, the schools appear to be a 'closed system', affected very little by development in other sectors.

DECENTRALIZATION

In this chapter we start with the assumption that most Western countries are in the process of abandoning the most centralized reforms for management of the educational systems and that decentralization is here to stay. The decentralization efforts of recent years would suggest that this is no passing fad but rather that this approach is becoming a natural framework for the management of educational systems. Through this framework a new balance and distribution of roles between the centre and the periphery is emerging.

This is not a common trend, however. There are countries with long-standing traditions of decentralization that have become more centralized. The most typical example of this is England and Wales under the former Conservative government. In these countries a national curriculum (the first ever) has been introduced, along with a system of national testing and reporting, and the option of choosing *not* to be subject to municipal administration but rather be financed directly by the Department of Education. On the other hand, there are examples of countries with a strong centralized past that are carrying out policies of radical decentralization (or at least municipalization). Perhaps Sweden is the example that springs most readily to mind.

We are talking about neither a uniform wave of decentralization nor a one-sided decentralization. Where decentralization occurs, there is also a redefinition of the role of the centre, which can result in a stronger role. Decentralization and sharper central control may be occurring in the same system at the same time, resulting in a more 'tightly knit' system. More fundamentally, it is a question of what serves best to promote the quality and objectives of the schools in general: a decision-making process that most closely resembles actual practice ('bottom-up'), or one that is governed from above ('top-down').

What represents the best balance between school-based, district-based and state-based decisions – and within which areas? If the balance is altered, what practical consequences will this have for how the schools operate? What hindrances and what forces will support a decentralization process? What are the 'costs' with respect to a modified central role?

There is an innate tension between the demand for autonomy for the individual school on the one hand, and the need to document the results one obtains (accountability) on the other. The schools use public funds, and finding ways of managing and governing the efforts of the individual school is clearly a public responsibility. This tendency toward greater autonomy and increased responsibility for the individual school will necessarily lead to a different pattern for the overall decision-making process and is bound to have consequences for all the decision-making levels and all decision-makers, from the classroom to the Minister of Education.

In this process we are faced with a number of process challenges. Increased autonomy is not achieved by *fiat* but through a lengthy learning process. In reality, it requires a change in school culture, often a sensitive process that can clash with a governmental need for insight and control.

As we shall see in the 'strategic chapters' (Part III) of the book, there is broad disagreement as to what promotes quality in the schools. Representatives of the so-called 'Effective Schools' research claim that government should tighten the reins and exercise more consistent control. On the other hand, a number of researchers claim that the best strategy for enhancing the quality of instruction is to create 'learning organizations', which especially involves giving teachers responsibility (empowerment). This necessitates a 'bottom-up' strategy, because the solutions must be tailor made for each school and must command the greatest possible support from the culture of the individual school and the local community (Rosenholtz 1989). We will be taking a look at this and other important strategic questions in Part III. We feel that in the vast majority of countries today a conscious effort is being made to strike a new balance between the periphery and the centre, and that in most cases this means giving the individual school considerably more latitude and responsibility. Thus we will discuss what decentralization might mean before we discuss the strategies associated with the development of a system that works in a more decentralized fashion.

There are a number of different forms and definitions of decentralization. We have chosen to describe a number of concrete examples, and conclude by analysing what decentralization involves and what grounds there are for the fact that educational systems are decentralizing significant tasks.

In this connection we shall use the three Scandinavian countries (Denmark, Sweden and Norway) as examples of what is meant by the concept of decentralization. We use these countries as examples because in many ways they represent the broad scope of the term decentralization such as it is practised in the educational systems in the Western world, and thus they can be used as models for a further discussion of other countries. Finally in this chapter we shall discuss the experiences gained by the educational systems in countries such as the United States, New Zealand, the Netherlands and Germany where it concerns decentralized practice.

But first, some statistical data about Scandinavia. These three countries (including Spitzbergen) together are three times the size of united Germany, but contain only 17 million people (as opposed to over 80 million in Germany) – a population density only one-fifteenth that of Germany, in other words. Norway in particular, as well as certain parts of Sweden, are thinly populated. Moreover, all three countries have a strong municipal tradition, in which local needs are looked after by municipal political and professional bodies.

These countries, while sharing a number of common features, are also markedly different. Denmark is heavily geared to agriculture; Sweden is the only one of the three whose base is primarily heavy industry. Norway is largely an exporter of raw materials; it is also characterized by a number of niche industries.

Reforms in public services

During the past fifteen years, even in Scandinavia there have been extensive reform efforts aimed at developing 'the new state'. The Scandinavian countries are known for their welfare states, and public expenses have risen so precipitously in recent years that all these countries have had to tighten their belts considerably. The intention has been to reduce the role of the state by directing it toward highly prioritized tasks, and to engage the public sector at lower levels (as well as the private sector) in tasks for which the national government was formerly responsible.

As in other OECD countries, in Scandinavia we also find developmental characteristics that are based on a 'revitalization of democracy' in which public services are brought closer to the client. Other features of the development have all the hallmarks of deregulation and municipalization. As a rule, this is related to demands for increased efficiency (Reichard 1992).

Developments in Denmark

Here the decentralization of the schools has come the farthest. In all probability, this is due to a long historical process that has unfolded over the past 100 years. At present, the 'School Boards' of the Danish public schools – where the users (the parents) command a majority – have the right to make basic decisions about an individual school's development, within the framework of broad national pedagogical goals and a municipal economic framework (Lindbom 1993). In the Danish debate, the term 'self-administration' is often used for this form of user influence. Here the terminology is often unclear. Self-administration can mean that the individual school receives a large measure of autonomy; but it can also mean that each citizen has the right to administer his or her school resources, through such means as free choice of schools. In Denmark, self-administration means that each school's governing body (in which the parents are in the majority) has significant power.

This development toward user management is probably historically grounded in the strong position that *Grundtvigianism* has had (and continues to have) in Denmark (Haarder 1983). For *Grundtvigians*, it was essential that the schools not be centrally governed (which might involve the promotion of a certain ideology or system of beliefs). Parents had to be allowed to 'choose against' (for example, by being allowed to change schools) and be heard (for example, in the schools' administrative bodies). In addition, a strong free school movement was created, particularly through the 'folk high school' tradition (influenced by *Grundtvig*).

From 1814 to as late as 1933, supervision of primary schools in Denmark was the domain of the local government official – namely, the priest. At the same time, throughout the past and present centuries, the folk movements in the Danish villages have been sceptical of the governing elite. Moreover, in Denmark the struggle for parliamentarianism was bitter and protracted. 'The fight for the constitution was an economic-social and cultural power play between merchants and government officials on the one hand and the peasant class on the other' (Lindbom 1993).

The Danish Left party, which came to power in 1901, had a strong municipal and *Grundvigian* grounding. An attempt was made to provide for direct parental influence at the individual school level. This did not win a majority, but in 1920 Southern Jutland was reclaimed from Germany, and it was in this area that radical

7

efforts were made that opened the way for the so-called 'school commissions' at each school – commissions where parent participants had advisory power.

The battle for influence over the schools was also a struggle between ecclesiastical and regional-administrative supervision. In 1932 it was decided to introduce a more pedagogical academic supervision and simultaneously strengthen parental influence. The model was Southern Jutland, which had acquired a rather unusual status during its time under German rule. The local priest's automatic place in the school commission disappeared, and a teacher's council at every school was to be established. The office of county consultant as *pedagogical counsellor* (not as inspector) was created. There was strong political disagreement about whether to give the central administration so much power at the regional level. The Social Democrats wanted to go further and invest the office with the authority of inspection. Parents still had only an advisory influence in what was now called school committees.

The development toward larger municipalities (from 1,300 to 275 municipalities) led to greater academic competence locally in the municipality. Eventually, and especially since 1975, the school committees were invested with a growing range of tasks and responsibilities. In the municipalities a conscious effort was made to delegate and decentralize decision-making authority. The aim was to give individual schools a larger degree of self-government under more user-friendly conditions.

The Public School Act of 1989 gave each school a strong administration that could prioritize and that was so constituted as to safeguard the interests of the users and not (first and foremost) the 'producers'. The municipalities have been given broad scope to decide for themselves how their own schools shall be governed. The school commissions, with their 175-year history, were abolished, the counties' work with the folk high schools has ceased, and the body of legislation has been vastly simplified. Instead of teachers' councils, the Danish public school now has pedagogical councils with less influence than before. Instead of school committees, there are now genuine school governing boards in which the parents form a majority, and the head teacher's position has also been strengthened (Ministry of Education *et al.* 1990).

This entire development – over a period of more than 180 years – has been one long battle over who should have the power in the public schools. That the schools were to be *municipal* institutions was taken for granted, but the argument was about whether this meant they were to be governed by the municipal authorities or by the parents.

What is happening in the Danish schools nowadays with respect to decentralization? The question is virtually irrelevant, because Denmark has had strong, decentralized public schools for several generations. Henrik Larsen, who has carried out a number of empirical studies of decentralization in the Danish schools, found the following development traits:

- More than 85 per cent of all the municipalities practise school-based allocation of resources in one form or another; some also have full control of the salary budget. Most of the reports have been positive. Better use is made of resources, it is cheaper to operate in a school-based manner, and it gives the schools better control of their own operations.

- To an increasing extent, municipal administrative tasks are also decentralized to the level of the individual school, together with the municipalities' costs in implementing them. Each school can now decide for itself whether it wants to execute the administrative tasks, hire them out privately (if that should prove profitable), or purchase the service from the municipality.
- The role of the head teacher has changed in one significant respect. He/she is no longer a colleague among colleagues. The head teacher is now more of a co-ordinator between the school board and the municipality on the one hand, and the staff and pupils on the other. To avoid having the head teacher become a bottleneck in the system, a training and counselling programme has been established in such areas as user-orientation, communication, and change management.
- The changes in Denmark have also led to changes in the state and municipal administration. As more and more tasks are devolved to individual schools, the administration becomes thinner; in large measure, it becomes a *consultant* with respect to budgeting, administrative tasks and pedagogical tasks, for example with respect to the schools' annual development plans.

Larsen sees a number of problems with the developments in Denmark. For instance, a number of schools feel overtaxed. In several studies, users say that the total amount of resources has been reduced. This is particularly the case where the school budget is fused with the cultural and social budget and the school is given a lower priority by local politicians than it once enjoyed. Furthermore, a number of teachers and head teachers are having trouble coping with the extensive ongoing changes (Larsen 1992).

Developments in the Swedish schools

Developments in the Swedish schools are markedly different from those in Denmark. This can probably be explained largely in terms of Swedish history and traditions that have taken many generations to become ingrained. Even though Sweden today is also governed by the principle of decentralized management, direct user influence in the schools has been rejected by the Swedish parliament (Lindbom 1993).

One of the key factors in this historical debate has been how to define democracy; and here a distinction is made between *full citizenship* on the one hand, and *partial citizenship* on the other. The term 'local democracy' has been an important concept in all three Scandinavian countries. In Denmark it has led to user influence in sector-specific bodies (e.g. the school board, or 'part citizenship'), whereas in Sweden, on the contrary, municipal bodies were established that crossed sectoral boundaries (or 'full citizenship'). The Norwegian researcher Johan P. Olsen (1990) puts it this way:

Do schools, for example, primarily concern pupils, parents and teachers, so that these groups should be regarded as 'demos' and have special potential for influence ('partial citizenship')? Or are the schools a common, national institution where everyone is to have the same potential for influence through representative bodies ('full citizenship')?

Developments in Sweden have largely been characterized by the *equality ideal*, which has led to the development of a strong state that could compensate for the weaknesses that a fragile and variable municipal economy could represent. But the Swedes, contrary to the Danes, had much more faith in governing authorities. Lindbom explains this by what he terms 'administrative corporateness' in Sweden. Among other things, this meant that workers could be represented in administrative corporative organs, and this happened long before universal suffrage became a fact of life (Lindbom 1993).

Sweden has a long tradition of public office. In 1842 a law was passed which stipulated that the school house should preferably be situated near the mayor's residence in order to facilitate his job of inspection! Also in Sweden, public schools were a municpal concern, but the federal government had the right and duty of inspection. However, as early as 1858 it became clear that the state would play a significant financial role, for ideological (the principle of equality) and pragmatic (financial) reasons.

The liberal breakthrough in Sweden did not result in the same radical manifestations as in Denmark. The pronounced distrust of the federal government that Danish farmers had come to have did not arise to the same extent in Sweden – probably on account of that country's slow but steady development toward democracy. The official views on federal intervention were also radically different: during the 1880s the Swedish government introduced duties on agricultural products to placate Swedish farmers. In Denmark, however, farmers were free traders in their outlook, because they were highly competitive in the international market and thus did not relish federal intervention (Lindbom 1993).

Developments in this century have seen the establishment and entrenchment of a strong Swedish system of public office at all levels, until the radical reforms of the 1990s. From 1904, this system was built up and rapidly increased the amount of regulation. Also federal support for schools increased from 30 per cent in 1900 to 63 per cent in 1940 (Wennås 1989). Bureaucracy flourished to such an extent that *Skolöverstyrelsen*, the major official centralized body, was so weighed down by a proliferation of issues that its work of inspection and its pedagogical function were neglected.

The debate was also ideologically based. Those who belonged to dissenter churches wanted the right to excuse their children from catechism instruction. On the other hand, there were those who defended the role of the state on the basis of the view that pupils ought to have such instruction so that in time they could determine their own religious standpoint, which in turn meant that the state should guarantee children this right (Algotsson 1975). The federalization of the public schools increased during the 1930s – in fact, it continued until as late as 1975.

Confidence in the Swedish schools and in officialdom was strong during this period. Sweden was also, on an international scale, a bright and shining example of a country with a successful welfare state and its attendant school policies. Gradually, however, the technological features of the Swedish school became more pronounced, especially with a one-sidedly rationally grounded research and development strategy for school improvement initiated by *Skolöverstyrelsen.*

During the course of the 1970s, there were signs that something was amiss. Swedish school improvement was in a crisis. The Swedish research group 'The Schools' Inner Workings' (SIA) began its work, and quite a different story began to emerge from this committee. It was true that school commissions before the SIA committee had pointed out the paralysing bureaucracy and the need for user-management (cf School Commission of 1948), but the SIA report was the primary dividing point.

Toward the end of the 1980s, the Ministry prepared a report of its own, which neither *Skolöverstyrelsen* (SØ) nor other interests could sway. This report gave rise to a number of radical decisions which had the effect of ushering in a new era for Swedish schools. The federal government decided to shut down the *Skolöverstyrelsen* and to municipalize the teachers' working conditions. *Skoleverket* (The Central School Administration) was established; about one-third the size of SØ, its task was to develop and co-ordinate a national school system and work out a foundation for school improvement. Six county offices have been established, each with responsibility for *Skoleverket's* work in several counties. Each municipality now has full personnel responsibility for teachers. Moreover, a new system of federal grants was introduced which was more clearly in the nature of financial support and was not intended to be regulatory (The Government's Bill 90/91:18: 'Responsibility for the Schools').

Has Sweden finally abandoned its centralistic past? There is no easy answer to that question. Suggestions have led to a clear municipalization of school activities, but developments have neither led to self-administration nor any form of user-orientation. Instead, suggestions in a number of counties and municipalities have given rise to a system in which services are 'bought and sold'. The county (or municipality) 'orders' certain educational services, and the schools 'submit bids' and are given 'contracts', as it were. In principle, this leads to a form of market control of services.

More fundamental is the question whether or not Swedish schools have abandoned their positivistic past. Ingrid Carlgren did a critical analysis of the so-called LUVA ideology in her 1986 dissertation. The local development work (LUVA) was conceived in a school reform of 1982 vintage (Carlgren 1986). She feels that despite the fact that there was a desire to abandon the traditional R & D model, a technological mind-set nevertheless persisted, which was based on a positivistic legacy that guided LUVA. There were still researchers that 'had the answers' and who saw it as their job to develop the new knowledge.

Carlgren feels that the LUVA ideology rests on the unspoken notion that local development work should take place 'in line with the guidelines'. If only teachers would follow the syllabus guidelines, there would be no problem. The schools have a problem, *but the solution already exists* (in the curriculum). Carlgren feels that it is only when local problems are *defined as problems of knowledge* – i.e. as questions that need answering in practice in their actual context – that there can be any guarantee that 'the quality of activity in any deeper sense will improve' (Madsèn 1993).

Even though both deregulation and perhaps decentralization were important elements of Swedish reform in the late 1980s, the financial problems remained the biggest hurdles to overcome. A powerful impetus toward greater efficiency was an important rationale (cf Parliamentary Bill 90/91:18: 'Responsibility for the Schools').

Developments in Sweden also involve a consistent decentralization of management which, among other things, implies a major practice of evaluation in which the new *Skoleverket* plays a major role. Another feature is that the municipalities which before the reform controlled 15 per cent of the school budgets, now control 100 per cent. They also negotiate with teachers' organizations about salaries and work conditions (Ekholm 1992).

Municipalization also means that the schools come to be regarded as a part of a larger whole in which the growth conditions for children and young people is the unifying theme. Both on account of this development and what we described above as supply and demand ('contracting out'), the head teacher is forced into a new and much more active role. The so-called 'annual plans' enter in here, as do internal school assessments and a more superordinate responsibility for resources. Today's head teacher is also responsible for hiring teachers, after consulting with the school's other teachers.

Developments in the Norwegian schools

We shall describe Norwegian developments relatively briefly. Norway was united with Denmark for more than 400 years and with Sweden for nearly 100 years. The democratization process that occurred during the 1880s must in many ways be regarded as a national fight for independence from union with Sweden (1814–1905). Parliamentarianism was established as early as 1884.

Gruntvig played an important role also in Norway, although not as strong as in Denmark. Like Sweden, Norway has had a strong workers' movement that has assumed a major responsibility for the development of the Norwegian school system, where equality of opportunity has been a major theme.

In Norway there has been a long-standing controversy about the role of the counties in school life. In 1860 the office of School Director was created which, along with the 'County Commission' was supposed to lead the development of the public schools in each diocese. Dokka claims that this was, in reality, a test of whether public schools were a federal matter in a highly 'pregnant sense', or whether the various municipalities had both the right and the duty to govern themselves with respect to school improvement (Dokka 1967). Also in Norway, federal funds were earmarked for municipal support (the so-called diocese funds). One prerequisite for contributions was that the municipalities had to fulfil minimum requirements for teachers, salaries, number of teaching hours, etc., and furthermore that they allocated as much as they received in federal support.

In 1884, under the leadership of Sverdrup, the Left party took the initiative in revising Norwegian school legislation, with particular emphasis on a renewal of school administration. In the spirit of the liberalism of the time, the power of the County Commission was to be cut back in favour of stronger popular control, especially with regard to teaching positions. A heated debate in the Parliament, where the language question was uppermost at the time, resulted in full victory for the Left party, which in turn led to a large measure of freedom for the individual municipality. This debate gave rise to the Law of 1889, which was written in the spirit of local public government.

In many ways, Norway finds itself situated somewhere between Sweden and Denmark in the development of a decentralized school system. Throughout the twentieth century, Norwegian schools have had a strongly centralistic tradition; but developments in the post-war years have moved in the direction of decentralization. A number of attempts at decentralization were made, both with respect to localization issues (of major importance in Norway) and to pedagogical and admini- strative issues (Karlsen 1991). Typically, during the past twenty years, as Karlsen points out, the federal government gives with one hand and takes away with the other. Alongside decentralization, a process of centralization has also been going on, in many ways.

The most important decision in Norway with respect to decentralization came in 1986, when the country changed the system by which it earns income and transfers funds from the federal government to the municipalities. Instead of earmarked funds bound by a complicated set of regulations, the municipalities were now given block grants. This means, for example, that the federal government can no longer make decisions about common norms (e.g. teacher concentration) for the country as a whole. The individual municipality (there are 450 in all) is now empowered to make decisions on a number of personnel matters as well as the total amount of instruction time. It is now the general municipal laws that regulate the relationship between the municipality and the schools. One result of this is that the municipalities have decentralized a significant portion of the budget, leaving it to the individual school. The hiring of teachers has also changed character. Before 1986, the regional, federal school director (*Skoledirektør*) had to approve all hiring of teachers, head teachers and municipal superintendents. This is now the task of the local school board. There is, however, an outlet for appeal that involves the school director. More important, perhaps, are the pedagogical tasks that are now delegated to the schools, especially with the introduction of the Curriculum Framework Agreement of 1987. Also in Norwegian schools, an annual plan must be drawn up each year by the school and be submitted to the municipal school board for approval. The role of the municipal school board, however, is somewhat unclear on this point.

Nowadays, the individual school has a broader responsibility than before; however, it is not more user-governed to any significant extent than it used to be. Teachers' working conditions in a more decentralized school day have occupied a

13

central place in the Norwegian debate. The traditional agreements seem outdated, and new agreements are emerging that allow for more common time and thus more co-operation between teachers. You also find global budgets in many Norwegian schools, where it is now possible to move around budget items.

In 1997, the Norwegian government in many ways reversed this development and tightened the reins on a number of key points. The government has become more heavily involved in curriculum development, and the federal administration has in a sense become 'decentralized', in that it must now be located in nineteen places throughout the country. The nineteen federal offices, on the other hand, now have a more centralistic profile because, to a much greater extent than they once did, they now keep watch and examine the results. One of the main reasons for this development is probably the desire for a stronger academic profile in the Norwegian schools. There has been anxiety in the workplace and in the business community alike about the quality of the schools. Moreover, there has been a desire for stronger political control. The balance between centralized and decentralized decision-making has altered, and at present we do not know all the potential ramifications.

Decentralization in other countries

Scandinavia is not alone in decentralizing the decision-making process to the municipal and the individual school levels. In the *United States*, all through the 1980s a reform movement was active that had decentralization as one of its key elements. True, a country with over 110,000 schools, 15,000 *independent* school districts, 50 states – each with its own body of legislation – and a federal level is such a complicated system that it is difficult to draw general conclusions.

There is a chapter in the book *From Risk to Renewal* that is devoted to an appraisal of decentralization within the major reform movement called 'restructuring' (*Education Week* 1993). One of the key motivations here was to create 'ownership' with respect to the individual school by giving parents, pupils, teachers and the head teacher a lot more influence over school improvement. Typical of the developmental optimism that fuelled this trend is the following comment by Colorado governor Roy Romer: 'I want everybody to look down the street, and see the school building and say, "That's ours. We are responsible for it"' (*Education Week* 1993).

One of the strong motivations for school-based decision-making is that the parents, teachers and the school leaders are the ones who best understand the contexts and cultures of the school, which is why it is important to give them real power and to enable them to become jointly responsible for student learning.

Thousands of attempts were made, most within 'site-based management', for a decentralization of decision-making in favour of the individual school. This could take place by giving the school administration more power (which actually happened in a number of states); but it could also involve 'collaborative decision-making', or an extensive collaboration between teachers and management on school improvement. This was largely what happened, for example, in such states as Colorado, Florida,

Kentucky, North Carolina and Texas. Parents were directly involved in the decision-making process in far fewer instances.

It is becoming increasingly understood, as we argue in this chapter, that we are talking about a new balance of power between the school and the school owner (district). The question then arises: Who decides what? Schools belong to a larger system – district and state – that must provide a strong centre of decentralization if it is to create something other than anarchy (David 1996). Parents must be given real power and responsibility over decisions that are important to them and their children. In some cases nearly all resources spent are encumbered, the school has little flexibility, and we are just toying with people. In an interview with Michael Strembitski, O'Neil reports of long experience of decentralization in the Canadian province of Alberta. The balancing act was there to give people 'at the school level the freedom and the flexibility that they needed to do their jobs, yet within a framework that included a district perspective and district accountability' (O'Neil 1996, p. 67). In Alberta the result was a closer working relationship between the schools and the district, and each understood what the other was up against (p. 68).

Those tasks over which the schools in the USA came to have greater influence included the allocation of funds within a budget framework, personnel policy (including the hiring of new teachers), and far-reaching tasks in curriculum development and pedagogical matters. There are examples of schools with virtually full autonomy (e.g. the so-called 'Charter Schools', see Sarason 1998); likewise, there are examples of schools where nearly no form of decentralization has taken place.

The results are mixed. Rhetoric has often outpaced action. Very few development projects are independently evaluated, and no connection between higher levels of decentralization and better pupil achievement on standardized tests has been proven (Collins and Hanson 1991, Bryk et al. 1993). In many projects the schools have partly been confused about their powers and have not known how to make use of them. Intensive training for new roles has been lacking, for the most part. But even more ominously, many schools have no clear vision and don't know how to use more power and influence. If decentralization is to succeed, an all-around development of school culture and organization will be needed.

One major aspect of the restructuring has been to give teachers a bigger say in school affairs. The theory is that this will develop empowerment and a sense of duty and thus improve the quality of the schools (Conley et al. 1988). Data from the study entitled *High Schools and Beyond* (US Department of Education 1988) shows that American teachers in the upper secondary schools have a significant degree of control over instruction; but there is a desire for more participation in areas such as the budget, hiring, evaluation practices, and staff development (Bacharach, Bauer and Shedd 1986). Many reports of 'site-based management' tell us that little has been done to give teachers greater influence, in spite of the fact that research has shown that schools with a large measure of teacher influence enjoy better staff motivation, increased efficiency and an extensive 'we-feeling'. When the atmosphere is more open and participatory, teacher satisfaction rises (Miskel and Ogawa 1988).

Michael Fullan (1991) discusses a research report by Levin and Eubanks (1989), who have studied site-based management in a number of schools in the United States. The report is an analysis of the problems a decentralized school reform encounters in the face of American realities. They identified a number of problems, including insufficient time, training and assistance, diffuse lines of responsibility, problems in the decision-making process, resistance from leaders at all levels to yielding power, regulatory limitations, and state and federal agreements (Levin and Eubanks 1989, pp. 4–8).

They are particularly concerned with three dangers of decentralization. First, we must not confuse satisfaction with results. There is little so far to indicate that decentralized school reforms lead to improved pupil performance (as measured by standard tests), although teachers feel more satisfied. Second, we must not forget (in a spirit of decentralization) that the centre also bears responsibility for supporting extensive school reforms. Third, site-based management initiatives should focus on modifying instruction and not be concerned solely with management and organization.

Elmore (1988 and 1992) is concerned that decentralization might stop at the abstract school level; he feels it should go on to foster development in the classroom, in the schools as a whole, in the relationship between the schools and school systems and in the relationship between the schools and the local community. In other words, it is no longer a question of carrying out specific projects, but of modifying school culture; it is a question of interaction between the centre and the periphery.

Americans often become enthusiastic about innovations and are eager to change practices almost overnight. But that rarely ever succeeds. An attempt has been made to compare studies done in the school sector with corresponding studies in American industry that have proved successful. The striking contrast is that, while industry enjoys a satisfactory salary system associated with such organizational changes, this is lacking in the schools.

In the more long-range and professional systems, two results become apparent:

- The head teacher gets another, more important role. More is required of him/her as an institutional leader. More creativity is required, along with the ability to unite the school society (teachers, pupils, parents and others) in a common vision and to maintain the ongoing development work that is necessary where the schools no longer enjoy central protection.
- The status of teachers is improved. This is important in the United States, where teaching as a profession is held in low esteem. When schoolteachers actively draw parents into the decision-making process, a kind of partnership emerges. An example of this is the projects that are being carried out in the State of Florida (*Education Week* 1993).

Developments in the United States were initially beset with unrealistic expectations; disappointments were inevitable. It soon became clear that decentralization is not a decision, but a learning process (Lieberman and Miller 1990). David Squires and

Robert Kranyik who report on the 'Comer Programme' argue that the changes envisioned 'in reality require deep cultural changes in the school and in the district' (1996, pp. 30). Clearly, a change has taken place, particularly in the bureaucratic cultures, and there is virtually no turning back. In the United States, realistic development plans for decentralization have begun to emerge, qualifying of leaders and teachers has taken place, and realistic budgets and necessary support for implementation have become a reality.

Lessons from North America are not very different from the experiences in Scandinavia. Guidelines for the 'new generation' of restructuring projects include:

- A clearer vision and more explicit goals for the decision-making process.
- An understanding that restructuring is not a goal in itself but a process for bringing about a broad set of reforms.
- A will to include parents in a real way and be responsive to their concerns.
- A change in teacher incentives and the organization of the work day to provide time for collaborative decision-making.
- An understanding that high-quality professional development is a must if reforms are to have any impact.
- An effort to establish a collaborative school culture focused on improvement.
- A comprehensive effort to change the central office and the relations between the schools and the district.
- A concentration of efforts around real needs of students, and a structured learning climate (Guskey and Peterson 1996, Squires and Kranyik 1996).

Developments in *New Zealand* are an attempt at radical decentralization coupled with a strongly governing central role. We shall have a look at the consequences at the system level in Chapter 8. Here we shall describe and discuss the reform at the school level.

Each school (2,666 state schools and no districts) has a board of trustees that is responsible for all aspects of school operations. The board has a special responsibility for ensuring that the interests and needs of the local community *vis-à-vis* the schools are met. The board is legally responsible for all school operations, including budgets. All in all, school boards have charge of operating budgets to the tune of 500 million NZ dollars – not, however, the salary budget of 1,500 million NZ dollars (Cameron 1992). In a sense, all schools have become 'Charter Schools'.

Fifty per cent of the board members are parents – followed by the head teacher, an elected teacher representative, a student representative and (in special cases) two representatives for those who own the school grounds. Thereafter up to four 'resource persons' can be elected from the local community in order to strengthen the board's academic profile.

Each school must develop its own 'charter' which, within a broad national scope, describes the school's distinctive character. The charter is to be approved by the Ministry and is signed by the Minister. After such approval, the charter becomes a contract between the school, the local community and the Ministry. The board reports regularly both to the local community and the Ministry, and central authorities assess the school's development every other year, through the central Education Review Office. This process of evaluation is particularly concerned with whether the board can handle its function as a responsible governor for the school, and whether it is operating within its proper bounds, laws and guidelines. Next, the evaluation concentrates on the academic development of the pupils. The reports are public (Lange 1988).

Every charter must clarify the manner in which the schools intend to work toward general national goals, and especially the manner in which the country's minority groups (e.g. the Maori culture) will be ensured equal educational opportunity.

The new school board, strongly represented by parties outside the schools, was welcomed by parents, teachers and head teachers alike, and the interaction between school and local community has, since 1989, taken a positive turn (Mitchell *et al.* 1993). There was keen interest in participating on the board (somewhat less interest at the second election), and within eighteen months all the schools had developed a charter, a process in which the head teacher has played a major role in most schools. The value of the charter and the process of creating one together was regarded by most people in a very positive light; but many felt that it did not contain anything essentially new about the schools and thus did not represent real school improvement.

The school boards were supposed to focus on learning. While most boards follow the school activities, property and financial decisions occupy their time. The Ministry of Education reports (1995) that 35 per cent of elementry schools and 61 per cent of secondary schools were in the red for the 1993 financial year. Nevertheless, the fact that parents have a real say in the governance of the schools has produced many positive effects. The communities now 'have a better understanding of how schools work and what helps their work' (Wylie 1996, p. 68).

The central evaluation process (see above) was looked upon as 'supportive' and not as 'control'. Almost all 3,000 schools have already been through an external review process. From the perspective of the schools, there appear to be two negative factors in particular associated with the reform: teachers being overworked, and the fact that the head teacher is forced into more administrative tasks and has less time for his/her pedagogical managerial functions.

Overworking has been discussed in a number of reports. In a study of primary schoolteachers in Christ Church, Bridges (1992) shows that the teachers are forced into a work week of at least 50 hours on average. Even though about half felt inspired by the reform, a majority of the teachers were nevertheless negative toward it, on account of work burdens, financial problems, and altered lines of responsibility. Many teachers felt powerless in the face of this extensive reform. They are disappointed in a policy which seems to 'put the system ahead of the person (the pupil)' (Bridges 1992, p. 34).

In this reform, the head teacher plays a major role. In a study of the system of management, Gordon (1993) states that the most important task the board has is hiring a head teacher. The head teacher is the party with the academic responsibility, whose job it is to 'apply' the board's decisions. In practice, there is no clear-cut distinction between governance and management (Gordon *et al*. 1994), and each school finds a 'pattern' in which the roles are more or less clearly defined. In the first phase of the reform, the focus was on local management control, where the cultural and demographic factors played a vital role. Then it was deemed important that the board, whose members are primarily external, should have overall control. In time, competition arises, finances and efficiency are put on the agenda, and the role of the head teacher grows ever stronger.

Which model is most appropriate in the distribution of power and tasks between the board and the administration? Relatively rigid preconceptions have arisen, which the central Education Review Office reviews for each school. But such a legalistic interpretation hinders the individual school from arriving at a workable system of management. Good management, like good teaching, is largely dependent on the local context.

Many are concerned that equality of educational opportunity is threatened by reform. A number of critics claim that the gap between schools is widening (Nuthall 1993). In Gordon's study (Gordon *et al*. 1994), we see that local financing plays an ever-increasing role. Even though the Ministry has built in a number of warning systems and report functions, the first few years have already shown that this system is less capable of ensuring equal educational opportunity for all than the rule-governed system it was meant to supplant. In a market system there will, by definition, be 'losers', or schools that are unable to attract their fair share of pupils. The consequences are reduced income, fewer teachers, and – most importantly – a negative reputation that the board is responsible for changing (Gordon *et al*. 1994).

After only five years of work, we are unable to say with certainty what the consequences will be at the school level of the extensive reforms in New Zealand. A number of criticisms have been raised, and several research reports have highlighted some of the dilemmas. For example, will parents necessarily have more say because a few parents are managing the schools? That depends first and foremost on how the board works, and whether it pays heed to the parents and takes its task and parent representative seriously.

The reform is permeated with modern management philosophy. This has, among other things, led to the head teacher having to work on administrative tasks far more than before, with less time for pedagogical leadership. Increasingly, critics are starting to feel that the entire reform is an attempt to cut the federal budget, and that the various initiatives have little to do with the pupils or good teaching. The system has, in particular, with its bulk funding (or block grants) created uncertainty and aroused the ire of teachers, because they see their workplace being threatened.

The New Zealand decentralization effort is another example of simultaneous centralization. The introduction of a new central curriculum, a comprehensive set of standards in all curriculum areas, and central inspection and review are but a few examples of a very strong central role. Again it is a question of striking a balance.

If we were to summarize some of the effects at the school level, we could best do so by quoting from the large follow-up study of the New Zealand Council for Educational Research (Wylie 1994):

- 41 per cent of teachers and 46 per cent of head teachers feel that the quality of pupils' work has improved after the transition to self-management.
- 81 per cent of parents are satisfied with pupils' learning and with the information they receive about the school's work.
- 85 per cent of the schools enjoy good relations between teachers and the board.
- Most board members feel that they can cope with their role, but show little interest for more power and more tasks.
- 55 per cent of the head teachers now feel that budgets are too tight, whereas in 1990 just 21 per cent felt the same. Only 16 per cent of the schools did not apply for extra funding in 1993.
- Schools in low-income areas have greater financing problems than others, and they also lose pupils to other schools more easily.
- Options for pupils with special needs have increased, but in about half the schools there is no change.
- Competition between schools raises the marketing budget, but rarely changes the actual scope of teaching. For that matter, 63 per cent of the parents of 5-year-olds have already decided which school their child(ren) should go to.
- The workload is, as we have seen, a big problem. The head teachers have, on average, a 59.85-hour week, and teachers a 48.18-hour week.

It is still an open question whether the new balance arrived at in New Zealand supports meaningful quality improvements. There are trends which indicate that school-based management is taking place in a vacuum, 'devoid of external interest, support, initiatives and well-grounded information' (Wylie 1996). If that is in fact the case, it does not augur well for school improvement.

School reform in New Zealand is perhaps the most extensive and fundamental of all the OECD countries. In Chapter 8 we shall discuss these reforms at the system level and take a special look at the central role.

In the *Netherlands*, developments have come a long way in recent years, and resemble the development in New Zealand. The Dutch have created very radical reforms that have fundamentally changed the state of affairs at the individual school level. The Dutch reforms involve the following:

1. Each school 'owns itself'; it should virtually be regarded as a foundation, and bears complete responsibility for the instruction and teaching that goes on at that school. The leading question has been the following: 'What is it that the school itself *cannot* do?' The reformers have put great stock by what the individual schools themselves are capable of doing.
2. The state has laid out a very broad framework for all pedagogical activity. The

private schools (70 per cent) and the public schools are, in principle, treated alike with respect to goals and general conditions.

3. Each individual school is assigned a general budget (in principle, dependent on the number of pupils that take their exams within expected time frames). When pupils take longer to complete their examinations, the school loses resources. Special compensation is given for pupils with various kinds of handicap.

4. Each individual school is completely independent with respect to the development of its syllabus and pedagogical options within a very broad national framework. The school management hires and fires teachers after consulting with the teaching staff.

5. The school board is elected by the school's users; as a rule, these are highly regarded, highly influential citizens. They are responsible for drawing up broad guidelines for school operations and for hiring management (which in turn is directly responsible to the board).

6. Parents are free to choose the school they want their children to attend. Thus a genuine market situation is created, and today schools must compete for pupils. As a result, much emphasis is placed on the school's 'pedagogical profile' and upon marketing the school.

Here we see a radical example of decentralization coupled with *user involvement*, much like the New Zealand system. The Dutch example is clearly the most radical reform project in the European schools today. It is too early to tell how it will turn out. Even in the Netherlands, there is more talk than action; nevertheless, there is no doubt that each school faces a new world.

We have experience from other countries with a longer tradition of centralization and bureaucratization. We are thinking first and foremost of *Germany*. Here it has been shown that decentralization in public administration has proven extremely difficult (Reichard 1992).

We also have experience from a smaller German state, Bremen, where a radical attempt is being made to modify the school system both from above and below, at the same time. The schools have organized themselves in an 'innovation forum' on a voluntary basis – a network in which ideas are discussed and developed. Over twenty school improvement consultants (with an emphasis on process consultancy) have been educated over a period of two to three years, and a number of schools are involved in independent development work, often supported by a consultant. At the same time, the Ministry is working with extensive internal restructuring, which includes a comprehensive delegation and decentralization process. In this programme there is a plan for extensive supplementary and continuing educational programmes for teachers, head teachers, school inspectors, and different categories of staff internally in the Ministry. A separate commission has been given the task of working with the substantive aspects of reform, and has submitted suggestions for a framework for pedagogical reform.

It is too early to say for sure how much genuine decentralization will ultimately take place in Bremen. Despite the many traditions and legislative rules that bind the system, we find a significant motivation at all levels for creating a more flexible, decentralized system (Rolff 1994a).

WHAT ARE THE REASONS FOR DECENTRALIZATION?

When we see decentralization in those countries we have described and analysed, we find the following possible reasons for the decentralization process:

1. *Productivity:* In most of the cases we have analysed, increased productivity plays a role, which is expressed in terms of deregulation, management development, new personnel policies, 'contracting out' (school buildings, for example), global budgets with built-in flexibility, etc. The crucial thing is that this greater flexibility be handled by those closest to the challenges.
2. *Democratization:* The intention here has been to bring the decision-making process closer to the users of the public services – and preferably involve the users directly, either as 'exit' (electable) or 'voice' (co-influence). In the United States, creating ownership *vis-à-vis* school improvement has played an important role. In Denmark, the rights of the individual citizen have been regarded as a matter of course and as best safeguarded by the rights (and participation) of the parents.
3. *Relevance and quality:* The schools' technology, or the wealth of knowledge that forms the basis of good teaching, does not exist on an abstract, scientific level. Pedagogy is more of an art than a science and is understood by experienced teachers in their encounter with a vast array of pupils and various day-to-day challenges. Quality does *not* increase just because decisions are made centrally on the basis of rational research data about what constitutes good teaching, or what constitutes a good school. *Quality increases when well-informed, well-educated and experienced teachers draw on theory and practice to reflect over the dilemmas of teaching.*

Lauglo and McLean (1985) have arrived at a similar justification for decentralization in those countries where they have studied the phenomenon (political, administrative and ideological rational), and Weiler (1990) has a nearly identical typology (redistribution of authority, increased productivity and improvement of the teaching culture).

Karlsen (1991) has made use of three analytical categories for discussing decentralization in the Norwegian schools of the 1970s and 1980s. We shall apply them here:

1. *Political or professional power:* In other words, does decentralization result in politicians or professionals accumulating more power? In Denmark, the users have indeed received more power – at the expense of the professionals. This is also the case in the Netherlands; but there, a strengthening of school management has also taken place. In Sweden, the trend is far less clear-cut. It could appear that

a balance has been maintained. In the United States, developments are so varied that it is difficult to say anything unequivocal. But the trend is that the head teacher has more power. The head teacher's role is interesting, because he/she is no longer a 'leader of colleagues'. Does he/she represent the political element (the board) or the professional element (the teachers)? In New Zealand, the users (formally, at any rate) have acquired a lot more influence. Also here, the first years of experience have shown that the head teacher's role is strengthened, but administrative responsibilities appear to detract from the pedagogical leadership tasks.

2. *The relationship between the market and official regulation:* In centralistic systems, the public administration has largely regulated the supply of educational services. With decentralization there is a chance for the market to gain greater influence. We see this in all countries in this discussion: in Sweden, the municipality purchases 'units of studies' from the schools. In Denmark, the schools can purchase services from the private sector or from public institutions, and parents are free to choose schools. In the Netherlands, all schools are organized like 'companies' in a market, and all services are privatized, with open competition for pupils. And in Norway, which has the least market element, schools can offer their educational services in an open market (for example, they can offer upper secondary schools courses in data processing on the open market).

The development in New Zealand is meant to create a market. The development of a market within upper secondary education has been studied by High Lauder and his colleagues (1994). They find, along with Willms and Echols (1993), that a free choice of schools reinforces differences between pupils from dissimilar socio-economic classes, and that those who are already privileged gain even greater advantages. Also pupils from typical working-class homes use their freedom of choice, but end up choosing between schools that usually recruit pupils from the working class. Pupils from academic homes or financially well-off homes are more mobile and often choose schools far away if they have 'a good reputation'. Lauder and his colleagues also find that it is in fact the best schools that choose among the best pupils who apply, and that parental choice is far from effective. They also raise an ethical question as to whether the very foundation of the market model is tenable, because it assumes that some schools will not succeed or will develop in a negative direction. This means that one assumes that the pupils who go to these schools in all probability will not succeed either. Finally, we find that pupils' assessment of the schools and their own potential is far more realistic than their parents' assessment, which raises questions about the parents' influence in the upper secondary school.

3. *Stability or change:* Does decentralization lead to change or to stability – perhaps even some new form of rigidity? A number of schools and local communities tell of difficulty in creating a consensus, and other environments are dominated by strong personalities or groups. It is no matter of course that decentralization will lead to development, or (preferably) to renewal. We will be looking at this very

thing in the next four chapters. Whether or not school improvement becomes a reality in a decentralized system depends on the way the system works.

DOES DECENTRALIZATION HAVE A FUTURE?

To conclude: is this but one of many passing fads, or is decentralization here to stay? There are so many problems associated with this inherently significant reform that success is not automatically assured.

Decentralization will take many shapes and will assume many forms; in fact, that's part of the idea behind it. The grass roots have a broader playing field, which means that solutions will vary. Decentralization cannot be dictated by centralized governing bodies; only the framework can be defined.

If the individual pupil, parent, teacher, head teacher, and others who work in the schools are to experience a new reality – that they are in fact participants in an exciting learning organization – then everyone, both young and old, must commit themselves to enter into a personal and social learning process. We will discuss 'individual strategies' in Chapter 6.

What is certain is that decentralization will never be an effective force unless the individual school culture is changed. Elements such as the annual development plan, internal evaluation and similar exercises can easily become just that: vain exercises, and not strategic tasks for a school in development. If decentralization is to be experienced and its potential exploited, this must take place in terms of the unique way in which each school functions. Decentralization to the municipal level will only be perceived as a new form of centralization, because the control aspect has moved closer to home. We discuss the development of school culture in Chapter 7.

As we have seen in our work in a number of countries, and most recently in the state of Bremen, we will not be seeing much decentralization at all unless the central authorities start thinking afresh. What is required is a 'new state', a new balance between the centre and the periphery. Courage and the will to think decentrally is required, and this in turn requires learning at all levels and practice in taking on new roles. We discuss central strategies for change in Chapter 8.

In reality, we are faced with a process that requires negotiation and co-operation between all parties in the system. Henrik Larsen (1992) put it aptly:

> *If* the highest levels of management set many detailed guidelines, *if* the central administration only exercises administrative control, *if* institutional management and personnel are bound by tradition, professionally and attitude-wise, and *if* the users remain passive, the institution will have little room for maneuver. The production of services in such an institution will be relatively fixed and determined by circumstances that are relatively unaffected by the users served by that institution . . . (pp. 10–11)

If a systematic process of change can be created, one in which every link acts in unison to create a new system, *then* there is a potential for genuine renewal.

Part II

Theories of School Improvement

Introduction

Our ambition in this section is to set forth theories that we believe represent important contributions to our understanding of how schools improve, and how systems change. School improvement studies have been going on for more than 50 years. If we include the studies of organizations and management as a necessary theoretical base for understanding change in organizations, this represents about 100 years of research.

Although it is, of course, important to include contemporary research in this section, it is equally important to include earlier work that has proved useful to our understanding of school improvement. The reader will find, in chronological order, models of thinking, perspectives on change and on organizations as these have grown out of various research traditions over time.

Theories of organizations and theories of leadership and management are fundamental to our understanding of change. Much of the way schools are organized has its roots in early industrialization and the organization that was seen as 'productive'. Many schools are still striving to 'get restructured'! Other school systems are toying with new management concepts, sometimes with an insufficient understanding of what that implies, where the models come from, and what they normally produce. But it is important that we raise the question of *what constitutes a good learning organization,* or more fundamentally, what constitutes productive learning (Dalin and Rust 1996; Sarason 1998), through the presentation of various models of organization and management.

The last chapter deals with change theories and, more specifically, school improvement theories. The research tradition here is younger and based primarily in North America and (partly) in Europe. Our aim is to present the main theoretical schools of thought and relate them to theories of organization and management.

Owing to the volume of research that is relevant to this section, we have been forced to limit the items of research that we can report. We have, however, included a full list of references which, hopefully, will prove useful for those who would like to study a particular theory in greater detail.

Chapter 2

Theories of Organizations

Organizations are like the landscape: complex and varied. Moreover, they change with the seasons, with the weather, and with our observational perspective. We can return to the same terrain and still feel like it's the first time we've ever been there. Our experiences are so varied, so different, depending on our perspective.

Our outlook on organizations is based, in large measure, on hearsay, long-standing beliefs, and the force of habit. It's like traipsing along the same marked paths on familiar forest trails. We 'nod in recognition', as it were, as the landscape unfolds before us.

Let's take an example. We've often heard it said that an organization must formulate goals, and that these should be clear and concise. The clearer the better, and the easier it will then be for us to reach them. And so we make the groundless assumption that organizations are concerned with reaching goals. This conclusion is based on a kind of 'rational model' thinking, an approach with deep roots in political science.

While it may be true that under certain circumstances some organizations could be regarded as goal-oriented systems, it is just as true that many other organizations cannot be so regarded. Organizations are complex, diverse and tangled systems that often surprise us. A formal, rational, bureaucratic view of organizations can in no way explain the many anomalies that arise. What can be observed, experienced and developed in organizations is far too complex to be explained from any one perspective.

An exciting contribution to the understanding of organizations was presented by Gareth Morgan in his book *Organizational Images* (Morgan 1988). Morgan makes use of a number of different metaphors to describe and analyse the many and diverse phenomena associated with organizations. We give a brief rundown of his 'images' to stimulate our imagination and to help us steer clear of a constrictive cognitive point of departure in our discussion of organizational theory. Through his images, Morgan develops theses and antitheses, enriching our ability to understand what is essentially a very complex phenomenon. Here are Morgan's eight 'images':

1. *Organization as a machine:* At the beginning of this century, during a period of rapid growth for natural science and engineering, many thought of organizations

in terms of machines in which each part had its special task and a specific role in the overall scheme of things. The goal was to make organizations as efficient and effective as possible. As machine parts, human beings also fill the role of 'parts' that fit into a whole of some sort, parts that can be changed and replaced.

2. *Organizations as an organism:* This image emerged gradually, as it began to be understood that organizations were dependent on their environment. Organizations came to be regarded as entities that were 'alive' and that underwent various stages of development in an evolutionary sense, entities that interacted closely with the environment of which they were a part.

3. *Organizations as a brain:* Here the focus was on the ability of organizations to process data, on the cybernetic processes, on 'learning to learn', and on the ability of organizations to govern themselves. According to this image, organizations have great flexibility, a marked capacity for innovation, and they work like computers.

4. *Organizations as culture:* This image regards organizations as social constructs, created for the express purpose of reaching specific goals. Key words in this image are values, norms and rituals, all of which organizations 'administer'. Organizations can have different subcultures, and for this reason it is important to make a conscious attempt to promote a common company culture.

5. *Organizations as political systems:* With this political metaphor, Morgan illustrates various conflicts of interest and power plays in organizations. According to this image, it is important to understand conflicts, to be able to use power and govern pluralistic organizations.

6. *Organizations as inner prisons:* According to this image, the question is raised as to which unconscious emotions organizations might represent – e.g. anxiety, suppressed sexuality, patriarchal or matriarchal patterns, and death. Psychodynamic and ideological thought patterns characterize this perspective.

7. *Organizations as entities in a constant state of flux:* In this image, 'dialectical analysis' is in the foreground, and a key perspective is organizations as self-producing systems. It is important to understand the fundamental (often unconscious) dynamic that shapes the organization, and to understand the dynamic of change – not as linear lines, but in terms of 'loops'.

8. *Organizations as instruments for supremacy:* This is an expansion of the political metaphor and shows how an organization can exploit individuals and groups for its own purposes. Organizations are looked upon as instruments of domination and exploitation; among the matters discussed are work environment problems, drug problems at the workplace, stress, and international companies as world powers.

Morgan's images show that organizations can be viewed from a number of different perspectives. To be able to understand a given organizational theory, we must first understand the position from which the theory has developed.

In a number of studies, the Norwegian scientist Paul Moxnes has helped shed light on the nature of groups and organizations. Among other things, he works with different roles, which he perceives as 'mythological roles'. He gets his images from fairy tales, legends and mythology, and has come up with new and exciting perspectives on what is going on in the way of human interaction in organizations (Moxnes 1993).

Many researchers have sought to develop organizational theories. Common to them all is the fact that each investigator has had his own special interest. They have either worked with a certain type of organization (industrial firms, for example), or they have represented a certain perspective (for example, being concerned with the decision-making process). The inevitable result has been a theory in which attention has been directed toward certain types of organizations under certain types of conditions. And so we have theories concerning decision-making processes, concerning conflicts, concerning communication, concerning leadership, and concerning power and influence, to name but a few examples.

No one theory has been developed that can be said to encompass all aspects of all kinds of organizations and that would thus tell us why organizations act the way they do; but in recent years some theories have been developed that have aspired to understand all the essential aspects of an organization. (We will return to the St Gallen group's theory later in this chapter.) A number of excellent research projects have been conducted, but all of them have certain limitations, which will be looked at more closely in this chapter. In this and following chapters we will attempt to apply the current body of knowledge to schools as organizations. In doing so, we hope to extend our reach as broadly as possible – that is, to include examples from a number of 'schools'. On the other hand, we also wish to be critical in our selection, because it is unlikely that all organizational theories are equally relevant to schools.

However, this approach involves many dilemmas, which should be highlighted. First, we know so little about schools as organizations, that it is unclear what is relevant and what is not. It is far too easy to claim that a theory is irrelevant merely because it happened to be developed within the context of an organization other than the school. I assume that schools can be described, in organizational terms, in much the same way as most other organizations; but the characterization, significance and relationships of the individual factors can often vary greatly. Second, how is it possible to find criteria for the selection of existing theories? I have chosen to present certain primary perspectives and discuss theories that appear to have the best empirical basis.

In choosing these primary perspectives I have once again been faced with a number of dilemmas. Within the organizational literature there are a number of orientations. It is true that a number of approaches have much in common, and it would be natural to group them under one primary perspective. This is the case, for example, with 'classical organizational theory' in which a number of traditions have been developed in Germany, France, the United States and other countries. Even though they stress different organizational aspects, they have so much in common – for example, in their view of humanity – that it is natural to treat them under the same primary perspective.

The aim of this chapter is to outline various perspectives on organizations and their application to schools. I am convinced that if we cannot 'see' organizations from the viewpoint of different perspectives, our chance of understanding them – and changing them – will remain limited. One of the most important limitations in school improvement has been our lack of understanding of schools as organizations. We have taken it far too much for granted that schools function in the way that their formal structure would suggest. We have made a number of assumptions about schools as organizations, and in doing so have based our school improvement work on false premises.

It has become customary to present organizational theory in terms of three distinct traditions: classical theory, humanistic theory, and system theory. As I have worked with *school improvement theory*, however, I have developed doubts as to whether these general theories are useful for understanding organizational *renewal*. Therefore, in this chapter I will review four perspectives on organizations: structural, humanist, political and symbolic perspectives (in which the traditional theories are included; see also Bolman and Deal 1984). I will then discuss the integrated theories of Mintzberg, Senge and the St Gallen group which in principle bridge the gaps between the four perspectives.

1. THE STRUCTURAL PERSPECTIVE

This regards organizations as 'rational systems', concerned with realizing set goals by means of the most effective structure and procedures. The following theories belong under this perspective: classical organizations theory, system theory, contingency theory and socio-technical theory.

Classical organizational theory

This originated with Max Weber, a German sociologist from the turn of this century; Henri Fayol, a French industrialist; and Frederick Taylor, an American engineer who developed their thoughts at about the same time. They were all primarily interested in creating new organizational and management forms, as industrialism with its new technology and mass production began to make major inroads into society.

As far as schools as organizations are concerned, Max Weber's thinking has probably had the greatest impact. He defined a number of set organizational principles which he assumed could be applied universally. He claimed that as long as these principles were followed, they would inevitably lead to higher productivity:

1. *Hierarchical structure:* The organization is a pyramid in which the one on top always has authority over the one under him. Orders are communicated systematically from top to bottom in the organization.

   Most countries have organized their school systems on a national basis, with varying levels of decision-making down through the system, all the way down to the individual pupil. To a great extent, the 'higher-ups' have power over those who are lower in the system. Power largely rests on legitimate authority. Rolf Haugen (1977) has pointed out how complicated the Norwegian school bureaucracy is, how powerless teachers and pupils feel with respect to the system, and how information – when truly vital – flows outside official channels. Above all, he regards the bureaucracy as an impediment to learning. In previous works, I have shown that, to an increasing extent, the schools appear to be centralizing knowledge (for example, central research and development work), that 'horizontal' interaction is complicated by the hierarchical structure, and that central authorities still play a governing role in daily teaching.

2. *Specialization:* Since it would be too complicated for everyone in an organization to learn everything equally well, greater efficiency is achieved if tasks are distributed on the basis of each individual's competence, skills, experience, and specialties.

     The traditional school, with its breakdown of subjects, classes, grade levels, and various kinds of schools, is structured on a specialization model. This development quickened pace in countries such as the United States and particularly Canada, whereas European countries (especially Great Britain and Norway) have been reluctant to back this trend – except for vocational specialization; Norwegian schools have had great difficulty breaking free from academic specialization.

3. *Rule structure:* Decisions and actions are governed by clear-cut rules. There are rules and procedures that safeguard the rights and duties of employees; these also assure uniformity and stability.

     In countries with strong centralized authority, regulations and ordinances are an important means of governing schools. Norwegian schools have a long-standing tradition of being governed this way. In other countries, handbooks are written with precise instructions to teachers and pupils alike. Head teachers are taught to handle all sorts of questions and conflicts in terms of the rules that have been laid down. Until very recently, both teachers and pupils had to accept rules for normative behaviour that were laid down by central authorities.

4. *Impersonal relationships:* It is easier to keep tabs if personal relationships, emotions and irrational reactions are eliminated. Each employee is therefore under strict discipline, and their work is closely monitored. This is a principle in Weber's philosophy that has not really caught on in schools. In my opinion, this is primarily because teachers' academic code of ethics looks upon a personal relationship to one's pupils as being of overriding importance (indeed, for many teachers it is the primary motivation for their work) (Dalin and Rust 1983). This shows perhaps more than anything else the conflict that exists, as I see it, between the schools' bureaucratic structure and the schools' professionality.

5. *Career possibilities:* Promotions are given on the basis of seniority and/or achievement. Pay is closely connected to the hierarchical level. There are pension arrangements. On the whole, this promotes the establishment of a stable career-oriented class of workers and staff.

     The schools' promotion system is built exclusively on seniority. It is also the case that the highest positions in the bureaucracy are the best-paid ones. Therefore, to a certain extent, the school system is such that success and status are related to one's place in the hierarchy. This can have unfortunate consequences: for example, a very good teacher can become a head teacher, even though there is nothing that says being a good teacher automatically guarantees that this person will make a good head teacher. In fact, the opposite is sometimes the case: good teachers sometimes become bad head teachers. It is reasonable to assume that even though career possibilities in the school system are fairly minimal compared to other sectors, the system undoubtedly creates a basis for a relatively stable professional group. For a number of years, Brooklyn Derr has been studying motivational factors in a number of professions, and has found that teachers are primarily interested in 'security' and a 'balanced' lifestyle; and some are very concerned with 'academic interests'. There are relatively few who – in Derr's words – are 'getting up', i.e. interested in a managerial career (Derr 1986).

6. *Goal orientation:* An organization is regarded as a rational, systematic, and goal-oriented organism. For such organizations, a rational problem-solving process is needed (Weber 1964).

    The schools are formally a goal-seeking organization. The results are measured in terms of pupils' achievements. But in reality, the schools have very generalized, diffuse and overlapping goals which often conflict with each other. Teachers are often more concerned with the means than with the goal itself. Furthermore, there is greater prestige attached to 'internal knowledge' than to 'external knowledge'.

Assessing the use of classical theory in today's schools is no simple matter. In many ways, classical theory belongs to a bygone era. That being the case, what kinds of pedagogical goals can best be realized by organizing the schools according to 'classical principles'? We have seen that *effectiveness* (often in a narrow sense) and *control* over management from above are the guiding principles of classical theory. There is also reason to believe that *uniformity* and *standardized solutions* can be realized by the application of principles such as the foregoing.

For a number of years now, European schools have been moving away from centralization, hierarchical control, standardization and a fragmentation of the learning process – which is why classical theory almost seems like an anachronism. Nevertheless, I feel that several fundamental characteristics of the schools are still contributing to bureaucratic solutions.

Open system theory

This is concerned with the dependency that exists between an organization and its environment. To describe this interaction, it was necessary to move from a static to a dynamic description of organizations. Since the environment is always in a state of flux, there will always be give and take between an organization and its environment. Allport speaks of a 'recurring cycle of events' (Allport 1962). As in nature, according to this perspective there are constantly recurring processes that are necessary for the survival of an organization.

Along with theorists within the humanistic tradition, system theorists claim that it is more expedient to study what actually happens in an organization than to start out with formal goals. Then it is only natural to look at what an organization receives from its environment: input, what it does with its resources: throughput, and what it gives back to the environment: results (output).

Resource factors can be both human and material resources – for example, teachers, pupils, textbooks, buildings, expectations and attitudes; from teachers, pupils, parents, the local community and the community at large, and more general 'structural' influences; and thoughts and ideas promulgated by the mass media.

Throughput in schools has, first and foremost, to do with the teaching process in the classroom. But other activities also take place in the school which can be looked upon as 'supporting processes' to the explicitly instructional work: planning, meeting activity, decision-making, evaluation, development of materials, communication, management, etc. There is practically no limit to all the activities and processes that characterize a school.

Results from a school are characterized, first and foremost, by what the pupils have learned, by the concrete knowledge and skills they have acquired, by those attitudes and norms which the school has helped shape, and by the contribution that the pupils themselves can subsequently make to society. The parents' attitudes toward the schools are also an important result of the schools' work which, in political terms, have significance for the working conditions schools enjoy in society.

There are a number of circumstances about schools as organizations which, in this context, are worthy of note: in most organizations there will be a relationship between what an organization receives (resources) and the quality of its work (results). The schools are practically guaranteed new resources every single year, regardless of what they 'produce'. And precisely because it is of little consequence to the schools whether they function at peak efficiency or not, it is not vital that they accommodate the expectations of their environment. The problems of the pupils rarely pose any real problem for the schools (until such time as these become a disciplinary problem for the classroom teacher).

It can be very difficult to determine whether a school has achieved its goals; likewise, we have very little proven knowledge about learning and instruction. Consequently this can easily be used as an argument to continue current practices and shy away from changes that are challenging. It can also be used as an argument against unsolicited and unwelcome criticism. And when the teachers in a school are labouring under work conditions that practically make it impossible to take any disciplinary action against them (except in cases of gross negligence), it is reasonable to believe that many schools are not all that interested in an open relationship to their environment. A number of scientists have discovered that schools are approaching what we could call 'closed' systems (Carlson 1965).

Contingency theory

Contingency theory, like open system theory, is concerned with the relationship between an organization and its environment. To the extent that significant changes take place in the environment, this can entail changes in the organization's 'response'. Contingency theoreticians are eclectics – that is, in a given situation they choose solutions based on different theories. There is no one way to organize one's life that is superior to every other in every situation. So too with organizations. The way in which they are built up, the way in which management acts, depends first and foremost on the situation.

An example of this theory is the work that two Scottish scientists, Burns and Stalker, published at the beginning of the 1960s (Burns and Stalker 1961). They found that organizations could be categorized as 'mechanistic' and 'organic', respectively.

As shown in Figure 2.1, mechanistic organizations are represented in relatively stable societies. They are complex, with a clear-cut hierarchy where rights and duties are strictly defined. Their tasks are specialized, few have any overall control, power is concentrated at the top, and communication, as a rule, is vertical. These are all features we recognize from Weber's bureaucratic model.

		Organizations that are:	
		Simple	Complex
Societies that are:	Stable		Mechanistic
	Dynamic	Organic	

Figure 2.1 *Two forms of organizations (according to Burns and Stalker)*

Organic organizations usually arise in situations in which there are rapid environmental changes. As a rule, they are relatively small and simple in structure. In organizations of this kind, the goals of individuals are largely accommodated. Power and influence are shared maximally (which leads to a common sense of responsibility for solutions), and communication (both horizontal and vertical) is encouraged. It is thought to be natural that one person can carry out more than one task, there is often an overlapping of roles, and all do their part to make sure that everyone views the organization from an overall perspective.

Burns and Stalker find that an organization's size and the degree of change in the environment are the factors that can explain the justification of the two different organizational forms. In another context, I have pointed out that an organization's tasks also, to a certain extent, determine the form of organization (Dalin 1973). In research and development organizations there will be a greater tendency, for example, toward 'organic forms' than, say, in military units.

Much of the development we see today in organizational development in the schools has 'organic ideals'. This can be seen in such notions as 'the Creativity of the School' (1975) and 'Changing the School Culture' (Dalin and Rolff 1993). In this connection it is important to pose questions such as the following: Are the schools autonomous? To what extent are they bound by the goals and ordinances of society? Who 'owns' the schools? Is the school a 'simple' organization in the Burns and Stalker sense of the term? In other words, is it possible for the school *itself* to reflect the demands of its environment, and – perhaps even more important – can it choose which demands it will take into account?

The latter is a question of values, as well as a question of politics. Most people would claim that it is not up to the individual school in any society to decide which demands it will relate to: this is decided by the political authorities. In other words, the schools are limited in their freedom. But this does not provide a satisfactory answer to the question that 'contingency theoreticians' are asking. For them, school authorities are but *one* of the groups that influence the schools and that schools must take into account. If they do not, they will run foul of their environment. Most curricula are so loosely defined that schools can interpret them rather freely. I would suggest that, in many ways, the schools have greater freedom than most other organizations, because they are not dependent on the quality of their results. A firm in the so-called free economy is most likely just as bound in relation to its environment as the schools are, because the market will determine its chances of survival.

Precisely because schools in many ways are so unbound and needn't fear the reprisals of their environment to any large extent, and because management and teachers have power over pupils, a great responsibility – politically, academically, and morally – rests on the adults in school life.

Socio-technical theory

I group this under the structural perspective, even though this placement is not a perfect one. Socio-technical theory derives some of its concepts from system theory; but, as its name implies, this theory also has its roots in the humanistic theory (see below). Representatives of socio-technical theory are Trist and Rice.

Rice developed an open socio-technical theory in which he sought to combine elements from open system theory and humanistic theory (Rice 1963). Rice assumed that every organization has a primary task that it must perform in order to survive. At the same time, to succeed in this, it is crucial that the organization be in a position to offer its members meaningful work. But the members' need for meaningful work must not be allowed to pre-empt the organization's primary task. Thus it becomes a manager's task to create equilibrium in the system, so that both task and human needs are safeguarded. For this to happen, the manager must also be able to 'negotiate' with his environment so that the organization receives the resources it needs for the processes required to produce what that environment expects.

2. THE HUMANISTIC PERSPECTIVE

This is concerned with the individual's contribution in organizations, and with the interaction between all the organization's members. Human needs and the placating of those needs occupies a central place in this theory. Typical representatives for this perspective are Mayo, McGregor, Argyris and Herzberg.

Fundamental to this theory is the question of what *motivates* employees. Until Elton Mayo carried out his famous experiments, the accepted view was that rewards and promotion were the only motivation for effort. But now researchers began to discover that group norms, climate, relationships to management, and a sense of personal accomplishment were factors just as important for productivity.

'Human relations' theoreticians assumed that organizations in which members were most content would also be the most effective organizations. So it was only natural that these theoreticians began to favour democracy in the workplace, maximum participation in the shaping of assignments, and a high degree of open communication.

The humanistic perspective is founded on research from a number of disciplines and upon the following premises:

1. Organizations exist for the purpose of satisfying *human needs* (people do *not* exist for the purpose of serving the needs of their organization).
2. Organizations and people need each other. Organizations need the ideas, the energy and the talents that people possess, whereas people need the career, the salary and the employment opportunity that organizations can provide.
3. When there is a major mismatch between the needs of individuals and the organization, one or both will suffer: either the individual will be exploited, or she will try to exploit the organization.
4. When the individual and the organization are well matched, this is to the advantage of both. People are capable of carrying out meaningful and satisfying work; this enables them to provide the organization with the resources it needs in order to fulfil its role.

However, there were those (for example, Etzioni, 1964) who felt that the humanistic perspective was founded on a fallacious understanding of human nature, or that scientists were attempting to impose on everyone a kind of academic middle-class value system. They were also criticized for overlooking individual differences. And above all, they were criticized for disregarding power, structure and politics in organizations. Ideological conflicts and 'organizational politics' are considered more as problems that need solving than as natural and fundamental phenomena in organizations.

We have chosen to include two theories of organizations under the humanistic perspective which are only partially related to this perspective, namely collectivist theory and 'clan perspective'. We could also have defined them under the 'symbolic perspective' (see below), because they also contain elements that belong there.

Collectivist perspective

The collectivist perspective has been described as follows by Rothchild-Whitt (1979).

Ideal description of collectivist-democratic organizations:

Dimensions	*Characteristics*
1. Authority	Authority is associated with the group as a whole. Delegating seldom occurs (and only temporarily, at that) and can be withdrawn at any time.
2. Rules	A minimum of rules; as a rule, *ad hoc* and individually adapted. Each person is free to act on his own with a general knowledge of the group's ethics.
3. Social control	Social control is based primarily on personal trust and moral appeals, as well as careful selection of members.
4. Social relations	The community ideal. Connections are all-encompassing, personal, and have value in their own right.
5. Recruitment and promotion	a. Hiring takes place via friends, political and social values, personal characteristics, and informal evaluation of knowledge and skills. b. Career and promotion have meaning in their own right. There are no hierarchical positions.
6. Rewards	Normative rewards are the most important. Material rewards are of secondary importance.
7. Social team-sharing	Equality ideals. Reward differences (if any) are carefully regulated by the collective.
8. Differentiation	a. A minimum of specialization. Administrative work is combined with academic work. The division between intellectual and manual work is reduced. b. The generalization of jobs and functions. All-encompassing roles. The demystification of expertise. The ideal of the amateur.

In Scandinavia there are several schools of research whose ideals derive from the collectivist perspective. The Oslo Experimental Gymnasium in Norway is but one example. The socio-pedagogical alternative for the study of pedagogy at the University of Oslo could also in many ways be said to have values that are consistent with this perspective. In the general school system it is practically unthinkable that such a perspective could catch on, particularly in view of the bureaucratic rules for hiring, personnel policy and management. But even in the regular schools, many working groups are organized in this way. The smaller the groupings, the easier it is to win acceptance for this form of organization.

The clan perspective

The clan as an organization has been under considerable scrutiny the last few years. Ouchi defines the clan in the following way:

1. Agreement between members about what constitutes acceptable behaviour.
2. Agreement about legitimate authority, often traditionally justified.

3. An information system containing rituals and ceremonies that reflect the norms and values of the organization.
4. A stable staff.
5. Selective recruitment, intense socialization, ceremonial forms of behaviour control and ceremonies associated with results (Ouchi 1980).

A number of schools and other institutions of learning share features typical for clans. Certain recent studies also show that schools which approach a form of organization with clear rules of behaviour, clear lines of authority, and respect for mutual norms and values can show good school results (Rutter *et al.* 1979).

At a time when norms and values are more relative than ever before in modern history, when schools are struggling with disciplinary problems, it is hardly surprising that many educators regard the clan perspective with interest. The clan perspective has traditionally been associated with an accepted leader. As far as the schools are concerned, a development toward a clear perspective is possible only if the legitimate leader is also a charismatic leader, someone whom everyone can support. There are head teachers that have in fact created such schools, which have produced good results – at any rate, if we apply behavioural criteria and traditional character. The fact that there might be a price to pay for such 'solutions' was another matter. The manager often tends to be too much of a key figure. It can be difficult for others to advance their ideas – at any rate if these do not coincide with the interests and values of the leader.

3. THE POLITICAL PERSPECTIVE

This regards organizations as scenes for battles and conflicts of interest, illustrated through a fight for resources and exemplified and highlighted through the dissimilar values and interests of individuals and groups. Representatives of theories within this perspective are Marx, Baldridge, Cyert, and March and Gamson. This perspective is also represented in Norway, as well as in several studies by Berg and Wallin at Uppsala University. Under this perspective I also include the marketplace model, developed by Chester Barnard, which in reality is a negotiation model in which contracts are the object of a bargaining process.

The conflict perspective

Baldridge (1971), Aliniski (1971) and Cyert and March (1963) have all supported the conflict perspective. They see organizations as coalitions of individuals and interest groups. Because organizations consist of many different interest groups, they will have many contradictory goals. It is the distribution of power within the organization that determines which goals are given priority. Bolman and Deal (1984) have summed up this perspective in the following way:

1. Most important decisions that organizations make involve the allocation of resources that are scarce.

2. Organizations are coalitions that consist of a number of individual interest groups (for example, hierarchical levels, departments, professional groupings, ethnic groups).
3. Individuals and interest groups have different values, preferences, beliefs, information, and perceptions of reality. Such differences are usually stable and change only slowly, if at all.
4. The goals and decisions of organizations develop by means of an ongoing process of negotiation and jockeying for position among individuals and groups.
5. Because resources are scarce and because there are lasting dissimilarities and differences, power and conflict will always remain central elements in the life of an organization.

The *political perspective* assumes that management seeks to safeguard 'the goals of the organization'. But there is very little truth in this. By virtue of their needs and interest, everyone in an organization has a part in advancing their goals. Each person acts on the basis of his/her own personal interests. The goals of an organization are the product of an interest struggle and power struggle at all levels, where those with the greatest *actual power* have the strongest likelihood that their goals will be achieved. But as a rule it is extremely uncertain whether it is those who are at the pinnacle of power who have the most power (Cyert and March 1963).

The marketplace model

As far back as 1938, Chester Barnard claimed that organizations were not goal-oriented. According to him, they existed for the benefit of the individual, which he regarded as the strategic element in an organization (Barnard 1938). He claimed that behaviour is tied to incentives, that organizations are 'markets' in which incentives are traded, and that the goals of an organization are subordinate, at all times, to the demands, needs, personal satisfaction, and rewards of the individual.

According to Georgiou, power in an organization depends on the ability of one person to provide incentives to others (Georgiou 1973).

According to Barnard, schools exist for the benefit of teachers, not pupils. In recent years he has been supported in this view by other organizational theoreticians who have studied what has taken place in school systems whose budgets have been drastically cut back. Most observations suggest that the schools have done whatever is best for the staff, and not necessarily what was best for the pupils.

There are other examples that support this perspective. It would appear, for example, that renewal projects that are the easiest to carry out are the very ones that afford advantages for the teachers (for example, those that save time, are easy to employ, etc.). Projects that call for extra effort on the part of the teachers (for example, more time, more academically demanding) are the hardest to carry out. Teachers have also strongly opposed projects that might rob them of their teaching monopoly (data technology, for example) (Clark and Wilson 1961).

In Norway it is first and foremost the teachers' unions who represent the teachers in this way. It would not be unreasonable to say that the academic work of the

41

organizations has been relatively weak, while the organizational effort has been given a high priority. Naturally, there is nothing unreasonable about this. Even in oil-rich Norway there have been suggestions for cutbacks. Studies by the Norwegian Association of Local Authorities, which recommends a rationalization of the governmental structure at the municipal level, have stirred massive opposition within the teachers' unions. One of the main arguments of these unions has been the equal opportunity throughout the country with respect to education. Teachers feel that their own work interests are best served by a centralized system in combination with a separate school board (and superintendent, i.e. a Director of Education of the school district) in the cities, which gives them more control over 'earmarked' funds.

The schools are among the country's largest workplaces. It would be naive to believe that personal goals, incentives, and group pressure were not pivotal factors in school improvement. Since the 1970s, the Norwegian Union of Teachers has demanded negotiations as a condition for teachers' participation in trials. When one party in the schools (the teachers) can promote their own interests *vis-à-vis* the government in this way, it will become more important, in time (as in other countries), that pupils and parents also find organized forms for their demands.

There is an aspect of this development that is often overlooked: it has a tendency to weaken the teachers' academic status. The reason for this is not merely because most people have begun to realize that teachers, through their organizations, are very powerful spokespeople for their own interests (which is, of course, completely legitimate), but eventually, classroom skills will no longer be the crucial factor in their influence but rather their belonging to the power centres of those organizations that are in control of important assignments. This development has already been at work for quite some time now, with respect to political power. Political membership increases one's prospects for assignments and promotion. It also helps weaken the view that working with children is important. Incentives are associated with influential work in the adult world, not to work in the classroom.

Criticism of the political perspective

The political perspective has provided us with an insight into the major significance that conflicts and political processes have in organizations. In fact, some of its advocates go so far as to suggest that the political perspective is the *only* perspective that represents the truth about organizations (Aliniski 1971).

The political perspective is a clear alternative to the structural and the humanistic ways of looking at the world. But the political perspective can also be a trap, because it can blind us to many other aspects of the life of an organization – aspects that are crucial to understanding these organizations properly. The political perspective, as I see it, underestimates the degree of rationality and the significance of collaboration within organizations.

By the same token, this also suggests a *pessimistic* view of the potential for renewal. In reality, there is nothing that can be categorically defined as renewal. There is only what we can call change. The process we call school improvement simply consists of turning our attention and resources from one interest group to another.

This represents the extreme in the political perspective – whereas in reality it is a consequence of a particular way of looking at the world. So the political perspective has little to teach us about *strategies for renewal*, except for reminding us about all the conflicts of interests and struggles for the distribution of power that exist – no mean contribution, to be sure.

4. THE SYMBOLIC PERSPECTIVE

This represents a view of reality which, more than any other, is an alternative to rational thinking. What is important is not what actually takes place, but the meaning, or significance behind it, which, in turn, depends on the 'symbolic value' that an organization's members ascribe to what takes place. The symbolic perspective is represented by a number of scientists from several disciplines – Selznik, Blumer, Corwin, Weick, March and Olsen, and Moxnes, among others. Spokespeople for this perspective are concerned with myths, rituals, ceremonies, organizational culture, and metaphors. Within this perspective I include organized anarchies and loosely connected systems.

The symbolic perspective, as discussed by Bolman and Deal, operates primarily with the concepts of *meaning, faith and trust*. There is much about life that cannot be explained rationally. Contradictions and dilemmas are all an integral part of our daily lives. Viewed from the symbolic perspective, it is first and foremost *the meaning behind the actions* that serves as the point of departure for the analysis. Does the planning process really benefit planning, or is the whole process merely a ceremony that gives the organization and its environment an *impression* of order and enterprise? Are meetings truly problem-solving, or do they merely serve as a forum for airing opinions? The symbolic perspective helps us 'to get under the skin', so to speak, or break inside the shell (it is in stark contrast to the three perspectives we have been discussing up to now) as we search for some meaning behind the actions – without taking the rational explanations of the organization's members for granted. In the symbolic perspective, the world is neither *safe, rational* nor *linear.*

Through the eyes of the symbolic perspective, the world looks different:

1. The important thing about every action is not what happens, but the underlying meaning.
2. The meaning of an action is not merely determined by what happened, but also by the way we *interpret* what happened.
3. Many of the most important actions and processes in an organization are both vague and uncertain – it is often hard (if not impossible) to know what is actually taking place, why it is happening, and what it will all lead to.
4. Vagueness and uncertainty undermine rational methods of analysis, problem-solving and decision-making.
5. When we are face-to-face with vagueness and uncertainty, we create *symbols* to minimize the uncertainty, clear up the confusion, increase predictability, and provide a sense of direction. The events themselves might still be just as illogical,

coincidental and meaningless, but our symbols make them seem as though they weren't (Bolman and Deal 1984).

Many actions and processes in organizations can *appear* to be illogical and irrational. Only when the symbolic value of these actions is made clear are we able to see that they are nevertheless logical and serve a purpose. Once again, let us take planning as an example: few planning processes yield results of any significance for the future of an organization. Why, then, do organizations spend so much time on the planning process? One important reason is that planning serves to draw the organization's members into a process where opinions can be aired, members can get acquainted, values can be discussed, and where a sense of solidarity can be developed. This is an important element in the development of a common culture. But for the outside world, the organization behaves like a modern, forward-looking company that is laying its strategic and operational plans.

Organized anarchies

This concept originates from Cohen *et al.*, who applied it to educational institutions (universities) which in their view could hardly be said to act 'rationally'. Another concept that Cohen *et al.* often use is 'The Garbage Can Model' – which describes, in their opinion, what really takes place in the decision-making process. Organized anarchies have the following elements:

1. *Ambiguous preferences.* Preferences are discovered by acting, instead of people acting on the basis of preferences.
2. *Ambiguous technology.* Even if an organization manages to survive and even be productive, its own processes are not understood by its own members.
3. *Variable participation.* Participation varies, both as to time spent and the work expended on different areas (Cohen *et al.* 1972, p. 2).

Decision-making in organized anarchies is often inconsistent with a well-ordered problem-solving process.

When I read works by March and Olsen, especially their work entitled *Ambiguity and Choice in Organizations*, I am struck by how 'different' their thoughts are from traditional system theory (March and Olsen 1976). Quite a few axioms are turned on their heads, and the way these authors express themselves forces the reader to make a critical reappraisal of 'rational truths' that many of us thought were sacrosanct.

My guess is that the 'anarchy model' can more readily be applied to institutions of high learning than to pre-college schools. One of the reasons for this is the decentralized form of organization characteristic of universities and the conflicts between a central bureaucratic system and academic preferences – which, in my view, are better expressed at the universities.

Loosely coupled systems

The idea that organizations are systems that 'stick together' in some rational way, so that changes in one part of the system have consequences for the other parts, has been a fundamental one in system theory. As an alternative, the theory has been put forward that organizations are not as 'tightly knit' as they might seem at first glance; rather, they should be regarded more or less as 'loosely connected'.

Organizations, according to this train of thought, consist of entities, processes, activities, and individuals that are relatively loosely connected (Weick 1980). In other words, what actually takes place in an entity (or is initiated by a single person), is not consistent (according to any predictable theory) with other parts of the organization.

Loosely connected systems go through times when the resources are more plentiful than the requests, times when different initiatives will lead to the same goal. They will also experience a relative lack of co-ordination, very few rules, conscious independence, planned situations where there is no accord, the casual monitoring of activities, and discretionary delegating (Weick 1976).

A common reaction to such a state of affairs is that this must be a sick organization in need of reform. But that is far from certain. It could be that the relative freedom that certain departments in an organization enjoy might help other units adapt to the requirements of their environment while the rest of the organization remains stable. It can also protect the entire organization from collapse. But it can also, of course, impede necessary changes in the organization as a whole, impede vital communication between sections, and protect individuals from criticism by their colleagues.

The important thing to note is that *all* organizations vary in terms of how closely knit they are. When we realize that this is an important variable, it will help us understand certain features of schools as organizations. And schools have certain features in common with loosely connected organizations. How often does a head teacher take her counselling responsibility seriously and listen to teachers teach? Is what happens, for example, in Norwegian language classes being co-ordinated with what is going on in the social study subjects? Are there are common norms for behaviour? Do committee reports have any practical consequences for what goes on in the classroom? Are experiments spread to other schools?

Most schools are characterized by a number of units (classrooms) that are isolated from each other, by teachers without guidance, by initiatives that have no practical consequences, and by guidelines that are not followed. The question is whether all this is good or bad.

The symbolic perspective gives us a number of new impulses in the understanding of organizations. It raises questions about the meaning behind actions and processes, and helps us draw on a broader range of human behaviour. It also helps us achieve a greater openness, helps us discuss 'what is actually going on', increases our creativity, and helps us be and make use of ourselves to a greater extent than is the case when we are forced to live with the 'party line' about what is happening to us.

The symbolic perspective encourages us to take a fresh look at what we have previously regarded as 'just a bunch of ceremonies' and investigate processes we thought were ineffectual or infelicitous. In my work with developing countries, I have begun to appreciate the significance of the symbolic perspective. I have gradually come to realize that ceremonies are crucial to the identity of the participants, to the legitimizing of their activities, and to the development of a project culture that can be viewed from the perspective of the nation's cultural values. For all these reasons, ceremonies give security and meaning to the participants.

Criticism of the symbolic perspective

The symbolic perspective is the 'youngest' of the four perspectives. Few empirical studies have made use of it as a frame of reference. Clearly we must reckon with the production of studies that differ in nature from the traditional quantifiable studies. Qualitative methods based on a phenomenological perspective will probably prove to be the most fruitful.

The symbolic perspective is, to a lesser extent than the other perspectives, *one* theory. It unites a number of ideas – relatively loosely connected – and more time is needed before it can be regarded as a fully-fledged perspective. And that is assuming that this is even possible – let alone desirable, in view of what this perspective stands for.

The symbolic perspective contains a dilemma: a symbol can involve a clouding of realities; it can confuse the issue by deliberately being cynical and disingenuous. The myth that a teacher whose formal qualifications are in order is automatically a *qualified* teacher can, in some cases, result in protecting incompetent teachers and hinder urgent reforms in teacher education.

Another way of using symbols is to look upon them as expressions of true meaning. The symbolic perspective tells us that what we regard as *hard facts* is, in reality, what people have chosen to create. This gives us hope for the future: we ourselves are able to create a world which, both academically, politically and morally, is in harmony with our innermost values.

5. INTEGRATED THEORIES

In recent years a number of new 'organizational theories' have appeared on the scene. The following scientists, among others, have rendered significant contributions to the study of organizations: Henry Mintzberg from McGill University in Canada, Peter M. Senge from MIT's Sloan School of Management in the United States, and Peter Gomez from Hochschule St Gallen in Switzerland (cf Mintzberg 1991, Senge 1990, Gomez and Zimmermann 1992).

While Senge has come up with one specific systematic perspective of organizations and developed his theory of 'the learning organization', both Mintzberg and Gomez take a broader approach. The fact that I still choose to present Senge in this context (and not under the humanistic perspective) is because his thinking goes deeper and encompasses more than one specific perspective.

Mintzberg

Mintzberg's point of departure is that all organizations are influenced by both internal and external forces, and that a balance between them is essential for achieving effectiveness in any given situation. There is no one way of achieving this effectiveness, but many.

But Mintzberg goes beyond the 'contingency theoreticians' (see above), who virtually claim that 'it all depends' on the situation in each case, without stating clearly what effect various remedies might have in given situations. Mintzberg attempts to clarify which strategies are best for *developing* an organization, what makes an organization *outstanding when it counts*, and what it takes to maintain and *perpetuate* an organization that is already functioning well.

In Mintzberg's first works, the concept of 'configuration' played an important role. He sought to group organizations according to specific patterns, each 'form' being effective for its particular purpose. Later, however, he discovered that a number of very effective organizations did not fit into these patterns of his. Today he prefers working with concepts such as 'forces' and 'forms'.

He feels that most of what goes on in organizations can be understood as an interaction between seven different forces (see Figure 2.2).

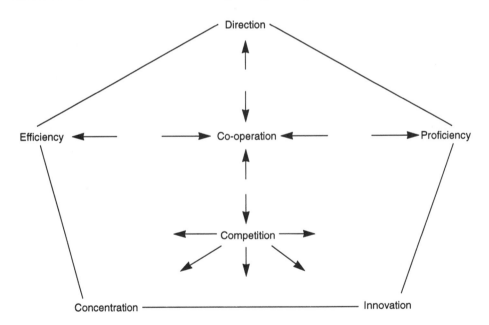

Figure 2.2 *Mintzberg: A system of forces in an organization*

1. *Leadership or direction:* Gives us an indication of where an organization as a whole is headed. Without such a 'strategic vision', it is difficult to get every part of an organization to move in tandem.

2. *Efficiency:* Seeks to optimize the relationship between cost and results. All organizations, apart from the most shielded ones, have to be concerned about their productivity, which often leads to cutbacks.
3. *Proficiency:* Involves the performance of tasks with a high level of knowledge and skills. Without academic expertise, most organizations would not survive.
4. *Concentration:* Certain parts of an organization concentrate on serving specific markets. Without this kind of specialization it would be difficult to manage complex organizations.
5. *Innovation:* Makes it possible for an organization to discover and develop new methods, services and products for its customers and for itself.
6. *Co-operation:* Seeks to find and utilize a common ideology for the purpose of moving together. By 'ideology', Mintzberg means more than an organization's culture in the traditional sense. His use of the term includes such concepts as norms, traditions, conviction and values. For Mintzberg, these factors are valuable energy, and serve as 'glue' in the organization.
7. *Competition:* As opposed to co-operation, organizations are also up against competition – or what Mintzberg calls 'politics': and 'each to his own' attitude, the fact that competing interests are vying for power, often by means of unacceptable or illegitimate attitudes and behaviour.

Mintzberg's theory states that all these seven forces are potentially active in every organization. If one of these forces is allowed to predominate, in time a unified form will take shape, which he describes as a *configuration*. If an organization develops in a lopsided fashion according to one particular pattern, this will have the effect of repressing other vital forces in that organization. The danger is lopsided dominance and what Mintzberg chooses to call *contamination*.

Where no single force predominates, organizations will function as a combination of forces that are in equilibrium. Such a pattern can easily lead to *division*.

Both *contamination* and *division* call for management that can successfully cope with *disparities*. Then what Mintzberg calls 'the catalytic forces', co-operation and competition, play an important role. However, these are contrasting forces, and in an effective organization these must be in balance. Regardless of the form (or 'configuration'), the balancing of forces remains the basic issue.

Configuration
By a given 'form', Mintzberg means an organization that is consistent and integrated. This is an organization in which everything 'fits together', as it were. There is no single form that is effective for every purpose in all organizations. There are a number of forms, each with their own special features:

1. *The entrepreneurial form:* Appears when 'management and direction' pre-dominate in an organization, usually when a manager plays a decisive and dominant role. This often happens in the start-up phase, when a strong vision and a strong leader are often essential before an organization can really start moving.

2. *The machine form:* Appears when the demand for efficiency and productivity is important. This form is typical of large manufacturing or service companies, and for organizations with a strong need for control.
3. *The professional form:* Usually develops when proficiency and academic quality are the predominant forces – as, for example, in hospitals and high-tech companies. The tendency is to extend the existing base of knowledge and methods, instead of developing new ones. Established, high-skill procedures predominate and make it possible for individual professionals to enjoy a considerable measure of freedom with respect to their colleagues.
4. *The 'Adhocracy':* Created in response to the need for innovation. In this form, as well, we have a team of professionals, but because they are under pressure to constantly be creating something new, they usually work in teams on a cross-platform, interdisciplinary basis. Something new is always being created – either in-house or in close co-operation with customers.
5. *The 'diversified' form:* Present when the need for concentrating on specific products and services becomes so pressing that these must be developed and handled separately. Such organizations are characterized first by a significant degree of delegating, and second by 'divisionalism'. Each department is given a large measure of autonomy, governed by norms and guidelines laid down by a small, centralized staff.

Mintzberg also regards 'ideology' and 'politics' as forces which, in certain cases, can dominate an organizational form. In this connection he mentions the Israeli kibbutzes as an example of a type of form that is ideology-based.

None of these forms exist in a 'pure' state; there are, however, a number of examples of organizations that share features with a certain form. Mintzberg compares having a form with having a personality. Without a 'form', any organization will experience a crisis of identity. The fact that an organization has a certain form is effective as long as the situation is static; but as soon as dynamic changes begin to take place, an established form will inevitably become ineffective – it is just a question of time.

When a specific form predominates to the exclusion or detriment of other forces, or when an organization does not react adequately to external changes, the seeds of self-destruction are sown. A 'machine organization' might be unable to renew itself because innovative forces have been consistently quelled. Professionals can wind up dominating things without taking sufficient account of the issue of productivity – and do so to such an extent that their organization ultimately strangles to death. An entrepreneur can wind up exploiting his own organization to go on an ego trip. A divisionalized organization in which common values play a minor role easily breaks apart. Likewise, an *ad hoc* organization that is incapable of exploiting the potential for innovation (before it develops something new) will not be able to survive.

An organization cannot, in other words, be effective in a 'pure' form unless it is kept in check by other forces in the organization (Mintzberg calls this 'containment').

In those cases where it is possible to have a 'pure' form, this is just fine; but most organizations, instead, have to cope with *competing* forces. Naturally, an orchestra requires a high professional standard for its players, but it also needs clear-cut, competent leadership. Just as a lopsidedly 'pure' form can easily destroy the equilibrium of an organization and eclipse all other forces, organizations that enjoy a combination of strong forces will often have to resist centrifugal forces that would break up the organization.

Mintzberg claims that most organizations go through several transformations during the course of their lifetime. He exemplifies this and points up the danger of splintering. To manage a divided organization, or one that works with deep and latent divisive tendencies, is a great (and highly relevant) management challenge. Mintzberg points out important aspects of the processes of change that must be taken into account if these periodic transformations are to succeed.

Traditionally, organizations have tried to tackle this challenge in one of two ways: by renewed *co-operation* or increased *competition*. In Mintzberg's mental image of an organization (see Figure 2.2), these two forces have been placed in the middle. They have a tendency, not to pull an organization toward some extreme form, but rather to put their stamp upon the organization as a whole. Mintzberg calls these the *catalytic* forces.

Co-operation is a crucial catalytic force that helps hold an organization together. Whether a co-operative atmosphere is created by a charismatic leader or is the fruit of common efforts, organizations with a highly co-operative culture are able to resolve the structual conflicts inherent in a lopsided form of organization.

Mintzberg points out the limitations of co-operation. In the first place, it is difficult to develop a co-operative culture, let alone maintain it once it has been established. Karl Weick once said: 'A culture is not something an organization *has*; rather, an organization *is* a culture' (quoted from Kiechel 1984). This is why it is so hard to change organizations.

An ideology of co-operation risks becoming too inward-looking, morbidly preoccupied with itself, and might (directly or indirectly) reject internal criticism that seeks to take a critical look at the company culture. Even though a co-operative culture does make it possible to renew the organization within established norms, it nevertheless resists fundamental change.

Competition represents the force that encourages the individual to pursue his or her own interests (often at the expense of the common good). In other words, competition encourages an organization to move in many directions at once, which would ultimately lead to the death of the organization. However, if an overly assertive ideology has been obstructing fundamental criticism over a long period of time, increased competition can help bring about important and necessary changes in an organization.

Thus it is important that these two forces be kept in equilibrium: *co-operation* on the one hand, and *competition* on the other. Both forces are essential: co-operation helps secondary forces to keep a dominant force in check, whereas competition tends to promote confrontation. Mintzberg claims that it is only by striking a happy medium between these two forces that an organization can develop and survive in a dynamic world. Organizations need a sense of direction, true; but they also need a balance.

Mintzberg has tried to integrate several theories within the structural and the political perspectives. It is not clear to what extent the humanistic perspective plays a role in his analysis. The forces 'co-operation' and 'competition' point up the significance of different types of cultures and can thus be said to represent Mintzberg's version of the humanistic perspective. The symbolic perspective, not being explicitly represented, can almost be regarded as an extreme consequence of lopsidedly dominant forces (for example, 'loosely connected systems' can be said to be a version of Mintzberg's 'diversified form' – which can be a positive thing where the market calls for concentration, but which can easily lead to a break-up.) In addition, Mintzberg is very strong on *contingency theory*.

Another interesting feature of Mintzberg's theory is that it couples open system theory (organizations are completely independent of their market), with the need to understand those internal processes in organizations that are important for determining the type of configuration they have.

Peter M. Senge

With his book *The Fifth Discipline – The Art and Practice of the Learning Organization*, Peter M. Senge introduced a new integrated theory of the 'learning organization' (Senge 1990). His main perspective belongs to the humanistic perspective; however, he does go beyond it.

Senge introduces a *systemic perspective* on organizations. He is particularly concerned about the fact that the reason it is hard for us to understand how organizations live is because we are bound by our established 'mental images', and because we do not understand the long-term effects of what takes place in a social system. Our understanding is only partial, and we often misinterpret events because organizations rarely conduct themselves 'logically' in the short term.

Thus Senge also lays down a challenge to the contingency theoreticians, whose concern is about organizations reacting to short-term market variations. Senge feels that organizations, naturally, depend on their environment, but that 'the environment' is neither an unambiguous concept, nor does it react unambiguously – nor does it distinguish clearly between *short-term* and *long-term* needs.

Senge mentions five 'disciplines' as being essential to understanding organizations:

1. *Systemic thinking*, which for Senge is the key discipline. It helps us understand things in context, to understand the whole pattern and not just bits of the whole, and on this basis to sway organizations in the direction of meaningful changes.
2. *Personal mastery*, which is the learning process that continually seeks 'to clarify and broaden our personal vision, focus our energy, develop patience, and take an objective look at reality' (Senge 1990, p. 7). Senge sees a deep, personal learning process on the part of the individual organizational member as a prerequisite for a sound organization.

3. *Mental models*, or 'images' are deeply established conceptions, generalizations, hypotheses and assumptions that every one of us has and that colour our understanding of the world in which we live. They exert a strong influence on us and can often hinder us, for example, in choosing new, promising alternatives because our impressions serve as mental blocks. For Senge, common planning and development is a crucial learning process in sound organizations.

4. *Development of a common vision*, or the process that draws 'images' and experiences together into an integrated process toward a common image of 'why we are all here', is absolutely essential to the success of an organization, as Senge sees it. No facile 'Five-step rule' will beget such a vision, only long-term common development work carried out in an atmosphere of openness and transparency.

5. *Team learning* (or dialogue) is closely related to the previous discipline; but it has a deeper meaning as well. It concerns the general learning situation in an organization in which members succeed in laying aside their own mental images and 'think together'. The Greek term *dia-logos* signifies a free exchange of opinions in group work, which enables the group to discover new insight that no individual acting alone could achieve; and this is the process that Senge has in mind.

Senge stresses that this 'fifth' (here, the *first*) and most important discipline is *systemic thinking*. This discipline helps us to integrate the others so that they will not be relegated to a 'life of their own', so to speak, and become mere gimmicks. Nowadays it has become popular to talk about the need for a 'vision', but often this winds up being some flashy image without any deeper meaning for the employees. Often, teamwork is looked upon as a goal in itself; the result is often an inconsequential and unproductive process that does no one any good at all. It is important to Senge how individuals see themselves, likewise that these same individuals experience their organization as a place where they can continuously find out how to create their own reality.

This is why the concept *metanoia* occupies such a central place in Senge's theory. This is a Greek word that means 'fundamental change', or close to what we might call 'conversion' – i.e. a completely new way of perceiving oneself and the world. In the deepest sense of the word, this is what Senge believes learning really is: a fundamental means of 'recreating ourselves'.

Then what exactly does Senge mean by 'systemic thinking'? He has come up with a number of 'laws' meant to serve as rules of thumb for systemic thinking in organizations:

1. The problems of today stem from the 'solutions' of yesterday.
2. The harder you push and the more you try, the harder the system pushes back.
3. The situation often gets better before it gets worse (for example, giving food to the hungry does not help them become self-sufficient in agriculture).
4. 'More of the same' brings us right back to where we started.
5. The cure can be worse than the illness.

6. Quick action means slow or delayed solutions (the quickest method is not always the optimal one).
7. Cause and effect are not closely related in time and space (thus it is often difficult to understand cause and effect).
8. Minor change can often have major consequences; but it is often unclear where it pays to expend the most effort.
9. You might 'have your cake and eat it too', but not necessarily all at once.
10. To split an elephant down the middle does not necessarily yield two small elephants (living organizations have integrity, and their character is a function of the whole).
11. No one is to blame.

Senge shows us that organizations react on the basis of how processes affect the whole – in both the long run and the short run. Without a deeper understanding of an organization's culture and systemic conditions, there is a major risk that 'development', instead of working as planned, will prove self-defeating.

In contrast to Mintzberg, Senge reflects a basically carefully considered humanistic perspective. His contributions also have great significance for our own thinking about strategies for renewal in organizations. But above all, his perspective is important for school improvement – not only because it explains why organizational learning is 'required knowledge' for the coming generation, but also because the schools themselves have much to learn from Senge if they are going to realize these principles for a learning generation.

The St Gallen Group

1. *A comprehensive way of looking at things:* An organization is perceived as a system, in which the whole is greater (or something different) than the sum of its parts. Three dimensions of a system are analysed – namely, the *normative*, the *strategic*, and the *operative*.
2. *Integration and variety:* Dividing things into different dimensions does not mean that it is possible to separate components from each other. On the contrary: the dimensions are mutually dependent; they 'cut through', and are connected in a network.
3. *Developing a way of thinking:* in order to understand systems. The purpose is to help the members of an organization to understand the complexity, to enable them to develop a goal-oriented philosophy, and assist them in making concrete changes (Gomez and Zimmermann 1992).

The St Gallen group has had a 'management theory' as the goal for their work. In our context we will describe and analyse the group's perspective on organizations, which can be divided into three main areas:

A. *'Organizational profiles'*, which is the organizing of information around eight organizational dimensions, organized as four contrary dimensions. Here are the questions: What typifies an organization as seen from a broad perspective? What potential for renewal does it have?

B. *Organizational dynamics*, or which phases characterize 'the life cycle of an organization'? Typically, what profiles characterize which phases? Which profiles are desirable in a given phase in order to avoid a decline?

C. *Organizational methodology*, or which methods are most appropriate in the development of an organization in a given phase?

Below we shall discuss what the St Gallen group characterizes as 'organizational profiles', because it is by means of these profiles that we gain insight into the theoretical basis for further analysis. These four main profiles are called:

1. Techno-structure – Socio-structure.
2. Palace – Tent.
3. Hierarchy – Network.
4. Foreign organization – Self-organization.

While we do not discuss the methodological aspects of organization development in this context, we will return to the concept 'organizational dynamics', which is a theory about how organizations change in nature, in the course of time, with concomitant consequences for the development process.

Organizational profiles
The fundamental analytical instrument developed by the St Gallen group is 'organizational profiles'. Through a systematic analysis it is possible, with the aid of these very profiles, to clarify key aspects of an organization. Below we shall give a brief description of the profiles:

Techno-structure – Socio-structure
Figure 2.3 shows how this profile is constructed. It is in the shape of a rectangle in which both axes are characterized by two poles – in this case:

1. Formalized – Symbol-oriented.
2. Person-oriented – Issue-oriented.

As long as an organization is *both* markedly issue-oriented and strongly formalized, the organization, on the basis of this concept, is largely a 'techno-structure', as opposed to an organization that is both strongly person-oriented and symbol-oriented. It is then, very markedly, a 'socio-structure'.

How do we define the various dimensions?

Issue-orientation: Here the emphasis is on substance, on a rational division of tasks within an organization, both with respect to differentiation and the integration of tasks. It is the nature of the tasks that determines the organizational structure.

Person-orientation: This is where the individual's motivation, knowledge, skills

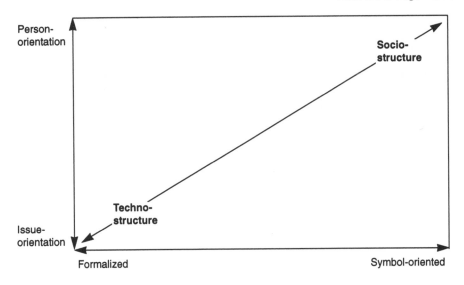

Figure 2.3 *The Techno-structure – Socio-structure organizational profile*

and potential become the starting point for the organizational structure. The individual worker is in focus; how groups work together as a team and how the company 'sticks together' is important. Management is co-operative and colleagues participate in the decision-making process.

Formalization: This means a written itemization of tasks, responsibility and work processes. Documentation is essential, especially in large and complex organizations. Formalization often takes place by such means as organigrams, function diagrams, job descriptions, guidelines, and contracts.

Symbol-orientation: Legitimacy is achieved through established norms and values that develop a specific identity. For this reason, symbolic activities that reflect the norms are important. Anecdotes and rituals help create identity. In such a climate, role flexibility is encouraged, as is participation in several groups and cross-functional learning.

The practice that the St Gallen group represents shows that strong issue-orientation is often coupled with a marked degree of formalization. They call this position 'techno-structure'. On the other hand, marked person-orientation is often associated with strong symbol-orientation, a position they call 'socio-structure'.

Techno-structure has its theoretical roots in the humanistic perspective (see above – for example McGregor, Argyris). Motivational theory occupies a central place in this aspect, on a par with 'subjective reality' and a cultural view of organizations.

Palace and Tent
Central to this perspective is a tension between preserving and developing. The two main dimensions are:

1. Efficiency – Effectiveness.
2. Established organizations – Temporary organizations.

Efficiency: The task is to reach the goal by using a minimum of resources, in the quickest and most rational way possible. As a rule, this involves making work more routine in nature; it also involves heavily programmed tasks, narrow limits for what is allowed, well-drilled procedures and routines, and a relatively inflexible organizational structure.

Effectiveness: The task here is to reach the goal as quickly as possible, even if this entails more costs than necessary. The principle is that 'structure follows strategy'. This principle works best in dynamic situations or where development is associated with high risks. As the individual enjoys a large measure of freedom, this often leads to overlapping assignments; but it also implies great flexibility.

Established organizations: These are organizations that are established, without a mandate limited in time, for the purpose of resolving a specific set of tasks. The energy is thus directed toward resolving these established tasks.

Temporary organizations: These are organizations that have been given the task of solving one or more specific problems; they know at the outset that their mandate is limited in time. The organization might be a 'project organization', one in which the need for communication and co-operation is acute. For this reason it seeks to develop a flexible interdisciplinary team in order to resolve problems in the best way possible.

'Palace and Tent' displays the pattern shown in Figure 2.4:

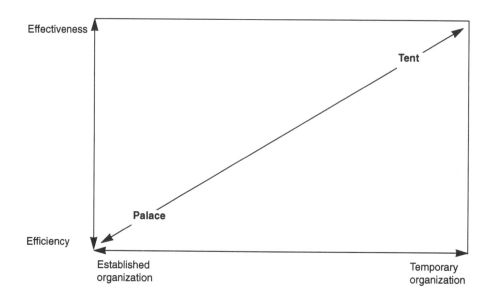

Figure 2.4 *'Palace and Tent'*

The Palace is a stable organization that has institutionalized an effective solution to routine tasks, an organization that is well suited to a stable, gradually developing world. The theoretical underpinnings are derived from classical organizational theory (e.g. Taylor).

The Tent is an organization that survives in a rapidly changing world. As such, it is flexible, adaptable, quick-witted, and capable of learning. Hedberg *et al.* originally developed 'The Tent Concept' (Hedberg *et al.* 1976). They feel that 'the tent' should be continually concerned with strategies of change – they even go so far as to suggest that the structure itself can also be regarded as a process. Gomez and Zimmermann describe a number of related theories (e.g. adaptive organizations, adhocracy, informational-technological structures, etc.), all of which in some measure justify the benefits of 'the Tent'.

Hierarchy and network

The dimensions of this model are as follows:

1. Monolithic – Polycentric.
2. Hierarchical configuration – Flat configuration.

Monolithic can have three meanings: geographical concentration of activities; a collection of similar tasks; and a concentration of control and management. As a rule, monolithic means a strong central organization where decisions are made at the very highest level.

A *polycentric* organization lets decisions be made at the lowest possible level. With a high degree of complexity and a demand for flexibility, time is saved. Being able to act autonomously has a positive effect when there is a need to react rapidly in a market. However, this requires a high degree of professional proficiency on the part of the members. In organizations of this kind, a 'centrifugal' tendency arises, and a need for control – which can, in part, be resolved by self-control.

A *hierarchical* organization has many levels of management in a hierarchical order. A large number of the staff work in supervisory and control functions, which often results in suspicion.

A *flat* organization has a minimum of management levels. Direct contact is established with the implementation units. A flat organization is especially important in a rapidly changing world.

Figure 2.5 shows the quadrant that arises when these two dimensions are combined.

The *hierarchy* has a number of decision-making levels and a strong central concentration (monolithic). The justification for a hierarchical organization is the concentration of forces with respect to a clearly defined goal with optimum utilization of resources. Theoretically, the model is based on the bureaucratic models (e.g. Max Weber, see above).

The *network* arises when the organization has both a polycentric and a flat structure. It is particularly well suited to organizations that work with innovations and which must respond to a rapidly changing world. Decisions are made throughout

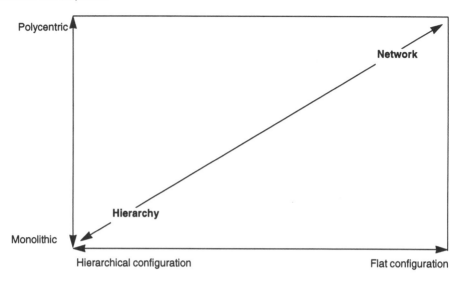

Figure 2.5 *Hierarchy and network*

the organization, and teams are often formed across established boundaries. There is often a risk of overlapping tasks, inefficiency, and conflicts. This model originally had its roots in the humanistic perspective; but eventually it sought models from a number of theories (cf Gomez and Zimmermann's discussion of the model).

'Outside' organization – Self-organization
The above title could have been 'From Dictation to Self-determination'. The dimensions in this model are as follows:

1. Exogenous orientation – Endogenous orientation.
2. 'Outside' management – Self-management.

Exogenous orientation is what Gomez calls an organization that is heavily influenced in its development strategy by the world around it. Dependency on the outside world, as it were, is justified partly in terms of the dynamics of a rapidly changing world, partly in terms of the need to be close to the market (customer orientation), and partly in terms of the requirements of new information technology.

Endogenous orientation means that an organization is primarily governed in its development work by its own inner needs. These are organizations that have a well-established culture and that depend largely on their own internal resources when making strategic choices. There is also a tendency to want to affect the environment (instead of the environment affecting the organization).

'Outside' management of development processes is characterized by 'top-down' organizational development. This often happens in organizations where there is a fundamental distrust of the lower echelons. Hence this development philosophy is also associated with a number of rules and monitoring systems. The strategy is that a

number of rules, procedures and plans should be able to 'regulate' the work of development.

Self-government of the development processes involves a 'bottom-up' model for development work. Organizational development is carried out with the full participation of all parties involved. Regulation takes place primarily through training and attitude improvement activities based on common sense.

The factors shown in Figure 2.6 constitute the fourth and last matrix in the St Gallen concept:

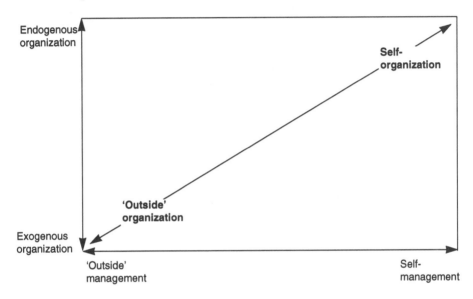

Figure 2.6 *'Outside' determined organization and self-organization*

An *'outside' organization* is one that largely turns outward to the world around it and depends on that world. The fact that the organization has adjusted to the market is a chief concern; so the strategy is often one of efficiency, sales, and customer orientation. Conflicts are often a function of the demands from the world around it in relation to the needs of its own employees. Development processes are 'top-down' and are perceived more as demands than as genuine development. This form of organization is theoretically rooted in contingency theory (see above, as well as Lawrence and Lorsch 1969).

A *self-organization* is typically an organization that 'regulates itself', with no hierarchical or external management. The perspective of the members is inward-looking, and the individual organizational units are given wide latitude for self-development. This perspective assumes that social systems are so complex that they cannot be predetermined in any detail, that a mutual tolerance among the departments is a prerequisite for integration, and that the best strategy is to work out common goals rather than issuing detailed instructions. Instead of hierarchy (where others have done your thinking for you), the creative thought process is central. The theoretical foundation springs from the humanistic perspective (see, for example, Emergy and Trist 1965).

The stabilizing organization

Through practical work and research, the St Gallen group has arrived at what appears to characterize different types of organizations. By a combination of the four matrixes in an integrated model, a pattern emerges for different types of organizations.

Figure 2.7 shows the forces that characterize an organization with a stabilizing structure. This is a formal, technocratic, hierarchically led organization under strong 'foreign' management. In large and complex organizations, this organizational form helps organizations standardize and achieve a productive utilization of resources. A prerequisite for this, however, is the planning of processes with a large degree of certainty, the manageability of those processes, and the relative stability of the outside world. This type of organization tends toward:

- Over-organization through autonomy-restrictive regulation.
- Bureaucracy through an array of formal rules and the introduction of monitoring systems.
- Specialization through a high degree of standardization.
- Maintenance of the *status quo* by the optimizing of existing activities.

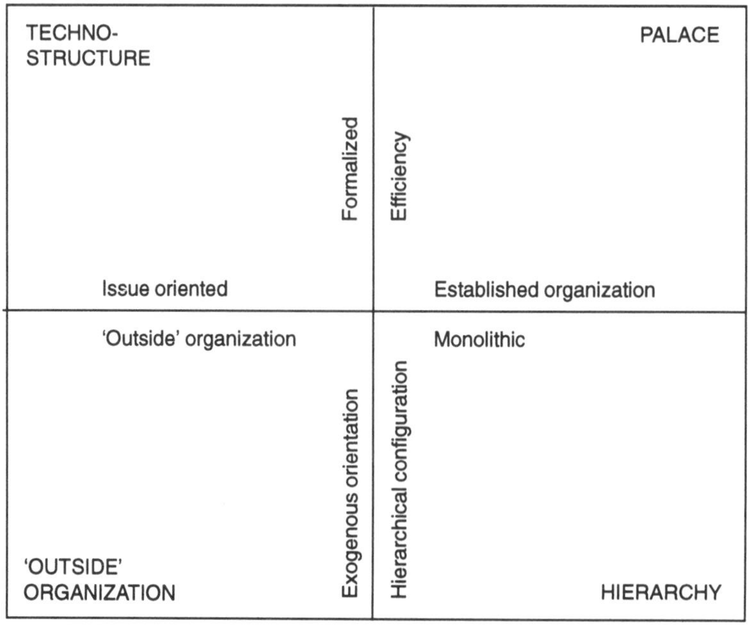

Figure 2.7 *Dimensions of a stabilizing organization*

The purpose of such an organizational form (in terms of business management criteria) is to optimize the use of scarce resources so that the organization can turn in a profit and have a chance to survive. This also gives rise to the impression that an organization, with the aid of authoritarian methods, can compensate for a lack of human orientation.

The development-oriented organization

The counterpart of the 'stabilizing' profile is the person-focused, symbol-oriented processor organization that is managed according to the self-management principle. Figure 2.8 shows the St Gallen matrices for this form of organization:

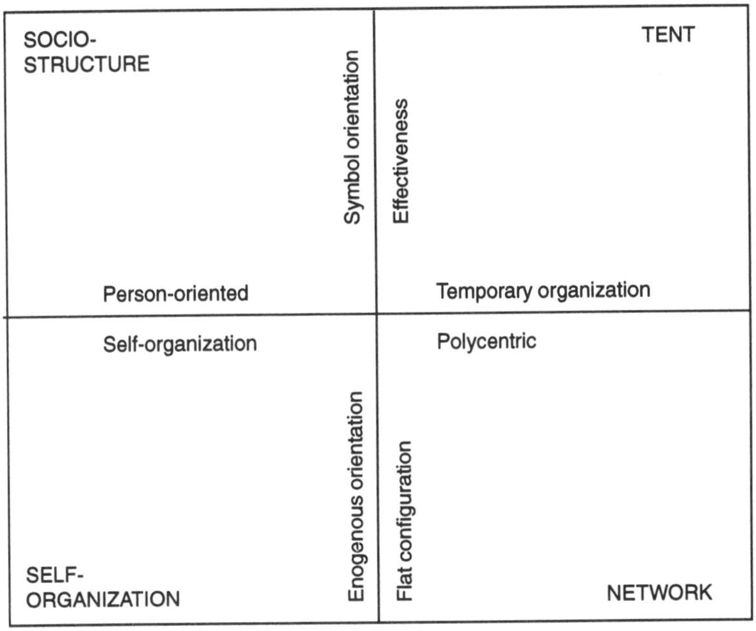

Figure 2.8 *Dimensions of a development-oriented organization*

The guiding philosophy here is to exploit the creative power inherent in the 'humane potential'. Human motivation is the driving force. Management in such an organization is 'distributed' and based on trust. This does not happen overnight; rather it is a reflection of a gradual development of the culture.

The purpose of an organization of this type is to overcome the *status quo* through visionary tasks and processes. The tendency in this form of organization is toward:

- Under-organization and a strong faith in symbol-oriented management.
- Ability to adapt by means of structural flexibility.
- Tension, clashes and extra work on account of many small, autonomous units.
- Innovations associated with healthy growth.
- Capacity for learning due to independence and motivation.

- Structural chaos.
- Organizational development based on the motto: 'Small is beautiful'.

The main strength of such an organization lies in its readiness for transformation in a complex, chaotic world.

Organizational dynamics

In concluding our description of the St Gallen concept, we will briefly touch on certain important aspects of the concept 'organizational dynamics' (or how organizations change character during the course of their existence). The idea did not originate with the St Gallen group; it is a theory that has been developed by a number of groups – albeit from a number of different angles (Lievegoed 1974, Greiner 1972, Elgin 1977 and Mintzberg 1989, to name a few).

The St Gallen group operates with four phases in an organizational development process:

- *The Pioneer Phase:* As a rule, a young and small organization, often with a strong, charismatic leader. Creativity is encouraged, and there are few formal procedures or structures. Odds of survival hinge either on the customer base or on an advantage in technology or human capacity.
- *The Growth Phase:* The market is exploited; a differentiation (and often an internationalization as well) occurs. Likewise, a development of internal culture and 'image' takes place. The organization is expanded, the manager's predominant position weakens, and professional management takes over. The founder assumes a normative function.
- *The Mature Phase:* The organization is well established and fully exploits its potential. This is partly due to previous efforts, but also to professionality and effective management. Toward the end of this phase, the benefits decrease and a certain amount of complacency sets in, as well as an orientation toward 'the good old days' and an increasing lack of flexibility. More extensive standardization and ever-higher levels of managerial energy are also used in the interests of harmony.
- *The Changing Phase:* The organization is at a cross-roads. It could be facing a phase in which the company trims down and eventually goes out of business. So no new investments are made in new product development, the organization shrinks, customers lose confidence in the organization, and profits are largely the result of previous investments.

The organization can also overcome recessions through renewal and a reorientation toward new possibilities. The establishment is called into question, and a restructuring becomes necessary. A partial break with tradition occurs, an effort is made to achieve greater flexibility and professionality, and attempts are made to strike a balance between being and changing.

Through practical organizational development work and theoretical studies of organizations of different kinds in various phases, the St Gallen group has developed a theory of organizations undergoing change. We will return to this in Chapter 5 (Theories of Change).

Criticism of the 'integrated perspectives'

It is not customary to regard Mintzberg, Senge and the St Gallen group's work as a unit. They are actually quite different; nevertheless, they all represent an attempt to understand the pervasive complexity of organizations. This comes across most clearly with Mintzberg and Gomez (St Gallen). Senge is more *normative* in his orientation toward the 'learning organization'.

Senge takes a normative approach as his point of departure. He sees the necessity of changing present-day organizations in the direction of 'organic', 'introspective' units in which a fundamental process of reflection and learning is the driving force in the organization. Actually, he represents a modern 'humanistic perspective'. His five 'disciplines' have a spontaneous conviction about them, and yet they are based more on an analysis of personal experiences and are to a lesser extent the result of empirical investigations.

His frequently unexpected and somewhat self-contradictory statements about 'systemic thinking' are also interesting, but they stimulate our thinking more than they define systemic thinking. We actually know very little about what it means in practice (despite the fact that his many examples from companies provide good illustrations). I am not sure that it all adds up – at any rate, not in every type of organization.

Senge's work is important because it has something to say about the important relationships of the processes that develop a 'learning organization', which should be of particular importance for schools.

Mintzberg, in many ways, is a 'contingency theoretician'. He has developed an interesting analysis model that embraces a number of the perspectives we have mentioned in this chapter. His model is rational and holds promise of a number of exciting analyses of the forces that affect an organization's life.

He has himself criticized a simplified interpretation of 'configurations', and no doubt feels that the seven forces work as a constant, dynamic process, and that it is the *balancing* of these forces (all of which are good and necessary) that produces a good organization.

The danger of his model is that it is based on one-sided rational thinking, with very little room for the symbolic perspective.

Gomez (St Gallen) contributes the most comprehensive analysis apparatus we have presented in this chapter. This apparatus deals with a number of organizational dimensions and represents, as does Mintzberg's work, an efficacious rational analysis. The difference is that in Gomez's model, 'symbol orientation' is also represented.

This model is based on a large body of empirical research. Nevertheless, the *composition* of the dimensions bear the hallmarks of *intuition*. The same is true, of course, of most models. Here, however, there is a vast potential for alternative interpretations. For example, it is not a foregone conclusion that all eight dimensions, in which each dimension is represented by two *polar* quantities, are truly unambiguously opposite dimensions.

We have a choice, for example, between 'person orientation' and 'issue orientation'. Are these necessarily *opposite* quantities? Or can they (as, for example, in Burns and Stalkers' contingency model) rather be regarded as two *parallel* forces (there can be a lot of both, a little of both, much of the one and little of the other). Consequently we will make use of the model guardedly. Otherwise we might fall for the temptation to believe that we have actually 'understood organizations'!

Chapter 3

The School as an Organization

THEORIES AS A FRAME OF REFERENCE

Each of the organizational perspectives just described are nothing more than tools, ways of looking at reality, kinds of windows. They let us look out, but only in one direction. Each new window broadens our perspective, but each window also has its limitations, or frames, which create blind-spots. As we give priority to one perspective, we will gain in one sense, gaining a deeper understanding from one angle; at the same time, however, we lose information and other insights.

Some people only experience life from one perspective. All their life they have looked at reality through one window. They know the view well. On the basis of their experience, they can intuitively interpret any change that takes place. The things that happen give these changes meaning. *They become reality*. Yet some people forget that there are other windows. For some, it is too threatening to view reality through another window. We act daily on the basis of our understanding of reality – on the basis of what we can interpret personally from our subjective point of view.

In my opinion, a study of school improvement should first and foremost provide us with new perspectives on the school system and society. If we are to infuse our experiences with new meaning, we will need to discover our own frame of reference – and take time to acquaint ourselves with alternative perspectives. That is why we are now going to use these alternative perspectives as a tool in our search for our own frame of reference, and as a means of gaining insight into the way other people think of schools and their development.

In the rest of this chapter I will refer to a number of research projects that have attempted to highlight characteristics of the school as an organization. I will also use the organizational theories previously presented as a point of departure for the analysis.

What do I mean by the term *characteristics*? First, that there are aspects that can be said to be typical of most schools; second, that these characteristics represent stable, long-term trends; third, that they are central aspects of what we mean by the term 'the schools'. In previous works I have pointed out a few such trends (Dalin 1978).

1. *Unclear goals.* The goals are often general, unclear and frequently in conflict with each other.
2. *Vulnerability.* Schools are heavily dependent on financial support, and seldom have recourse to self-determination.
3. *Low integration.* Teachers work on their own in their classrooms. There is little co-operation between classes, levels and schools.
4. *Weak knowledge base.* We know little about classroom teaching and learning. Unlike some other organizations, the schools do not have a predictable technology.
5. *Lack of competition.* Schools exist no matter what happens (more or less), and their existence is not based on the quality of their 'production'; thus, schools do not compete for tasks (or only rarely, and then only among certain types of schools).

What this list of 'characteristics' shares with other lists of its kind is that it is only partly based on empirical research. There are several ways of arriving at a list of characteristic properties of schools. Sarason, for instance, used a method he called 'Naive observation', speculating how a being from outer space would perceive our schools if he were looking down on them from space (Sarason 1971). Others have employed a more speculative analysis. Elboim-Dror has come up with a type of 'dependency map' (see Figure 3.1) that indicates how certain variables appear to 'hang together' (Elboim-Dror 1970).

Several of the variables that researchers work with are the same. However, the point of departure often varies, a number of potential causal relationships are excluded, and the models end up with a number of dependent variables. If we had included models from other perspectives, we would have found even greater variation. The organizational perspective we use to view the schools will, in other words, characterize our own point of departure, the factors we work with and the 'characteristics' we end up with.

PERSPECTIVES ON THE SCHOOL AS AN ORGANIZATION

There are several aspects of the school as an organization that have been dealt with in the literature (see Miles 1980; Dalin and Rust 1978, 1996):

- Goal conflicts.
- Goal shifts.
- Standardization of teaching.
- Quasi-professional teacher role.
- Decision-making authority (administrative/pedagogical).
- Little student authority over decisions.
- Little parental participation.
- Isolated teachers.
- Loosely connected units.
- Strong supervision of students.

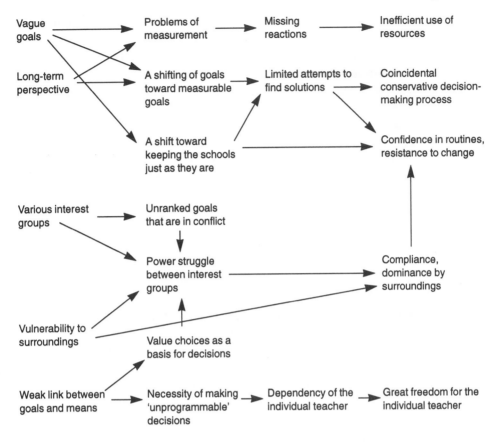

· Figure 3.1 *Characteristics of schools (from Elboim-Dror)*

- Little supervision of teachers.
- Little institutional control.
- Guarantee from the surroundings.
- Informal evaluation from the surroundings without direct consequences for the school system.
- The central role of ideology.
- The poor state of innovation.
- Lack of systemic thinking.
- Conflict between 'system configuration' and the individual 'school configuration'.
- The difficulty of evaluating school activity.

No single perspective on organizations can capture *every* aspect of the school as an organization. However, each perspective can *contribute* to an understanding of the school as an organization, as follows.

The *structural perspective* is concerned with the effectivization of the work processes. These processes will not change unless changes take place in the *surroundings* and/or in the *technology*. As it is, both things are happening, and in a somewhat dramatic manner at that. With the development of new microtechnology, society is undergoing rapid change. There is a demand for a better and 're-qualified' workforce, and there are demands that the schools 'follow up'. *Faith* in the new technology is about to create new conditions for change in the teaching process, at least in some subjects. There is still a long way to go, but computers are in use in most schools today, which will gradually bring about a change in a number of educational traditions – including the roles of teacher and student.

If schools were to oppose necessary changes in the teaching process, 'structuralists' would seek recourse in changes in the system of management. One option would be, for example, to give the parents increased influence. With this, 'market control' is introduced, for example through 'educational vouchers' that provide freedom of school choice, or a free system of options, as in the Netherlands.

The *humanistic perspective* is concerned with how human resources are utilized in schools, and recognizes the need for radical changes in the division of roles, influence and forms of co-operation, in particular to involve students in active, participatory roles. This will not happen unless a thorough change in attitudes and behaviour takes place first. It can only happen through school-based developmental work, where the parties develop ownership with respect to the various solutions. The work will also have to be on each school's own terms. Organizational development is the answer.

The *political perspective* is concerned with the distribution of resources and the power of the various interest groups over the school system. From being concerned with external circumstances (e.g. equality of supply), spokespeople for this perspective are more and more concerned with the *internal* distribution of resources and the dynamics which lead to a distorted distribution of learning possibilities. They are faced with a dilemma: while it is vital to defend the *teachers* in a society which, relatively speaking, is in the process of downgrading 'the soft sector', it is also vital to work for the rights of *students* internally (which can occasionally conflict with teacher traditions).

This perspective is not based on volunteerism. If there is to be a redistribution of power, it is going to have to happen by force. This can happen if society changes the internal rules of the game – which could lead to an increase in student power. Since we know that it is the most resourceful parents who influence schools, it is hardly likely that the political Left will favour increased parental power. (For conservatives, the opposite is probably the case.)

The *symbolic perspective* is concerned with the *meaning* of what is taking place, with whether important functions are being taken care of, and with what it is that activities and processes symbolize. The decision-making process in the schools is vague and unclear, and the results are seldom satisfactory. This is typical of institutions with unclear goals, undefined technology, and expectations from the surroundings which often conflict with each other.

What parents really want are *guarantees* that their children will be safe, that they are learning what they are supposed to, and that the adults in the school environment are qualified. What are controlled are the formal aspects of the organization's life (e.g. teacher qualifications in the guise of approved teacher training, building standards, etc.) – because these are necessary symbols. Nobody asks what really happens – whether there is any connection between formal teacher training and teacher competence, whether students enjoy themselves most in buildings that have been 'officially approved' or not.

The demand for increased rationality and effectiveness will be sabotaged. However, this is not important. What *is* important is to give an *impression of quality* – and this is best done by using symbols that everybody agrees on. When this has been achieved, a peaceful working environment will have been created, which is a prerequisite for renewal. What would the 'integrated perspective' say?

Mintzberg would claim that the schools suffer from weak management, partly because of unclear goals and goal shifts. Much has been arranged for the *machine form* (standardization), but there are also strong forces at work for a *split form* (divided decision-making authority, isolated teachers, little institutional control, etc.). There is very little to be said on behalf of a dynamic form of innovation, and there is little to indicate that the schools in practice are approaching the *professional form*. The two 'catalytic' forces will probably be held in balance, but the ideology is based on co-operation (see Chapter 2).

Senge would be concerned with the fact that the *conditions* for developing the 'five disciplines' are disfavourable. 'Personal mastery' is at best a random process, one that is dependent on people; developing new 'mental models' seldom occurs in schools; few have productive forms of 'teach teaching'; and few develop common visions (see Chapter 2). The base for the 'learning organization' in schools is the learning process itself, that is a learning process that develops the individual's ability to think, that moves the student from 'knowledge to understanding' (Dalin and Rust 1996), that helps the student to discover, to create meaning, and to develop motivation for further learning. Unfortunately, many will say that the context for productive learning does not exist in most schools as we know them today (Sarason 1998). If the goal is 'deeper learning', our context is the learning organization.

The last organizational perspective we discussed in Chapter 2 was the work of the St Gallen group. Figure 3.2 illustrates how one can perceive the 'profile' of a school (dotted line), and as a contrast how one can perceive the school system.

Schools differ, but in their culture there are dimensions that can be recognized from school to school, to various degrees. Figure 3.2 illustrates my perception of a typical Norwegian primary school. The dotted line indicates that schools are closer to a 'network' structure than to hierarchies, and the main emphasis is on 'socio-structure' and self-organization, with an increasing degree of instability ('tent').

The profile for the school system leans towards many of the opposite values. It is a stable, relatively rigid, hierarchical structure with an emphasis on techno-structure and bureaucratic organization ('Outside' organization; see Chapter 2).

If we now return to Chapter 2 and compare the school system profile with the two contrasting models (the stabilizing organization versus the development-oriented organization, see pages 60–1), we see that the school system resembles the stable model, while the school profile (primary school) resembles more the development organization. This illustrates that the greatest challenge is system changes, and that there might be considerable conflicts between the system and individual schools.

As far as I know no empirical studies of schools using this framework have been carried out, and my perception as illustrated in Figure 3.2 might be wrong. Nevertheless it illustrates the use of an analytical tool that might be useful as we try to understand schools as organizations.

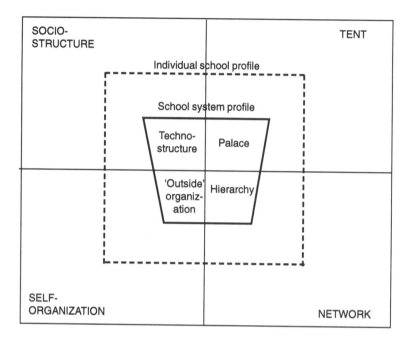

Figure 3.2 *The profiles of the school system and of the school*

A real-life situation built on empirical data would be more complex, more complicated. To understand a situation involving change, we need the ability to shift perspective several times in the course of the attempt. A specific perspective can be useful in one phase – while another perspective might prove more meaningful in another phase.

STUDYING THE SCHOOL AS AN ORGANIZATION

The five main perspectives discussed in Chapter 2 and in this chapter give us a glimpse of the dynamics that form part of the life of an organization. They are all simplifications – hence distortions – of reality. They can give us increased insight, but they can also blind us. In our view, there are three important principles in the study of the school as an organization:

1. *The school* – i.e. the individual school – is the point of departure for the study. It is also possible, and often useful, to study schools at the system level or at the individual level. In our view, the school is the unit for change. It is in the daily interaction between all the school's parties that the quality of the teaching is decided. Our focus must be the context of productive learning. However, it is important to understand systemic conditions, because they help determine the school's frame of action. Individuals are also essential to the analysis, because together they constitute the social community which forms the life of the schools (see the next chapter).

2. *Contingency theory* is our theoretical point of departure. We wish to study relevant aspects of the schools from the point of view of all five perspectives, but we do not want to make *a priori* claims that certain solutions are superior to other ones. Everyday school life depends on so many factors – some of which can be controlled, others cannot – that, in our opinion, it is impossible to maintain faith in 'the ideal solution'.

3. *Phenomenology* will therefore become the natural philosophy of science point of departure. Organizations must be viewed in the contexts in which they appear. Historical and cultural insight is crucial to an understanding of organizational phenomena. The external circumstances of the schools must be understood in the context in which they appear. Data only acquires meaning in the context in which it is created. Some of the knowledge thus gained will have importance beyond a specific case – but it is only when we understand the phenomenon that the theories acquire meaning.

FUNCTIONS IN ORGANIZATIONS

If organizations are to live, a number of functions must be safeguarded and developed. Not all functions are always equally important, nor is it the case that they must be performed in a specific way in order to achieve optimal results. But all organizations have certain tasks in common:

- *Production* – which deals with the way the work is carried out in order to achieve the organization's objectives. How productive is the learning process in our classrooms?
- *Management* – which deals with the way the organization is run, including planning, decision-making processes, co-ordination, guidance, development of an institutional culture, and communication between individuals and groups, the context of productive learning.
- *Development work* – which deals with the way needs are analysed, ideas are attended to, new things are discovered, and the way the development process is supported and carried out.
- *Information treatment* – which deals with the way information is obtained, how it is taken, accommodated and retrieved when necessary, how it is communicated, and how it is protected.

71

- *Evaluation* – which deals with the extent to which what is desirable is actually achieved, and whether what has been achieved is desirable, with what actually takes place, and with the extent to which what happens has the value we attach to it.
- *Legitimization* – which deals with giving a mandate to people and groups internally, and with working for general acceptance of the image of the organization we wish to maintain or promote.

MAIN DIMENSIONS

The functions briefly sketched above are carried out in relation to certain main dimensions within the organization.

Figure 3.3 illustrates the mutual dependency that we believe exists between five important dimensions of the school as an organization: *values, structures, relations, strategies* and *surroundings*. When we describe the relationship between these dimensions as mutual, this does not necessarily imply that they are connected in a mechanical, automatic or linear fashion. In some cases, changes in part of the system (e.g. altered work structure) result in changes within other parts of the system (e.g. relationships). In other cases the organization will, due to loose connections, protect itself from the consequences of change in one of the partial systems. Which connection releases mutual reactions, and the strength and direction of such reactions, can only be understood on the basis of a thorough knowledge of the dynamics of the individual school, among other things on how these functions are

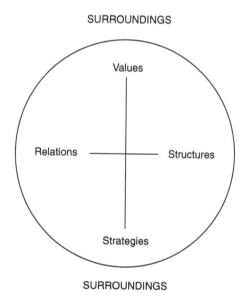

Figure 3.3 *The school as an organization*

safeguarded. In another context, we have discussed six schools that have been evaluated using this model as a point of departure. If the model is to be used in practice, a study of real-life situations (and preferably work with one or more schools) is required (Dalin and Rolff 1993).

We do *not* assume that the significance of some dimensions exceeds that of others. It is, for example, not necessarily the case that all changes have to start with changed values. It is just as possible that changed values, norms and attitudes are 'discovered' as a result of a new behavioural pattern. Likewise, crisis situations in the local community can lead to changes in the schools, but it is also possible that new thinking within a school can lead to reactions from the surroundings (e.g. the introduction of a new evaluation system). The individual dimensions in the organizational model have the following contents.

Surroundings

Where the schools are concerned, the term *surroundings* refers to both the local community and society at large, i.e. each person and organization in the surroundings that a school needs to have contact with in order to do its work. Schools are partly in a formal dependency relationship with certain institutions in their surroundings (the superintendent, the school board, the Department of Education, etc.); a mutual interaction is partly expected (e.g. with other institutions which are responsible for children and young people in the local community); up to a point, schools have an informal and non-binding relationship to people and organizations.

Most schools have a relatively large degree of freedom of action in relation to their surroundings. If a school generally manages to take care of the functions expected of it by parents and recipients, it will have great freedom to define its culture and form its day-to-day life. However, if a school breaks with expectations (often unspoken ones), with norms and traditions, and with our picture of what a school should be – then a counter-reaction will set in.

In relation to its surroundings, schools have to take a position on the following:

- How 'transparent' should schools be?
- Will a great degree of openness lead to influential forces 'taking over'?
- Should the boundaries to the surroundings be made so flexible that schools can 'open and close' as they see fit?
- Is there danger that the schools will isolate themselves to such an extent that they fall 'out of synch' with society?
- What can schools do to create a constructive relationship with their surroundings?
- What would the consequences be if parents and students had a free choice of schools?

A 'learning school' has creative and mutual links to its surroundings. This also applies to its relationship to the school hierarchy. We could regard the school administration as a kind of service organization. For example, it is possible to use existing rules in such a way that they *protect* a school from pressure from wealthy parents, and allow children from less privileged homes to take advantage of the school's resources. These children are usually not represented at parent-teacher meetings, and receive little support at home; they need school more than other children. If the schools were only to listen to active parents, the weakest children would probably have even fewer opportunities.

This illustrates the relationship between openness to the surroundings and the school's overall objectives. From the standpoint of short-term objectives, it would often be right to show a constructive openness to suggestions from parents and other people in the local community. The danger with this form of 'openness' is that one easily ignores the fact that different partners have a different degree of power and thus dissimilar opportunities for expressing their interests. School management (however we may define it) must be responsible for 'opening', or 'protecting' the schools from their surroundings. In our opinion, this should happen via open dialogue where, among other things, the dilemma presented in the example above is clarified.

This illustrates a major dilemma that non-profit organizations have in relation to market organizations. For the latter, the greatest possible openness and 'contact with customers' is crucial to the operation. The motto is 'The customer is always right'. For public institutions such as schools, which are meant to safeguard short-term and long-term learning needs, and which have clients who are often more concerned with the former than the latter, and which have as their aim the maintenance of *equality* of opportunities just as much as *high quality* standards, the task is far more complex.

School values

School values refers to the basic values (*Weltanschauung*) as they appear in ideologies, philosophies, ceremonies, and symbols. This dimension also refers to the formally expressed objectives as well as informal values and norms of school management, teachers, students, and others in the school community. This dimension has special reference to those values that are related to a view of learning and teaching.

As a rule, a broad range of values will be represented in a school. Often there are also conflicts between the formal objectives and the values that are represented, between practice and formal values, and between spoken values and practice. The real values of a school, the daily norms for behaviour, learning and upbringing are what actually drive school life. All schools should have as their goal to clarify values, appreciate differences in viewpoint and include all groups (also students) in the development of common values and norms. Any school depends on certain core common values (e.g. in the view of behaviour), while it can live with different views in a number of fields (e.g. the view of the teacher–student relationship). The task must be to clarify those areas where common values are necessary, creating common norms here, and understand and accept different attitudes and norms where the community agrees on freedom for each person or group.

The schools are also faced with a number of dilemmas in relation to *values*. It will be our perspective on organizations and change which decides our attitude to this dimension.

The *structural perspective* stresses the importance of value clarification and precision of goals. It is essential that there be no disagreement or conflict between groups, and that they all pull in the same direction. It is important to understand the consequences of values and goals, and that the organization is capable of assigning priorities to goals.

The *humanistic perspective* also stresses value clarification. Of major importance here is the fact that conflicts in values and goals can be resolved in such a manner that the human community is enriched, and that commitment, binding psychological contracts, and 'ownership' to the organization are created. With a basis in value clarification, it should be possible for everybody to define their 'membership' in such a manner that the energy is spent on the primary task of the organization. It then becomes unimportant to operationalize goals, because an open dialogue is a better aid when it comes to choosing direction and being flexible when necessary.

The humanistic perspective goes deeper into the values of productive learning. While the structural perspective is most likely to prefer standardized solutions to instruction (e.g. measured by standardized tests) because they appear efficient and can claim to measure 'high standards', the humanistic perpective will be concerned with the context and processes that stimulate motivation and creativity and will take into account the learning style of each individual learner.

The *political perspective* also stresses values and goals – but with a slightly different point of departure. Taking the schools as an example, we see clear differences: the political perspective with social democratic undertones stresses the fact that it is *society* that chooses the schools' values and goals. The task of the individual school community is to interpret the official objectives. In practice, it becomes important for values, goals and priorities to match the school's official objectives. This means that a number of interests must be 'held in check', or a local conflict of interest will break out that would harm the weakest members of the school community. These main points are probably shared by a bipartisan majority in Scandinavia.

The *symbolic perspective* is not concerned with official objectives. Rather, it is concerned with values that materialize through action. Value and goal clarification as a process can be seen as a ritual that may serve a useful purpose, because it brings the organization's members together; but clearer objectives do not cause organizations to end up with a better management tool. More important than discussing goals is *experiencing* values through action – and receiving confirmation that the organization is on the right track through the prevailing metaphors, symbols, and rituals.

The *integrated perspectives* we presented in the previous, as well as the present, chapter are concerned with different aspect of the 'value questions': from a 'non-profit perspective' it is important to assure that the needs and values of the members are

75

looked after. Is this at all possible without students and parents having more of a say? Can this be done without shifting the balance of services in favour of the more resourceful?

Senge would be concerned with the processes that clarify the actual values and the desired visions. Mintzberg describes organizations where ideologies take the upper hand ('missionary organizations'). He also shows how strong inner dynamics ('politics') can lead to a divided and 'politically-run' organization. In the former, values gain prominence and the map becomes more important than the terrain. If there is anything that doesn't fit, then at least it isn't the ideology that's the problem! In the latter, self-interest and power struggles gain prominence and create an intractable climate of conflict and unproductivity. A process that safeguards the debate on values and at the same time keeps an eye on these forces is essential in Mintzberg's analysis, and this is probably also of significance for several schools that strive with these very ideological conflicts.

Structure

This dimension refers to decision-making structure, task structure, and communication structure. The decision-making structure defines who makes decisions about what. The task structure defines how the work is divided between management, teachers and students. And the communication structure defines which people and groups will have dealings with each other (based on responsibility, tasks, schedules, etc.).

There is no ideal way for a school to organize its operations. Some structures are more useful than others under certain circumstances. It is only when we become acquainted with a school's objectives, its concept of learning, and its overall activities that we can assess the advantages and disadvantages of existing options. Every school needs to have effective structures that can organize its tasks. The structure must also maintain routines and traditions the school sets great store by. On the other hand, there must also be a flexibility that gives leeway for change. The dilemma lies in striking a happy medium between stability and renewal. Established structures often appear comforting. Too rapid change can appear to have a disintegrating effect. Any significant change requires a number of measures that protect the schools from unwanted negative effects, and which at the same time open the way for constructive measures that can create genuine renewal.

The schools are also faced with a number of questions and dilemmas related to *structure*:

- How rigid and how flexible should the structure be?
- What degree of dependency is necessary between teachers for the execution of their primary task?
- To what extent does the structure allow mutual learning and use of one another's resources?
- To what extent is it possible to work together and still leave room for autonomy?

- To what extent is the organization built on norms of competition or co-operation, and how does this affect the structure?

Although our term 'structure' primarily reflects a *structural perspective* on organizations, we also see the importance of questioning 'structures' that challenge a narrow definition of the term. It isn't until we see a *connection* between one dimension and the others that we will discover important ways of looking at the schools so that we can understand them as an organization.

Relations

This dimension refers to human relations in the school system as these are expressed in the informal organization (the power, influence, interaction, and norms of the individual and the individual group). This includes circumstances that contribute to the overall school climate (motivation, satisfaction, trust, support, collaboration, etc.). In addition, we include the individual person's sense of commitment to the schools and the quality of human relations, including the way conflicts are solved.

Circumstances in the schools are often reflected in the quality of human relations: relations between groups, including the relationship between teachers and students. Learning takes place through acting together. All schools should strive toward productive and good human relations. Often, however, problems in this area are easily regarded as *the* problem. The real problems might lie in unresolved value conflicts, in unsuitable structures, in relations with the local community or the authorities. So there are no simple ways to solve inter-human problems. The market is flooded with 'solutions' in these areas. The danger is that the symptoms alone will get treated, which doesn't help the schools on their way.

This area too has been fraught with problems and dilemmas that organizations must deal with:

- To what extent can the organization create a true sense of 'membership', even when the individual's values, personality and norms deviate from the usual ones (which is often the case in school)?
- How are emotions expressed? Are there emotions and forms of expression that are acceptable and others that must be suppressed, and is a difference made between boys and girls?
- Is it accepted that everybody can exercise influence? Are the members aware of how to do so, and are there acceptable and unacceptable ways of influencing events?
- Is the organization marked by a constructive openness and communication, or is energy blocked because people can't talk to each other?
- Have the schools established procedures for problem-solving and conflict-solving that are acceptable to everyone in the school community?

- To what extent have the schools worked actively with their own 'culture', climate, job satisfaction and responsibility?
- To what extent is it accepted that 'process questions' must have a place in the school's work just as much as 'product questions' do?

Strategies

This dimension refers to the way the school is run, to the mechanisms and methods for developing the schools, and to strategies for solving problems, making decisions, giving rewards and setting boundaries. It must be the school administration's task to find ways of creating a balance between the school's values, structures and human relations. It is also their task to find and develop suitable connections with the surroundings. In this book we are especially interested in school improvement. School administration has a unique responsibility here. In the next chapter, the topic of school leadership and school improvement will be examined more closely.

This dimension of organizational life also has a number of built-in problems and dilemmas:

- To what extent is the decision-making process clear to all the parties, and to what extent is it desirable that this process be clarified?
- What are the procedures and mechanisms for delegating decisions, and how are they followed up?
- Who has a real opportunity to influence decisions, and to what extent is the formal influence in accordance with the norms developed by the school?
- To what extent do the schools have the necessary expertise to carry out its tasks, to what extent is existing competence exploited, to what extent are skills appreciated, and to what extent are the schools ensuring development of expertise?
- To what extent are there sufficient resources for the schools to be able to discharge their responsibilities? Do the funds match the objectives, are the activities conducted where the funds are (and not vice versa)?
- Are the resources being used effectively?
- Have the schools established systems and procedures for school improvement that foster creativity, make room for changing practice, provide an opportunity for analysis and evaluation, and reward creative behaviour? And do the schools have a 'safety net' that can handle insecurity and conflict-ridden situations?
- Are the management functions being safeguarded (including the administrative, social and academic renewal functions), has the style of leadership been discussed, and is management promoting a positive view of co-operation and development?

It is sometimes useful to use all of the five perspectives presented in this chapter (and in Chapter 2) when looking into each of the dimensions in this model. This approach might suddenly reveal a possible relationship, a factor that may explain behaviour, or even a systemic meaning that explains organizational practices. And this level of understanding is often necessary to create meaningful interventions from within or from an external position.

Chapter 4

Leadership and Management Theory

Some of the studies we have been discussing in this book highlight the significance of leadership in the development process. In this chapter we will take a brief look at the role of leadership and its significance for school improvement.

'Leadership' is an ambiguous concept. The way in which leadership has been viewed in this century is closely related to the prevailing views on humanity in general, theories of organization, and theories of change. In this chapter we will begin by taking a look at various leadership and management theories in the light of the organizational perspectives we discussed in Chapters 2 and 3.

We will attempt to define, describe and analyse management at the system level and at the institutional (school) level. Our aim will be to clarify theories and concepts, not give practical guidance in management. Nevertheless, we will focus mainly on the head teacher, first by discussing the management functions that we consider central to a head teacher. Next we will provide a description and evaluation of the literature on the role of the head teacher in school improvement.

WHAT IS LEADERSHIP AND MANAGEMENT?

There are several definitions of leadership – all of which, as we shall soon see, are based on specific human and organizational outlooks. Most work is also related to organizations other than the schools (industry in particular). For each of the organizational theories we described in Chapters 2 and 3, there are one or more definitions of leadership.

Novotny and Tye distinguish between *leader* and *administrator* (Novotny and Tye 1973):

1. An *administrator* attempts to meet current goals and makes use of known methods.
2. A *leader* envisions new goals and encourages the use of new methods.

These two authors, whose work has primarily been in the field of school improvement, suggest that the following four dimensions are essential for a head teacher:

1. *Goal orientation:* The ability to focus on tasks and to structure one's work.
2. *People orientation:* The ability to create a healthy co-operative environment.
3. *Self-awareness:* The ability to appreciate one's own limitations while recognizing one's strong points, so that one can draw effectively upon one's own resources even while giving wide berth to others.
4. *Perspective:* The ability to project beyond one's daily work, understand the forces at work in society at large, exploit external resources, and have a broad view of one's work as a manager.

Lipham shares Novotny's and Tye's view on the distinction between administration and leadership. He defines leadership as taking 'the initiative in employing new approaches, so that organizations can reach their goals – or find new ones . . .' (Lipham 1964).

Milber and Lieberman point out the great expectations and the down-to-earth realities. A head teacher is supposed to:

* be a manager; in all probability he is an administrator;
* be a help; he is one who evaluates and makes judgements;
* share information with others; instead, he must keep information to himself;
* be democratic; in fact, he is authoritarian – at least at times;
* look after the individual; as a rule, he is only able to look after the organization;
* take a long-range view; as a rule, however, he thinks in an *ad hoc* way and acts in a spontaneous and context-specific way;
* be a renovator – one who renews; in fact, he is more like one who maintains the *status quo*;
* be someone with good ideas; instead, he is a master at working with specific issues (Milber and Lieberman 1982).

So it is more realistic to look at which *management functions* a school needs, and put together a team that will be able to satisfy them. At times, if the school is large enough, these functions can be filled by people in formal leadership positions. At other times it might be necessary – in fact, even preferable – to divide the functions among teachers and others. What management functions are important to fill in a school?

1. The administrative function

Organizing: Involves exploiting existing resources to the full (people, money, material, equipment) so that the school's objectives can be reached (the goals, that is, of both the organization and the individual). This in turn involves ensuring that the administrative rules and procedures are followed, that budgets are drawn up, and that routines are made increasingly efficient.

The decision-making process: Creating, developing and lending support to structures that create a common sense of responsibility for decisions that are made. Seeing to it that there is sufficient informational support for decisions, collecting information where that information is lacking, and knowing when it is necessary for a manager to make decisions on his own.

Delegating: Giving teachers, pupils and others a chance to develop by giving them responsibility. Entrusting certain matters to others so that the manager can concentrate on tasks he has to do. Creating a relationship of trust with others, which is a prerequisite for delegating.

Representation: Having contact with one's environment on behalf of the entire school, whether *vis-à-vis* the school system, other public administrative bodies, groups, or organizations where it would not be desirable to delegate this authority to others at the school.

2. The educational improvement function

Value clarification: Helping the school (teachers, pupils, parents and others) to clarify the various norms and objectives of individuals, groups, and the school as a whole. Clarifying one's own goals and communicating them to others. Assessing the school's *true* goals in relation to the school's *official* goals.

Development: Preparing a planning and development process that will be able to meet some of the needs that are brought sharply into focus in the debate on goals and values. Making sure that as many as possible are involved in the school's development work.

Guidance: Helping each teacher to master her own work situation and develop in the direction of those goals that teacher has set for herself and for the school. Observing the teachers in their work situation, responding to their behaviour, and comparing their work with the goals they have set for themselves.

Evaluation: Preparing plans for the evaluation of the school's activity (at all levels), or helping others to prepare the evaluation. On the basis of goals on which there is agreement (see above), criteria must be developed for achieving goals, different types of evaluation approaches must be prepared, and the information thus gained must be discussed, interpreted, and used in the process of renewal.

3. The social function

Motivation: Attempt to meet the individuals' needs in the school so that they will be inspired to do their best. Encourage and lend support in hard times.

Communication: Create structures and processes that lay the groundwork for an open two-way communication – on both the individual and group level. Ensure that each person has whatever information is necessary for working together, and create a climate in which the work of the school is perceived to be everyone's responsibility.

Resolving conflicts: Be able to discover and understand conflicts and find ways of resolving them. Be able to appreciate those values and norms that are at the root of conflict situations, when you are able to handle them.

Personnel care: Listen to individual problems. Try to be of help in personal crises, in difficult work situations and when hard choices must be made.

Leadership and management theories – a short review

Among the classical organizational theories, the 'Great man theory' was introduced by Thomas Carlyle (Carlyle 1910). He suggested that leaders distinguished themselves by certain traits, like physical strength, mental balance, energy, intelligence and creativity. During the First World War Ralph Stogdill, in a well-known study, found that isolated personal characteristics did not explain much, but a combination of traits, e.g. capacity, study skills, participation, status, and willingness to take responsibility, as well as the situation, could do so (Stogdill 1974). He later found that the factor he called 'situation' was the most likely to explain leadership. Eugene E. Jennings found that there was not a single personal factor that distinguished leaders from others (Jennings 1961).

With the humanistic perspective on organizations, a series of 'situation-dependent' theories of leadership was introduced. 'Leadership style' theories, for example the 'managerial grid' (Blake and Mouton 1964), were dominant. The main idea behind the grid was that the leader's style was dependent on the leader's concern for production on the one hand, and his or her concern for the workers on the other, the optimum style being high concern for both dimensions.

Another situation-dependent theory was developed by Tannenbaum and Schmidt (1957). It analysed the authority used by the leader and the amount of authority delegated to the group. The Midwest Administrative Center at the University of Chicago carried out a number of leadership studies (Getzels 1973) and distinguished between three leadership styles: (1) the nomothetic (rule and procedure oriented); (2) the ideographic (human relations oriented); and (3) the transactional (combination of the first two). Chris Argyris showed the dilemmas the leader could face if the distance between values and behaviour became too great (Argyris 1962).

With the work of Argyris the research field moved into behaviour theory, mainly influenced by the Ohio group, who among other things developed the instrument 'Leader Behaviour Description Questionnaire' (LBDQ). It built on the attitudinal model of Stogdill, but the orientation was changed from attitudes to behaviour.

A widespread contingency model in this tradition was developed by Hersey and Blanchard (1977), which related effective leadership behaviour to the 'maturity of the group', and thereby developed four major behaviour orientations.

In recent years 'role-theory' has dominated, for example as discussed by Mintzberg (1989). He has studied the relationship between what leaders do and the productivity of the organization. He has found that there are six mechanisms by which an organization is managed: (1) day-to-day informal co-ordination at the work level; (2) direct supervision; (3) standardization of work processes; (4) standardization of the product; (5) common goal orientation; and (6) standardization of knowledge and skills. Mintzberg finds that the management role depends on factors like the difficulty of the work, the way the organization is organized, and how co-ordination takes place. On the basis of his organizational theory, he develops ten different roles (see Chapter 2 for a discussion of Mintzberg, and Mintzberg 1989).

Paul W. Hersey, who built up the so-called Assessment Centres for school administrators (a project under the auspicies of the National Association for Secondary School Principals, NASSP), states that the following skills have been shown to be related to good school administration (Hersey 1982):

- The ability to plan and organize one's work.
- The ability to work together with others and to lead others.
- The ability to analyse problems and make decisions.
- The ability to communicate orally and in writing.
- The ability to understand the needs and anxieties of others.

School management is not just some *role* that can be exercised by one person. It covers a number of functional areas, in which the individual will have natural qualifications and development potential within certain functional areas more than in others. Much of the management training that has taken place has been a source of frustration for many school executives, because they have always returned with a sense of not measuring up. In fact, they don't, if the expectation is that they should be equally successful in all functional areas!

It is absolutely necessary to work with the concept of leadership teams, or a division of management functions in the particular group one is working in. However, this requires *trust*, the ability to *delegate*, and an appreciation of what *motivates* others to make an effort.

Trust, in this context, has a two-fold meaning:

1. *Motivation:* That I believe that the one I want to carry out an assignment for me has the right attitude – that is, that he or she will not abuse my trust or exploit it for their own purposes. I must feel sure that the one to whom I delegate does, in fact, share my objectives, or that I accept those of the other party.
2. *Competence:* At the same time, I must be sure that the one who gets the assignment is capable of carrying it out, that he has the requisite knowledge and skills, knows the limitations inherent in the situation, and knows how he should go about tackling difficult situations.

It sometimes happens that we delegate without first making sure that the foregoing conditions are present. It is sad indeed when a person in whom we have had personal confidence with respect to motivation turns out to be incompetent. It is not easy to come to grips with the situations which then arise. To take back an assignment that has already been delegated is a far more difficult thing than delegating it in the first place.

It can be just as difficult to assign a competent person a task if we should happen to find out that she is working toward other goals. Once more, it can be difficult to tackle such a situation. For most managers, it is just this kind of predicament that makes them reticent about delegating.

Delegating is a concept seldom understood, and we have already seen that it is hard to carry out in practice. It is possible, as we have shown above, to delegate tasks, including decision-making tasks. In certain situations it will be natural for someone other than the manager to make the final decision. In such cases, it is the decision-making authority that is delegated.

A school leader, one who leads an organization, has a certain formal responsibility. This involves, among other things, being answerable to superiors (for example, to a school superintendent). In actual fact, most head teachers have a wider degree of latitude with respect to their superiors than tradition would suggest; nevertheless, it is the head teacher who is formally responsible for what takes place in her school. *Responsibility cannot be delegated* – the formal responsibility in the hierarchical system, that is.

On the other hand, a school executive can delegate *authority* – that is, the right to carry out certain tasks and functions. She can give others authority to execute managerial functions, but she will, ultimately, be solely responsible to the outside world for all school operations.

If the head teacher is to delegate, she must not only be able to trust her colleagues, but these same colleagues must also be motivated to assume responsibility. One of the most well-known theories about motivation is Fredrick Herzberg's 'two factor theory' (Herzberg *et al.* 1959). He sought to determine the factors that led to well-being and motivation in work, and those that mitigated against need satisfaction in a work situation. Herzberg found that employees had two distinct types of need in their work situation. When people are unhappy with their job, they are, according to Herzberg, irritated over their work conditions. He called these 'hygiene factors'. When people are satisfied with their work, they feel as if they have accomplished something important, that they have developed something themselves, that their work is challenging, and that they receive recognition for what they do. Herzberg calls these factors 'motivation factors' (see Figure 4.1).

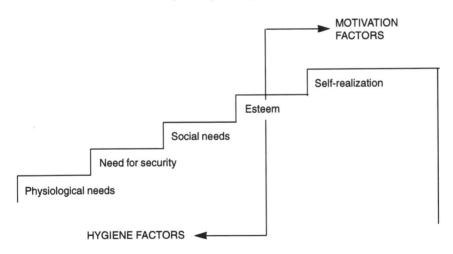

Figure 4.1 *Herzberg's two-factor theory and Maslow's needs hierarchy*

We have previously seen that teachers, as a rule, mention *external circumstances* in their work situation when they express what they feel should be changed (see Chapter 3). They mention such factors as greater resources, fewer pupils in the classroom, and other 'resource factors'. They seldom ever mention factors that have a direct bearing on their own work situation. Naturally, it is important to try to improve the external conditions (hygiene factors), because this can reduce dissatisfaction. But that is not to say that these same teachers will end up being happier with their work. This has to do with the need for self-realization, and this is influenced by those factors that Herzberg has called motivational factors (for example, recognition for work well done).

Being able to feel that you are in control of your own life is crucial to happiness. *So a functional division of leadership takes on double significance:* it helps implement the school management functions in a better way, and it provides more people with the potential for self-realization.

Some would object, saying that it's not quite that simple. Management will depend on whatever authority, power or influence one has. That is true, of course, but this is not necessarily related to people in hierarchical decision-making positions. It is essential to understand what these concepts involve:

1. Authority is the formal *right* to make decisions.
2. Power is the *ability* (not the right) to reward and punish.
3. *Influence* is the ability to have a decision carried out without resorting to authority or power.

As a rule, authority and power are related to positions, and influence is related to the personalities of individual people. This need not be the case, however. Certain pupils can have a great deal of power – so much, in fact, that they are in a position to block any and every attempt at carrying out decisions handed down by the school administration. Certain teachers might have a great deal of influence among their fellow teachers, perhaps because they carry a lot of academic weight.

Whereas authority is bound to specific formal positions, both power and influence are *distributed*. When delegating takes place, the pattern for who can exercise authority and power changes.

What conclusions can we draw, then, from our five organizational perspectives on management?

The *structural perspective*, more than any other organizational perspective, has been concerned with the importance of managing the organization. Most management theories, in fact, spring from this structural perspective. The primary aim is to develop a management role that can serve as a bridge between the organization and its environment, and between the different subsystems in the organization. The aim is more efficiency, better co-ordination, optimal use of resources, putting 'the right person in the right place', and making adjustments between the environment and the organization as both of these change.

The *humanistic perspective* is also very concerned with management and leadership roles. Here the main emphasis is on the significance management can have for personal development and interpersonal relationships. The manager should be able to release energy; therefore he should be sensitive, understanding, analytical, and should possess a number of interpersonal relationship skills. Those who have worked from the vantage point of this perspective are concerned with the processes that bind an organization together – or the glue that enables the organization to act as a unit. Management should, by its behaviour, bind the organization together so that it can better meet the needs of individuals, groups and the organization as a whole.

The *political perspective* has been concerned with the power dimension of leadership and management, and the search for a better balance of power in the organizations. There are, for example, schools without a head teacher. The purpose has been to distribute power, share leadership functions, and thereby utilize the leadership and management resources in the organization.

The *symbolic perspective* has been concerned with the symbolic value management has in the organizations, but we have seen very little in the way of management theory from those who have worked most actively with this perspective. The key element in the management concept is that the manager is a master of ceremonies. His main task is to understand which fundamental functions different ceremonies and myths have in his organization and manage these values in a confidence-inspiring way. At the same time, a manager must be able to exploit opportunities that might arise unexpectedly and exercise leadership.

The perspectives represented by Mintzberg, Senge and the St Gallen group are partly described by Mintzberg (1989), who also reminds his readers of the many myths that are connected with leadership (e.g. a high degree of rationality, effectiveness, use of information technology systems, and that management is a science). Senge is mainly concerned with innovative leadership and how management can encourage the learning process in an organization. The St Gallen group discusses various forms of leadership related to various organizational profiles and stages in the life of an organization.

The head teacher and school improvement

In the 1970s, the well-known American educational leader and scientist John I. Goodlad led an extensive research programme called IDEA. This was a research project that sought to understand the processes of change in American schools; a major part of the work was concentrated on the role the head teacher played in the development process. Goodlad concluded that: 'Basically, the principal was regarded as a strategic element in the development process. It would often happen that he or she was a *hindrance* to change, rather than a help' (Goodlad 1976).

A number of studies done in Great Britain show that the head teacher is a significant factor in school improvement. In a Department of Education and Science study of ten upper secondary schools, we find the following statement: 'The leadership provided by the head teacher was the one single factor that meant the most for the development of these schools' (Dept. of Education and Science 1977). Baker, too, shows the positive impact the head teacher can have on school improvement. He also shows that head teachers have ample opportunity to commit 'sabotage' – not by directly blocking the attempt, but by adopting a 'wait and see' attitude, by pleading neutrality and thus signalling scepticism toward those teachers who want to get cracking (Baker 1981).

The RAND researchers in the 'Change-Agent' study (see Chapter 4) came to a similar conclusion: the head teacher had a crucial influence on events in the execution phase. He or she had the power to stop an initiative (or, at the very least, set the stage for doing so), without necessarily having to resort to direct methods. But because the head teacher's control of resources and her power over personnel was so extensive, there was little that the staff could do to *counter* a head teacher's negative attitudes (Berman and McLaughlin 1975a).

In a study of 60 head teachers with 'very good reputations', Gorton and McIntyre found that the head teachers themselves felt that their prioritizing of development work came high on the list of important matters (in fact, they gave it the highest priority on a list of nine issues). Their teachers, on the other hand, felt that the priority was *not* that high; they rated it five out of nine of things their head teachers did (measured in terms of the amount of time they spent on each task) (Gorton and McIntyre 1975). Other results also show that the head teachers are not, in fact, as important to development work as they thought they were – *as seen from the teachers' perspective.* Both Aoki (1977) and Barrows (1980) found that head teachers play a peripheral role. In the first case, the issue was social studies; in the other case, the transition to more individualized instruction.

A number of studies show that the head teacher plays a modest role in school improvement. Other studies, however, show that head teachers do pass on ideas to their staffs. It would appear that the demands for stability and tranquility in the school force the head teacher into an administrative function, away from an academic managerial function (Crowson and Porter-Gehrie 1988).

This is confirmed by a number of studies of head teacher behaviour. Head teachers must often take charge of disciplinary matters and teachers' needs unrelated to classroom instruction; they must also concern themselves with practical details such as filling out forms, etc. on account of bureaucratic demands, as well as act as inspectors and supervisors, serve as liaisons to outside parties (Peterson 1988) and manage a turbulent school day.

Dan Lortie (1975) feels that there are many reasons why the head teacher at an American school (his subjects were head teachers in Chicago) tends to uphold the *status quo*: first, it has to do with recruitment and socialization. The head teachers are recruited from the ranks of teachers; they have very little alternative experience; they have learned that it rarely pays to stake out new paths; and they know that they must meet with acceptance on the part of their colleagues. Second, a head teacher has few reward options, and he or she is completely dependent on acceptance if any change is to take place. It is difficult to convince teachers that changing things will 'pay'. Quite simply, we know too little about what constitutes good teaching practice, and most teachers know that reforms mean extra work.

Third, the head teacher is under constant pressure from his or her superiors and local environment. The bias toward standardization is great. There is an unwritten rule which says that one must not do anything that would create an imbalance or the potential for disparity. But the fact of the matter is that most development processes do create 'imbalance', and restrictive rules mitigate against individual schools developing something that they really want.

Fourth, Lortie feels that the head teacher's career prospects depend on whether he or she is well liked in all quarters – among teachers, superiors, and parents. An innovative head teacher has to take chances; it is all too easy to step on toes, and doing so can scotch one's chances for advancement: 'Wasn't so-and-so the one who rocked the boat last year?' can be one of the factors that make advancement impossible. Lortie's conclusion is that head teachers are, by necessity, careful managers, and Fullan feels that at most, only one out of ten Canadian head teachers is a 'dynamic agent of change' (Fullan 1988).

Seymour Sarason, in an earlier study, came to a similar conclusion (Sarason 1982). He is concerned with the fact that head teachers have a narrow background and have been 'socialized' into a careful management role. He is also concerned about the fact that our perceptions of 'the system' and what it can do, regulates our behaviour. So as a rule, head teachers take few chances. Usually, however, a head teacher has a lot more freedom than he or she suspects, and empirical data show that head teachers (within the same system) differ markedly, which would suggest that 'the system' can accommodate far more than many head teachers believe.

Nevertheless, the head teacher can play a crucial role, especially by legitimizing a given school improvement process. Berman and McLaughlin found that one of the best indicators that a head teacher was genuinely interested in a project was whether he or she took part *together with the teachers* in seminars and planning meetings (Berman and McLaughlin 1975a). When a project did not have the moral support of the head teacher, it was in trouble.

Gene Hall has also done a number of studies of head teachers in schools in which he has observed teachers in school improvement. He puts it this way:

> In those cases in which the teachers manifested the greatest anxiety about the administrative sides of a project, their head teachers were not actively participating in the work . . . Execution is directly dependent on the head teacher's actions (Hall *et al.* 1980).

Hall points out the head teacher's role in the *administration* of a project. Some head teachers were too quick to delegate administrative responsibility, and the project ran into trouble ('delegating style', according to Hersey and Blanchard). Teachers mistook this for a lack of interest: 'Our head teacher doesn't follow up – in other words, he isn't very concerned with what we are doing' was typical of the reactions Hall observed.

In later studies, Hall took a look at the various roles the head teacher played in school improvement and also what roles other people in 'the management team' played (Hall 1988, Hord and Hall 1987). His criterion is the following: What can the head teacher do that will help teachers succeed in carrying out classroom reform? In an intensive one-year study, the head teachers of nine elementary schools were monitored, and the investigators found that the head teachers played one of three roles: *initiator, innovation manager,* or *supporter.*

In these studies they found (much to their surprise) that in each case there was at least one additional person who played an important leadership role alongside the head teacher (formally or informally). In schools that succeed with processes of change, there proved to be, in reality, a 'team of leaders' which – as a unit – represented the attitudes and skills required for the success of such processes in the organization. This is perfectly consistent with experiences IMTEC has had with school improvement over the past twenty years (Dalin and Rolff 1993).

Leithwood reminds us that the manner in which the head teacher participates is crucial to the results. He distinguishes between facilitative and directive managers. The former would set certain goals and then leave the follow-up and support to the teachers. The latter made most of the decisions where it concerned the content of the project and subsequently tried to bring the teachers on board. He shows that in a number of cases it was the first kind of head teachers that were the most effective, even though it might seem that they were not involved all that much (Leithwood *et al.* 1978).

Leithwood and Montgomery (1982) have conducted management research in schools for many years. They have come up with an extensive conceptual frame-work and a theory about the role of the head teacher. The so-called 'head teacher profiles' are detailed and comprehensive; the most 'effective' in the view of the authors, however, is 'the Problem Solver' – of whom there are few in the Canadian schools.

Matthew B. Miles, in a number of his studies, has investigated the role of the head teacher. Louis and Miles find, for example, that there are at least three main motives for the manager to work with changes:

1. To conceive a vision for the school.
2. To create a common sense of ownership for what is being changed, where the school should be headed and how.
3. Create a recurring planning process that can capture the learning that takes place in the development process (Louis and Miles 1990).

In an earlier work, Miles found that an effective 'change manager' was able to combine two contrasting attitudes: placing clear demands on one's colleagues and on oneself on the one hand, and giving relevant support throughout the entire process of change on the other (Huberman and Miles 1984).

In his studies, Michael Fullan has thoroughly discussed the head teacher's role in these processes of change (Fullan and Stiegelbaum 1991). He is particularly con-cerned with how the old theories about the head teacher as the rational and strong manager in an orderly world is an irrelevant paradigm. In the uncertain world of today, we need another paradigm.

Most of the studies done on the role of the head teacher are to be found in North American literature. However, studies are beginning to be done in other parts of the world – Europe and Australia in particular (see, for example, Chapman 1991). The most long-standing tradition is in Great Britain. Weindling and Earley, for example, have studied the first years of a head teacher's practice and find, in contrast to the North American studies, that British head teachers are quite active in attempts to revitalize the schools. They take initiative, make demands, and are supportive of the process. Weindling and Earley find, for example, that most British head teachers are at the highest level in the 'profile chart' that Leithwood and Montgomery have developed (see above). Weindling and Early explain the discrepancies between Great Britain and North America by pointing out that they have studied head teachers who have just started out; but they also point out that British head teachers have a great deal more power and room to manoeuvre than their American counterparts (Weindling and Early 1987).

This raises the question of how culturally dependent studies about management really are. We need *multicultural* studies to be able to answer this. Hofstede has carried out a fundamental study of employees' attitudes to management and to change, and shows that there are fundamental differences. We feel, for example, that there are basic differences between what is perceived as good management in Scandinavia compared to the USA, and that this is bound to have a bearing on the role of the head teacher in school improvement (Hofstede 1991).

It also strikes us that most studies about school management that we have mentioned are based on an image of the head teacher in a rational world. Perceptions of the ideal head teacher do not vary all that much. There are relatively few school management alternatives in the literature.

One of those who has helped create an alternative theory for management in the schools is Patterson. He starts with the assumption that organizations do not follow an orderly logic but rather that the development is often paradoxical and conflicting – albeit understandable. He suggests that managers must work with three strategies simultaneously: to lead the development of the school's culture, to carry out long-range stategic planning, and to motivate the teachers for the work ('empowerment'), (Patterson *et al.* 1986).

More generally, 'middle management' today labours under a strong pressure of expectations, and many feel that the job is impossible. And so Block has developed a radical concept that he calls 'The empowered manager'. The development, according to Block, is now away from a tighter control toward a more 'entrepreneural' spirit. This, in turn, means more responsibility, that one is held accountable, that one takes professionalizing seriously, and that positive visions are absolutely necessary for progress. According to Block, the choice is between maintenance of a system that does not work, and a new system in which management assumes responsibility for developments. He summarizes his viewpoints as follows:

... The key to 'positive policies' is to regard every contrast as an opportunity to support autonomy and create an organization the way we want it. This means that we look upon ourselves as agents for creating a better culture. Cultures change in many ways, but rarely by means of dramatic dictates from above. To await signals from above only causes us to lose our chance. If we are to have a better future, we must assume personal responsibility ... (Block 1987)

Our conclusions from this brief description and analysis of research into the head teacher's role is that the management style can vary, that 'effectivity' is context-sensitive, that *interaction* with others (and the sharing of responsibility for innovation) is essential, but that the most important thing – *what management ought to be in a world of rapid change* – is only now beginning to be defined. And as we have seen, it must be defined in relation to the dynamic reality that the schools as an organization and system are confronted with. Furthermore, it must be defined at every level in relation to the organizational concept that is to be the norm for the system's actions.

Chapter 5

Theories of Change

Discussions about school improvement usually revolve around the goals toward which it is aiming – or around *what* should be changed. The mass media have helped create the impression that something is wrong with the schools, that there is something in need of changing. The discussion is usually about what the tasks of the schools should be. The dividing lines are political; to some extent, they are also ideological and philosophical. This is an important debate.

In this context we shall take a look at another aspect of school improvement – namely, how it is planned, developed and carried out. For every suggestion for school improvement there are several views on how change should take place. Here too, among other things, it is a question of different values. Research that we will be presenting in this chapter shows unequivocally that quite a few proposals for renewal either remain untried, get altered in the process, or are simply resisted. The way in which school improvement takes place is often more decisive for the results than what the changes are all about.

Whether it is a teacher who plans to make changes in her classroom teaching, a head teacher who is working on changes in the organization of the school, a guidance counsellor who is working together with teachers to assist student learning, a superintendent who wants city-wide renewal, or a person situated in the political or administrative centre who favours reform – all are faced with the same basic question: how can change best be brought about in the schools?

The assumptions upon which school improvement is built are seldom clarified. They are often just as diffuse for those who are responsible for the work. Nevertheless, they are compelled to form opinions about a number of 'process questions' such as 'How will teachers/pupils react?', 'What are the most important factors in getting the job done?', 'Who should get involved?', 'How can we foster a collective sense of ownership with respect to the project?', and 'What will it all cost?'

These more pragmatic questions depend, in turn, on our attitude toward more basic questions, such as: 'Is a human being a passive individual that wants others to prepare the way for change, or is being involved in the development of a better future an expression of a basic human need?', 'Will we be willing to accept changes that do not serve our own personal interests?', 'Is participation a good thing, or does it hamper effective leadership?', 'Do we need more concrete knowledge about the daily life of the schools before we can change it, or do we know more than enough already?', 'Should we assume that most reforms are fraught with political and normative conflicts and that, as a result, power is a prerequisite for change?', 'Will central control of school improvement provide the best protection against pernicious effects?', and 'Isn't the whole issue of school improvement such a risky venture in the first place that it could wind up spoiling pupils' academic development?'

The answers we give to these and other questions will determine our views on what we wish to recommend, both on the *content* of reform, but especially the *manner* in which we proceed. In reality, we are up against a general problem: how do changes in social systems occur?

This chapter deals first with *definitions* of school improvement. Second, a number of general *perspectives* and *theories* of change are presented. Third, we review what empirical research can tell us about school improvement. And finally, we present our own perspectives on school improvement.

SCHOOL IMPROVEMENT – DEFINITIONS

Concepts such as 'change', 'renewal', 'innovation', 'reform', 'pedagogical develop-ment work', 'trials', and 'educational improvement' are often used interchangeably in everyday language. There is little agreement on clear definitions for these terms.

During the 1960s, Havelock made an attempt to distinguish between 'innovation' and 'change' (Havelock 1971). His main argument was that 'innovation' involved an improvement of the system, whereas 'change' only involved an alteration which did not necessarily imply an improvement. Even though at the time we agreed with Havelock that a clarification in this area was long overdue, we also pointed out that the kind of distinction he was making might easily lead to a superficial understanding of 'innovation' (Dalin 1973). Our own definition of innovation was 'a well-considered attempt at improving practice with respect to stated goals'.

What we were after was the kind of definition that defines 'innovation' in terms of *a renewal process*. But for us, it was far from clear that an innovation constituted an improvement for everybody. 'Better' for whom? It is just as important to understand who has benefited by a particular innovation as it is to define precisely what the improvement itself consists of.

This is an important discussion, because the term 'innovation' has positive connotations and is related to the technological sector. We are virtually convinced that next year's car models will be better than this year's! The fact that innovations – even in the technological sector – can result in serious, unforeseen effects, can have tragic consequences in the fields of medicine, pharmacology, chemistry and agriculture – not to mention the effects on the environment – has been amply proven in recent years. It is important for us to understand that most innovations entail costs.

This is especially the case in the field of education, where goals are often diffuse and mutually conflicting (cf Chapter 3). Short-term goals are not necessarily in accord with more long-range goals. For this reason it is very difficult to discover (and virtually impossible to measure) the unintentional effects of 'innovations'.

The consequences of this view must therefore be that it is problematical to distinguish between 'change' and 'renewal'. An uncritical use of the terms 'innovation' and 'renewal' could easily lend legitimacy to a development process on false premises. It has practically been taken for granted that the 'innovative' activity is bound to promote better schools because, after all, isn't 'renewal' what it's all about?

Many different attempts have been made, also in recent years, to define the term 'school improvement'. The most comprehensive definition appears in the book *Making School Improvement Work – A Conceptual Guide to Practice*, which is one of the results of OECD's International School Improvement Project, from which the following excerpt is taken:

> 'School improvement' is a systematic, sustained effort aimed at change in learning conditions and other related internal conditions in one or more schools, with the ultimate aim of accomplishing educational goals more effectively. (Velzen, Wim G. van *et al.* 1985, p. 48)

These authors stress that:

- In the matter of change, school improvement takes aim at the school *as a whole* (changes in personnel or in a single classroom don't qualify) – the programmes must be *systematic* and extend over a period of time.
- Changes apply to all aspects of the school (structures, processes, and climate).
- Changes must take account of the many factors related to a specific pedagogical change (circumstances within the organization, personnel, finances, equipment, and use of time).

This definition is strongly reminiscent of a *rational* view of organization and of change. The authors call our attention to the fact that the parties might well disagree about whether a specific change would be for the better, but they counter by saying:

> This question simply cannot be resolved ... It needs to be viewed as part of a broader policy for school improvement (and measured against it). A clear formulation of the goals of school improvement will help us in doing a better job of defining our strategies.

They also claim that a 'good school improvement process' depends on a consensus on goals, which should be clarified early on.

This is probably the most apolitical definition of school improvement to appear in recent years. Hans Tangerud and Erik Wallin, in another context, make a distinction between two different types of school improvement:

- Changes made within the scope of existing goals and that are made without altering basic values and goals. Changes of such a nature are directed toward technicians and methods and aim at increasing effectiveness under prevailing conditions.

- Changes whose aim and object is to alter existing goals and organizational assumptions (Tangerud and Wallin 1983).

In his studies of organizations, Pfeffer states that design (and change) are not a question of 'which causes', but of *'whose* causes' (Pfeffer and Salanick 1978). Bolman and Deal state: 'There is no such thing as permanent renewal. There are winners and losers today, and there will be winners and losers tomorrow as well. In such a world, change comes about when significant changes in the balance of power take place' (Bolman and Deal 1984).

The OECD project's definition of school improvement builds, as we have already said, on a *rationalistic* view of organizations (Chapter 2) and most closely approaches what Ernest House has called *the technological perspective* of change (see later in this chapter). The other definitions represent a *political* view of organizations and of change.

And yet it is not really clear just what the OECD Report is actually saying (the book consists of contributions from several authors). For example, in the concluding chapter, Mats Ekholm and Matthew B. Miles state the following:

- 'In general, the meaning of improvement varies not only according to the educational context of a particular effort, but also according to the context – the web of political, social, economic, cultural and demographic factors ... What is considered an improvement depends on the values of the participants ...' (p. 269).
- 'There is no universal norm that could define what is "better" for a school. It is a question of values, as well as other factors relevant to the situation ...' and 'that we must consider for *whom* the benefits of school improvement occur' (p. 267).

A number of scientists claim that organizations are neither rational nor political – they can best be described as symbolic (see Chapter 2). Adherents of this perspective say that changes occur for many reasons. The participants try to do things in a better way, and they are engrossed in a ceremony that is *called* change. When the ceremony is over, the participants are left to ponder the following:

- What went wrong?
- What was important?
- What gained legitimacy?

Furthermore, Bolman and Deal claim that the ceremony is often very satisfying: 'Old problems, new blood, outside expertise, and important questions are all brought to the mat, where they collide and merge to become new myths and new doctrinal tenets' (Bolman and Deal 1984).

Such a view of change differs from the rationalistic and the political. Although it closely resembles House's *cultural* view of change, it represents, first and foremost, what Bolman and Deal call the *symbolic* organizational perspective (see Chapter 2).

In other words, it is simply not possible to agree on a definition of school improvement without sharing a common view of organizations – which in turn is based on one's views of humanity, society, and learning. In the deepest sense of the term, school improvement is a question of *values*. And so we have to live with the fact that what for some people is truly meaningful, is of little importance for others. There are countless examples of teachers who are exasperated with meddling politicians. On the other hand, there are politicians who feel that 'the schools are at a standstill', even though the teachers are struggling with internal improvement efforts which they consider to be of major importance and yet difficult.

Attempts at renewing the schools must be weighed against the *values* which the schools are supposed to administer. These are found in universal goals and norms, but they are hardly ever *realized* in individual schools so that those concerned make these values their own. In Volume 1 of this series we pointed out the necessity of developing *visions* for the school system as a whole, and for the individual school. The schools' mission is *long-term*. They are supposed to prepare children and young people for a new and different world in the twenty-first century. Fundamental questions are at stake (see Dalin and Rust 1996).

The schools have had to cope with one wave of 'innovations' after another over the past 50 years – all of which, as a rule, were developed with the very best of intentions, whether they originated within or outside the system. But they have generally represented only a small part of the whole; they have served short-term interests and rarely ever been evaluated in terms of the school's basic value system. Professional teachers have often – with good reason – resisted so-called reforms (see our discussion of 'barriers' below).

School improvement has only one justification: that it should lead to a better school for pupils and teachers alike – in practice; and in our opinion, it is not all that important *how* this takes place. If we take a rational view of things, we will naturally try to arrive at as systematic a process as possible – and this has often produced results. If we look at the world from the perspective of conflicts, we will try to reach our goal in a political way. This, too, has led to renewal. As we shall see, there are also other ways of understanding the school as an organization – and subsequently also several alternative ways of developing the schools.

The School Improvement Research Group at the Institute of Education, University of Cambridge, has developed a pragmatic definition of school improvement which comes close to our perspectives (Hopkins *et al.* 1994, p. 3):

> [We] regard school improvement as a strategy for educational change that enhances student outcomes as well as strengthening the school's capacity for managing change. In this sense school improvement is about raising student achievement through focusing on the teaching-learning process and the conditions which support it. It is about strategies for improving the schools' capacity for providing quality education in times of change.
> (Hopkins 1994)

This approach leads to some liberating ways of thinking about change. Schools, and those who live out their daily lives within them, are no longer the victims of change, but can take more control of the process. By using the opportunity of external change as a stimulus, they can subject the specificities of change to their own professional scrutiny and judgement. They do this by finding ways of enhancing student outcomes through specific changes in teaching approaches and the curriculum, and through strengthening the schools' organizational ability to support the work of teachers.

In summary, this approach to school improvement regards it:

- As a vehicle for planned educational change; but it is also accepted that educational change is necessary for school improvement.
- As particularly appropriate during times of centralized initiatives and innovation overload when there are competing reforms to implement.
- As usually involving some form of external support.
- As having a dual emphasis on strategies for strengthening the school's capacity for managing change; whilst:
- Raising student achievement (broadly defined); through
- Specifically focusing on the teaching-learning process.

GENERAL PERSPECTIVES ON CHANGE

The literature abounds with studies on change. In this section we will attempt to give an overview of various 'theories' of change. It is not our intention to enter into an exhaustive analysis of each and every perspective. For this, the reader is referred to the list of references. We will primarily build our presentation on four sources: Chin and Benne's discussion (*General Strategies for Effecting Changes in Human Systems* 1969), Rolland Paulston's overview of theories for social change (1976), Ernest House's study on 'innovation perspectives' (1981), and Dalin's discussion of theories and models for educational change (1973 and 1978).

Chin and Benne's work contributed greatly to our understanding of the process of change. Until their work was available, there was no overall review (in the educational field, that is) of the various disciplines' contributions to our understanding of educational improvement. Chin and Benne grouped the different 'schools of thought' into three 'strategies' for change:

1. Rational–empirical.
2. Normative–re-educative.
3. Power–coercive.

Rational–empirical strategies, as defined by Chin and Benne, rest on the assumption that a human being is a rational being that can be persuaded by 'objective knowledge'. Those who wish to effect a change should therefore try to convince the potential beneficiaries of the advantages that such a change will entail. Much of the traditional research mentality is grounded in such a philosophy. It is assumed that an improvement project can demonstrate its strength through experiments, and the beneficiaries will be convinced because the new order is superior to the old.

Normative–re-educative strategies have another point of departure – namely, in how the user perceives his/her problem. Theories associated with this primary strategy have their roots in psychology, especially in the works of Sigmund Freud, John Dewey, and Kurt Lewin. According to the adherents of this strategy, the main question is one of whether or not changes take place in attitudes, norms, relations, and skills. To dig up 'correct' technical information, as rational–empiricists attempt to do, is regarded as being of lesser importance. Changes in attitudes and behaviour are just as important as changes in products. Defenders of this strategy also claim that the danger for manipulation diminishes when the user's values are the starting point. The essential thing is to activate forces *within the system* for desired changes. And for that reason, a lot of work is expended that aims at strengthening an organization's 'problem-solving ability', and at offering individuals in the organization a chance for self-development. The justification for such strategies is given by Chin and Benne (quoted from Dalin 1973):

> Intelligence is social, rather than narrowly individual. People act on the basis of social norms and a commonly accepted perception of reality – briefly put, a normative culture. On a personal level, we act on the basis of internalized experiences, habits and values. Changes are therefore not only changes on an external plane, but just as much on a personal plane – in terms of habits and values – as well as on the socio-cultural plane in terms of norms, roles and relations.

Even the normative–re-educative strategies also stem from an idealistic view of humanity and from optimistic notions about how the individual can contribute toward meaningful change.

Power–coercive strategies are based on a fundamentally different view of humanity. Here it is assumed that changes primarily take place by means of coercion or power. As Chin and Benne define 'power–coercive', it is *the way* in which power is used that distinguishes this strategy from the other two. Power, in the sense that one person or group influences another, is wielded in all kinds of human contexts. Power strategies are based on the assumption that people shy away from change, and that strategies which either coerce or entice are essential. As examples, we could mention the use of laws and regulations, financial reward and punishment schemes, and changes in terms of employment.

The discussion of theories of change was taken a step further when, in 1976, Rolland G. Paulston publicized his work entitled *Conflicting Theories of Social and Educational Change*. The strength of his work lay in his use of studies from a number of different disciplines. He didn't limit himself to just North American studies (which had been common up to then). Moreover, he was able to put the predominant American models into a broader philosophical perspective. Paulston distinguished between two main categories:

1. Equilibrium paradigms.
2. Conflict paradigms.

By 'paradigms', Paulston meant the way in which a profession regards a given field of research, the way in which one identifies problems suited for research, and the way in which concepts and methods are utilized. In other words, it is a matter of the investigator's overall 'point of view', or 'model'. Before we present and discuss Paulston's typology, we will let him speak for himself:

> As I set out to present this very selective overview, it is worth noting that I have a tendency to regard ideology, power and group interests as key factors in the planning and execution of fundamental educational reforms. Even though these three concepts might be off-putting to someone with a conservative-liberal view of life – a view that has long dominated American reform measures – there are signs that ideology is finally being considered as an independent variable in American reform studies. (Paulston 1976)

This long-drawn-out sigh touches on something totally essential about the research that has been – and to an extent still is – dominant in innovation research and organizational research. Since most of the theory developed in this field has also been American-dominated, much of the thinking in Europe and in other parts of the world has also been characterized by a pragmatic, rationalistic perspective.

The equilibrium paradigm

This paradigm encompasses a number of theories and 'schools', and yet contains a number of common basic assumptions. The evolutionary and neo-evolutionary theories rest, for example, on the biological theory of evolution and draw parallels to social change and educational changes. They explain development as a gradual process from primitive to more advanced forms (Persons 1950). Functionalist theory is more concerned with how development conflicts with amity, and emphasizes a gradual and continually accelerating development (Emerson 1954).

Those theoreticians who belong to the evolutionary and the neo-evolutionary schools have tried to find a basis for a mentality that thinks of society as developing according to a kind of naturally inherent development model, and that educational systems virtually automatically develop in tandem with society at large (Durkheim 1956). Durkheim's attempt to couple social development with school improvement has captured the interest of a number of investigators. Wilson has tried to compare the history of the most industrialized countries (socially and educationally) with the development of developing countries (Wilson 1973). Thomas identified four different types of educational institutions: those that stress learning by rote, training, intellectual development, and problem-solving (Thomas 1968). He feels there is a correlation between a country's economic and social development, on the one hand, and the 'maturity' of their school systems on the other. According to Beeby, the industrialized countries are doing less developed countries a great dis-service by saddling them with an educational system that doesn't fit their general level of development (Beeby 1966).

The structure–functionalists share many of the theory of evolution's stock of ideas. While evolutionists are primarily concerned with finding coherence in the developing stages between the schools and society at large, structure–functionalists are concerned with the mechanisms that create a balance between society's disparate social systems. Both 'schools' are conservative and perceive small, incremental changes as nothing but annoying 'disturbances'. Both schools are concerned with harmony. Every conflict within a system (e.g. the schools) is a sign of illness and calls for swift 'treatment' before the system can once again be brought into equilibrium.

Most theoreticians of these schools accept inequality in society; in fact, they look upon it as useful for maintaining the values of society. On this subject, Davis states: 'Social inequality is ... an unconsciously developed mechanism which ensures that society gets the best qualified people for the most important positions ...' (Davis 1949).

Theoreticians such as Persons regard education as society's most important mechanism for ensuring that individuals have control over their own development, while at the same time obligating them to perpetuate society's cultural traditions. Since the schools are completely dependent on society's resources, this enables society to keep close tabs on the schools' socialization process.

According to the structure–functionalists, innovations in the schools are created in the following way:

1. A need is created in society.
2. The schools are assigned the task of fulfilling that need.
3. The schools adapt structurally.
4. The schools internalize their new function.
5. Society changes gradually on account of the schools' altered educational programme.

Because the schools and society are so mutually dependent, according to the structure–functionalists it is simply not possible to change the schools in a fashion that is out of step with society. Most reforms in Western countries during this century have largely been based on an evolutionary tradition. This is also the case with a large number of attempts at school improvement in the Third World (Dalin *et al.* 1994).

System theory attempts to go one step further. While it rests on the same foundation as structure–functionalism, it also attempts to apply knowledge from biology, cybernetics, and information and communication theory to create a theory that has more explanatory value than structure–functionalism (Bartalanffy 1968, Cadwallader 1968).

This theory rests on an extremely rational problem-solving process; and, according to Bushnell, it consists of the following phases:

1. Problem diagnosis.
2. Goal formulation.
3. Identification of barriers.
4. Choosing from a variety of solutions.
5. Assessment of alternatives.
6. Carrying out the chosen alternative (Bushnell and Rappaport 1971).

Most of the strategies that come under Chin and Benne's 'rational–empirical' strategies rest on system theory, under which we also find the so-called research, development and dissemination model (R, D & D Model). It became clear in the early 1970s that those strategies which were based on system theories were beset with serious weaknesses. In the OECD study, the R, D & D strategy was the object of strong criticism (Dalin 1973). Herzog criticized this strategy on the basis of three viewpoints (Herzog 1967):

1. It is naively 'professional'.
2. It regards schools as objects that can be manipulated.
3. It does not understand that people do what they do, not because they are opponents of change, but because they believe in the values associated with their actions (quoted from Dalin 1973).

Development in the Western industrialized countries has followed an evolutionary course in which the schools and society have developed 'hand in hand'. The schools have been looked upon as an important component of development in society. Until the early 1970s there were few who critically questioned developments in society. Were we not all benefiting from a continuously improving standard of living? Didn't each stage of development provide all of us with better prospects? There were few who questioned who was actually benefiting from all this growth, or what the schools' functions in society really were, or whether the schools could play some other role.

We have no example of how the schools *alone* have led the way and taken positive steps to carry out radical reforms. China's primary schools, Cuba's boarding schools, and Tanzania's 'Ujamaa community' schools are often cited as examples of drastic school reform. But the question arises whether all these were expressions of the political will of the ruling class. School reform came *after* revolutionary changes in the political and economic system.

The conflict paradigm

This perspective on change embraces theories that emphasize the weaknesses, conflicts of values and conflicts of interests inherent in social systems. Marxists and neo-Marxists stress economic conflicts. The 'culture–reform theoreticians' and their devotees put the greatest emphasis on value conflicts and cultural conflicts; the anarchists are primarily occupied with conflicts that are created by oppressed institutions.

In Europe, Marxist-inspired theories of change found fertile soil in which to grow.

A number of studies have provided us with a new perspective on socio-economic conflicts in society. In a number of works, the Swedish educational researcher Donald Broady has established the significance that Marxist thinking has had for our understanding of the schools' function in society. He is principally concerned with education as reproduction, the political economy (in which the schools play an important role), and the teacher's role as 'salaried worker' in particular (e.g. Broady 1981a and Broady 1978).

The conflict theoreticians, as do the evolutionary theoreticians, also regard the schools as being dependent on society – and particularly dependent on society's dominant economic institutions. It is the *analysis* of this dependency that separates the equilibrium paradigm from the conflict paradigm.

This state of affairs is thought to be neither harmonious nor functional, neither self-regulating nor positive. On the contrary: this relationship is regarded as one-sided and dominating, and is looked upon as a pawn in the game for power played by society's elite. When the schools are unable to create equality of educational opportunity, this is not explained in terms of technical failure that calls for new pedagogical methods, as the functionalists would have done. Conflict theoreticians regard this as evidence that fundamental conflicts exist in society. The dominant elite are unwilling to turn over their privileges – without further ado – to those who do not have them. According to this mentality, the school system is structured in such a way that the socio-economic structure of society is confirmed. Pupils are trained to accept competition (which, according to this theory, is always unfair), to accept defeat, and to receive rewards – all of which are regulated by the ruling class.

Thus, educational reforms can only come about with the aid of social revolution, since they will always depend on radical changes in the economic and political system.

Conflict theories based on Marxist analysis applied to schools have had very little influence on educational reforms in the Western world. In point of fact, they have had very little significance in socialist countries such as the former East Germany and the former Soviet Union. Here, functional theories – not to mention system theories – have predominated. We believe the main reason for this is that Marxist theory is first and foremost an analytical tool. As such it can better help us understand the behaviour of society. Up to now, however, the theory has not been developed as a strategy for school improvement. Experience from socialist countries proves that the schools are not regarded as an instrument in the hands of those in power, an instrument that should have adapted the ideological principles on which society's economic and social institutions were based. Viewed from this perspective, the goal was to develop the most effective school system possible, i.e. a system adapted to society's needs as much as possible. In this regard, structure–functionalism (and perhaps system theory in particular) became handy tools.

Paulston regards 'cultural revitalization', or cultural grass roots movements, as another form of conflict strategy. In this he is supported by a number of investigators, such as Horton, who consider grass roots movements to be strategically important for educational change:

> We should have learned by now that fundamental changes do not take place on account of dissatisfaction with the way the system is working, nor as a result of the reform plans of the power elite. Opposition alone . . . has never brought about radical change. From the folk high schools, from Paulo Freire and others before him, and from the great 'grass roots movements' of this century, we have learned that we are motivated when we become personally involved in work that has a direct bearing on ourselves and our situation . . . The only way to bring about change in the educational systems is for pedagogues to ally themselves with common people, pupils, various ethnic groups and workers. Goals, curricula, and guidelines will also be changed to the extent that more people participate in the decision-making process and become supporters of fundamental changes in the educational system and changes in society. (Paulston 1976)

It is hard to find good examples of such alliances. At any rate, they have not played any major role in school improvement. Perhaps reform movements such as the Rudolf Steiner schools can be said to represent an alternative culture. Here an alliance between reform pedagogues and teachers has been forged – even though anthroposophy no doubt has a broader philosophical platform than what Horton had in mind. More commonplace – and especially relevant in Scandinavia – are general reform movements that point the way toward a new society – and toward a new school system. Folk movements such as 'The Future in Our Hands' (in Norway), which has its own views on how the schools should be, is but one example. Movements such as this, with a variety of ideologies, are commonplace in the United States, even though they have yet to play a crucial role in school improvement.

Closely associated with this orientation is what Paulston calls the anarchistic–utopian theory of change, illustrated by Illich's 'de-schooling' movement – with a Scandinavian counterpart in Nils Christie's work (Christie 1971). The 'de-schoolers' don't believe in any form of school institution because, despite their idealistic goals, such institutions would only be exploited by the strong. There is considerable doubt about this thesis, which Ian Lister in particular (one of the most active theoreticians of the 'de-schooling' movement), can confirm (Lister 1976).

In the wake of school criticism in the 1960s and 1970s, a number of alternative schools were founded, both inside and outside the public school system. There were several hundred such schools in North America alone, all with vastly different ideologies. Minority groups started their own schools. Reform pedagogues founded experimental schools. With the support of the teaching industry, everything from data-guided systems coupled to home telephones to 'street corner schools' were started, where pupils could take individual courses at small, specialized schools set up in 'your friendly local neighbourhood'. Toward the end of the 1970s, public school systems took up the challenge. Some upper secondary schools made room for a number of alternative schools under the same roof, so to speak, and certain municipalities developed a far more differentiated offer through the so-called 'magnet schools' (Silberman 1971).

A number of alternative schools were started in Europe, but the pace was much slower, probably because the schools were under heavy central control. Typically, it was in the most decentralized European countries, such as Great Britain and Denmark, that the most radical alternatives arose. The TVIND schools in Denmark could be regarded as an exponent for the European alternative schools. The Norwegian Experimental Gymnasium in Oslo is yet another example, a school that came to exert a great deal of influence on the democratization process in the upper secondary schools, both in Norway and other European countries. There is considerable doubt about what significance alternative schools actually have on the rest of the school system. Many would claim that the price one pays is sectarianism and isolation, with the system consciously attempting to distance itself from alternative practice.

While alternative schools during the 1960s and early 1970s were concerned with more 'internal' school matters (pedagogical methodology, in particular), the alternatives of later years have centred around the relationship between school and society. 'Youth Participation' programmes, or what we have called in another context 'Learning by Participating', or 'Community Schools' are all important in this regard (House 1981; Dalin and Rust 1996). They not only point to a broader relationship between schools, work and leisure, but also develop new, responsible roles for young people in society.

Paulston's analysis of the equilibrium and conflict paradigms enabled us to think of a number of alternative schools in terms of a conflict strategy for change. While Chin and Benne's work primarily gave us insight into various development strategies *within* the system, Paulston broadened the discussion to include processes of change that are not governed by the system.

Finally, in this connection we will consider a study by the American sociologist Ernest R. House, who sets forth three main perspectives on renewal: the *technological*, the *political*, and the *cultural* (House 1981).

House was one of the first in the American tradition of school improvement to point up its political dimensions (House 1974). House is concerned with the kind of knowledge we have about the process of change in the schools:

> Our understanding is not a mere conglomeration of facts, results or
> generalizations; rather, it consists of different perspectives that combine
> facts, values and assumptions which, in turn, form a kind of complex filter
> through which we view the processes of change. (House 1981)

The main perspective we have on change will thus influence what we see, what we emphasize, which actions are prioritized, which problems are uncovered, and which explanations are found. The primary goal of this chapter is, in fact, to shed light on certain main currents within innovation research. It is in this context that House's philosophy on perspectives is important.

The technological perspective

The *technological perspective* is concerned with *the product*. The innovation process is often seen as a mechanical thing. The relationship between the various people in the process is formed and fashioned by technological factors. The main goal is greater efficiency.

Earlier we described the growth of school improvement in the United States from the dawn of Sputnik at the end of the 1950s. To begin with, curriculum reforms were characterized by various university academics, who were specialists in their fields. At that time academicians enjoyed universal respect and authority, and there was general agreement about the schools' purpose. As we have seen, all this changed rather dramatically about the middle of the 1960s. Time-honoured pedagogical practice began to be called into question, and demands began to be made that school improvement should build on empirical knowledge based on material tried out in the schools. Thus began a major development toward a systematic, rational, and 'technologically' oriented innovation process.

What characterizes this perspective is the belief that solutions to the schools' problems are to be found in 'technologies' whose legitimacy and relevance can be applied in different situations. The important thing here, then, becomes a search for the most effective means of reaching a specific goal. 'The means' are usually regarded as a product, often in the form of a teaching aid or a method.

In a recently concluded work, Sashkin and Egermeier have sought to analyse various school improvement models in the United States (Sashkin and Egermeier 1993). They found that a typical strategy in the US has been the 'Fix the parts' strategy based on a rational–scientific notion that innovations are created by the distribution of innovative techniques. We recognize what we have called the R, D & D model for change and Chin and Benne's 'rational–empirical' strategies. Sashkin and Egermeier conclude as follows:

> After many years of experiment, we know that this is, at best, a *partial solution*. The more that distribution consists of stand-alone information, the less likely it is that potential users will actually adopt innovation. In contrast, the more that any dissemination efforts involve personal assistance and continuing support from skilled, knowledgeable and well-regarded persons, the more likely the innovation will be used (in some form), and the use will last. Educational reform involves much more than just 'getting the word out' about new and better practices . . .

In the present context we wish to point out that there were two main reasons why this perspective had considerably less impact in the 1970s than it had in the 1950s and 1960s. First, we were experiencing widespread mistrust of technological solutions to the problems of society. Even in sectors that were more technological than the schools, we were aware of a number of side-effects – particularly in the fields of medicine, agriculture and the environment. Second, social and political developments led to increasing doubts about the schools' place in society. The political unity which during the 1950s was practically taken for granted in the Western world began to unravel. Now that the goals were no longer clear, and the means more dubious than ever, the need arose for new perspectives.

It is not unreasonable to assume that the trend in recent years toward the widespread use of information technology (IT) represents a return to a belief in the technological perspective of school improvement. It doesn't have to be that way, but if IT is not put into a *pedagogical and social context*, there is a danger that technology and the schools will both come out as losers. Technology loses because it is rejected, and the schools lose because they can't make use of IT on their own terms. The schools, virtually as a matter of principle, have rejected technological options; just think of how little they have utilized radio, television and the telephone in their classroom teaching! The same fate could very well befall IT. The schools will end up on the losing end, because IT has the potential for contributing to the reform of our schools in a number of areas, not by making the existing school organization more productive, but by using its potential to create a new learning organization. Losers will also be the pupils themselves, particularly those who want a more relevant vocational education, or those with handicaps for whom technology can provide a richer life. The reality is that information technology reaches homes and young people long before it reaches the classroom.

The political perspective

The *political perspective* stresses that school improvement is a process in which power, authority and competing interests are in focus. Conflicts of interests can be witnessed on a personal level, the group level, and at the organizational level. School development becomes, more than anything, a question of the distribution of resources (in a broad sense). Thus it is important to shift perspective from innovation to the *consequences* of innovation *in a given situation*. Some of the key problems will be questions such as who will benefit from a given change, who supports a process of change, what rewards and costs will the change entail, and who is in charge of the development process.

The political perspective breaks with harmony models which, up to the 1970s, had most often served as the basis for understanding school improvement. Processes of change can involve problems, perhaps even conflicts of interest. Not everyone wants the same thing; not everyone benefits from the same development; and most people want to enjoy the benefits of whatever development work is going on. If development is ever going to be more than a set of minor technical variations of the means made available to the schools, negotiations between interest groups will have to take place. And before this can succeed, there must be enough common interests present to serve as a basis for compromise.

One consequence of this perspective is that attention is no longer focused exclusively on such issues as the 'quality' of a particular innovation, but is broadened to include the interaction between an idea and the organizations and environments that are taken up with it.

A number of studies of the execution of reforms during the 1970s showed that the characteristics of the school as an organization were of greater significance for whether an idea was carried out than 'the quality of the product' in a restricted sense. Thus it was possible to explain how the very same school improvement idea could succeed in one place and run into trouble elsewhere. This merely confirmed the doubt that had begun to emerge concerning the applicability of innovations across school boundaries. On a more general level, this in turn raised the question as to whether the knowledge we have of teaching has universal relevance and applicability.

In our study entitled 'Limits to Educational Change', we showed how characteristics of both *innovation, the schools, the school system*, and *society* (national and local culture) played a determining role in whether – and to what extent – innovation was carried out (Dalin 1978).

Michael Fullan also shows that what characterizes innovation ultimately has an impact on the follow-through. He also points out that what characterizes a local school system (along with the schools' characteristics and external factors) is crucial to implementation (Fullan 1993).

The cultural perspective

The *cultural perspective*, as defined by House, considers the values and norms that evolve in a group, an organization, or a community as crucial to the improvement process. Social relations are stable. One of the primary goals is to maintain and protect the organization's norms and values. Cultural autonomy is a basic prerequisite for being able to maintain cultures that have an inherently weak political or economic foundation. The cultural perspective focuses our attention on the organization that is affected by ideas. It is important to understand how norms and values are formed, how the work is structured, how interpersonal relationships are developed and maintained, and how a particular idea for change and renewal is interpreted in the school. The key point is the extent to which the norms and values represented by 'the development' are in harmony with the organization's basic values.

This is not a new perspective on the process of change. It is reflected in a number of studies – e.g. the fundamental work of Sarason entitled *The Culture of the School and the Problem of Change* (1971), Smith and Keith (1971) and Lortie (1975). But it can be traced even farther back – for example, to Jules Henry's analysis of the classroom (Henry 1963). The interesting thing to note here is that this perspective had little impact until the technological perspective began to unravel in the 1970s. This perhaps shows, in turn, that the way we see life, the various paradigms we apply in our research, are largely reflections of general trends and features in the development of society.

In some analyses it can be difficult to distinguish between the political per-spective and the cultural. While the political perspective presupposes a common set of values, so that compromise is possible, the cultural perspective presupposes a more fragmented society. It also presupposes basic agreement on values *within* organizations and groups, and less agreement *between* groups. And precisely because this perspective assumes that group norms, rather than political and economic interests, determine the process of change, it is possible to explain how different professional cultures affect the process. The example that comes to mind is the 'post-Sputnik' phase in which university teachers dominated school improvement. As it turned out, many plans (e.g. 'the new math') ran into a lot of trouble in the schools. Investigators who are firmly planted in the cultural perspective have shown that teachers in pre-college level schools represent another culture, with other norms and values, than university professors – which turned out to be a deciding factor in the implementation of these projects.

The OECD studies also showed (for the first time in a comparative study among Western countries) that the particular 'culture' that is represented in a development phase is crucial – not only for *what* is developed, but also for what is actually utilized of what *was* developed (Dalin 1973). This study also showed that 'teacher dominated' projects were strongly oriented toward reform of a subject's content, whereas projects in which others participated (pupils, for example) focused on other aspects of school life (for example, role changes). The traditional role of teacher is subject-centred. This also manifests itself in teacher training – and, to a large extent – in the teacher culture.

One who has shown the significance of the local culture is E. Farrer (Farrer 1980). In accord with the results which the RAND studies arrived at (Berman 1980a), he shows how local cultural norms and values alter a project in its implementation phase. He regards the changes that take place as a form of evolution, in which local norms figure prominently. In another context we have claimed that it is just as important to study how a system alters an innovative idea as it is to study the extent to which an innovation alters a system. The RAND studies show that, most likely, this is also a useful perspective on American school improvement (McLaughlin 1990).

Yet another perspective within the cultural perspective is the 'multicultural' perspective. A number of investigators, such as Goodenough (Goodenough 1978) and Bourdieu claim that the natural perspective on every nation is that each one exists as a network of several cultures. As a rule, individuals learn how to orient themselves on the basis of a specific culture. Their encounter with society (and the schools) requires that they learn to understand and work in a variety of cultures. The development of the schools is often dominated by elite cultures. The consequences are legion. For one thing, the farther away from the elite culture you were born, the harder it is to come by success. But it is just as important, perhaps, to recognize that gaining access to the elite culture becomes the very focus of change.

A fundamental study of 'cultures and organizations' has been carried out by Geert Hofstede. He showed that, on a worldwide basis and in a uniform company culture (IBM), there were *national, exclusive traits* crucial to the ability of a company to change (Hofstede 1991). Without a doubt we will need such *international, multicultural* and *comparative* studies if we are to succeed in developing an integrated theory of school improvement. We will return to Hofstede later in this chapter.

House has tried to compare the three perspectives (House 1981):

	Technological	Political	Cultural
Focus	The innovative in focus; its elements and effects.	The innovation in a specific context. Power and influence.	Situation and context. Meaning and values.
Values	Common values. Goals are predetermined. Find the best way to reach the goal.	Values not shared by everyone. Agreement is possible after negotiations.	Values shared within smaller groups. Values between groups differ and often conflict.
Ethics	Ethics are authoritarian. The innovation is in everyone's interests. There should be maximum striving for change.	Ethics are merely contractually binding. The innovation is not necessarily in everyone's interests. Compromises are sought.	The ethics are relativistic. The innovation could have unforeseen consequences. It is unfair to impose innovation on others.
Total impression	Production. Production-oriented.	Negotiations. Conflict-oriented.	Community. Opinion-oriented.
Fundamental principles and assumptions	Systematic. Rational processes. Explicit knowledge can be applied (cf R, D & D). Passive consumers. Efficiency and responsibility are essential. Common interests and values are assumed.	Fractions experience conflict and compromise. Influence is achieved by persuasion and coercion. Power plays predominate. Co-operation is problematical. Legitimacy is essential. There are conflicts of interest.	Participants are viewed in terms of cultures and subcultures. Innovation requires interaction between independent groups. The effects of innovation are diffuse and unnoticeable. Co-operation is not clear-cut. Changes have different 'meanings'. Autonomy is essential. There can be conflicts of values and interests.

He shows here how the main viewpoint and attention shift from the innovation itself to the context it is in, to a concentration on the organization's culture. Views on norms and values also differ, which is also true for the implicit ethical foundation and the 'image' the process aims at.

As we mentioned, there is a basic distinction between the three perspectives. From the vantage point of a technological perspective, everyone has a right to actively influence the schools. The basis for this is the fact that there is general agreement on the schools' development goals and on the fact that the important thing is to find the most appropriate methods of promoting common goals. Such a perspective provides a political and ethical justification for a centralized, national responsibility for the development process.

From the vantage point of the *political perspective*, external influences are more problematical. The ideological question is this: 'What is fair?' It is virtually impossible to find projects that benefit everyone, and external influence can easily come to mean one-sided influence. The only way of implementing school improvement from this perspective, on the basis of a code of ethics, is to wage negotiations that produce contracts, where compromise plays a natural role.

From a *cultural perspective*, general agreement is problematical. Two different cultures can easily end up misunderstanding each other, and most likely there is no common means of reaching an understanding. The risk of misunderstandings is great – and with it, the risk that innovation might cause unfortunate side-effects. The only foundation for school improvement on the basis of this perspective is that the individual school culture be in control of its own development. This is a viewpoint often espoused by teachers. The claim has been made that only teachers know what teaching is all about, which is why everything 'alien' to the teaching culture is consciously or subconsciously rejected, while that which springs from a genuinely felt need in this culture has a chance to make an impact.

One of the main questions confronting all school improvement is the kind of view one has of teaching as a profession. Is it a craft – perhaps even an art – or is it a technologically predictable profession? A craft is based on knowledge that is passed down from generation to generation. It is learned through practice, as a rule by interaction with a 'master'. A technology (e.g. the development of tests) is based on empirical knowledge. Technological knowledge is predictable. Many teachers would claim that teaching is a craft that can only be learned intuitively in the classroom. What *is* certain is that until now, we have *not* had much empirical knowledge that is generalizable in pedagogy. Those who represent the technological perspective usually claim that teaching can be based on predictable knowledge, that it is possible to arrive at good universal solutions, that experiences are transferable, and that rigorous trials and testing will lead to a better product, which in turn would improve the general teaching situation.

Those who regard teaching as a craft also regard the process of change as a slow process, one that must be controlled by the individual teacher. The opposite is the case with the technological perspective. Here, responsibility for development is relegated to investigators and 'developers', while the teacher is basically left in charge of implementing new solutions.

The past twenty years have not given us any clear answers to this dilemma. A number of different strategies have been developed that have tried to promote the various perspectives (see Chapters 6–8). My main concern in this book is to question all these perspectives (they all have their limitations), and yet at the same time to develop methods of analysing the development process so that we can identify more suitable strategies.

It could be useful to note the doubt that House himself betrays as he reflects on why he came up with the three perspectives:

> Why these, and not other perspectives? The answer is not completely clear. One could say that the technological perspective represents the interests of those who advocate innovation, the cultural perspective the interests of those who are being 'renewed', and the political perspective the negotiations between all these interests. But this analysis in itself implies a political perspective. It is important that these perspectives reflect the dominant institutions of society. Moreover, they have already gained entry in such academic disciplines as economics, engineering (technological), political science and sociology (political), and anthropology (cultural).
> (House 1981)

WHAT CAN EMPIRICAL RESEARCH TELL US ABOUT SCHOOL IMPROVEMENT?

During the past 30 years, many have sought to describe what actually takes place in a school improvement process and explain which factors determine whether the result is renewed and improved practice. Most published research, which is fairly well available, is in English-speaking societies – especially in North America, where English is a common language and where all school research has been organized and systematized in databases for years. I mention this at the outset of this section because the presentation will of necessity be biased. No doubt, a lot of interesting research on school improvement is being carried out in many countries (some of which we have had the opportunity of studying); nevertheless, many remain unknown to this author. So we see the importance of making more research public on an international scale, because there is now a need for cross-cultural studies before any further progress can be made in our understanding of school improvement.

The kind of research that has been done in the United States can probably best be grouped under the *technological* and the *humanistic* perspectives. Most major research projects on school improvement are funded by the United States federal government, which has wanted to renovate the American school system. So finding out which strategies 'work' has become a matter of some urgency. For many of the early research projects (especially during the 1970s), the following suppositions – whether conscious or subconscious – have been made:

1. Generally speaking, 'innovations' are improvements upon the practice they are replacing, and the aim of research is to discover the relationships and processes that influence planning, implementation and institutionalization.

2. Changes that are meant to lead to renewal must be based on *consensus*. Since it is taken for granted that a project will lead to improvements, the crux of the matter for the innovator is to sell, or to convince the user. The role of research is to bring improved strategies to light.

3. Processes of change can be *controlled*. It is taken as a given that the system acts rationally and that the way to manage a process of change is primarily a technical matter. The responsibility of research is to study the schools as a system and an organization, and chart effective organizational and management strategies.

4. Schools are *goals* or *objects* in the attempt by external authorities to alter everyday school life. Teachers are primarily consumers whose job is to *use* innovation so that it leads to innovative and improved practice.

Sashkin and Egermeier have called this the 'Fix the parts' strategy. In reality, much of the same mentality lies behind what they have termed the 'Fix the people' strategy (Sashkin and Egermeier, 1993). This is principally a training and development strategy. We know that traditional in-service training directed toward the individual teacher has a very limited effect. The reason for this is that the individual teacher most often fulfils the expectations of her colleagues rather than choosing her own path. This strategy can also wind up being a superficial 'Fix the parts' strategy, because it does not take the schools' culture seriously.

The American researcher Matthew B. Miles has spent 40 years doing full-time research on school improvement at the Center for Policy Research in New York. He has put his personal stamp on every phase of American school improvement research; he has also collaborated on many international projects. He stands for a broad and systematic perspective of research on school improvement. And perhaps more than anyone else, he has 'plumbed the depths' trying to find the 'critical variables'. At a lecture in 1992 presented before the American Organization for Education Research (AERA) he was invited to give his listeners a look at developments in retrospect. We have chosen to give a brief summary of the most important phases and the conclusions Miles has drawn (Miles 1992).

Miles' interest in processes of change began in *group training*, as early as 1948. Work with group processes and the influence of the National Training Laboratories in the 1950s and 1960s was potent. One result was the book *Learning To Work In Groups*, a perennial bestseller (Miles 1959, 1980). The most significant learning about development in this phase was that an open *process*, or the ability to be open and say forthrightly what is happening to you in a group, was essential for progress. 'Self-analysis' thus became an important driving force in the early school improvement projects that were based on the humanistic perspective; and until recently, a number of investigators have shown that strategies of change that are weak relative to process analysis will in all likelihood fail (Lieberman *et al.* 1991). Miles found that it was also crucial to the learning processes in the classroom (Miles 1964, 1971).

Miles called the next phase 'innovation distribution and adoption'. This was the phase with the most pronounced technological perspective. Two principal assumptions guided research: technical rationality and choice. Innovations were regarded as technically superior to traditional practice, and on account of the United States' complex public and private educational systems (which constitute 'the educational complex'), it was seen as important that each school should have a *choice*. Work with 'teacher-proof' innovations was conducted, and many good products were also developed. During this time the importance of *temporary groups* for the development and spread of innovations was documented. Such groups could mobilize on short notice; they could circumvent the system and 'flatten out' the hierarchy (Miles 1964).

Miles calls the subsequent phase 'self-renewal of organizations'. It was important to go a step further: from focusing on *the individual* to focusing on *the organization*. This type of thinking had already evolved for industry (particularly in Scandinavia by Emmery and Thorsrud), and the first organizational development projects saw the light of day. Miles started up the first project: 'Organization Development in Schools' (1963), along with the (perhaps better known) 'Co-operative Project in Educational Development' (COPED), which aimed at 'self-renewal' through the use of training, process consultation, data feedback, problem-solving, and structural changes. Miles feels that the long-range learning from this phase was the concept of 'organization health'. This notion, albeit with variable content, has played a major role ever since. Why, then, did organizational development (OD) lead to school improvement? According to Miles, it was first and foremost due to the notion of *normative change* (Miles 1969). OD exerts considerable influence on the rules that organizations play by, and improved communication helps change the way organizations function. OD was also having problems. Despite clearly positive results, this strategy was slow to make headway. Miles explains this in terms of too little emphasis on pedagogical and curriculum issues. The later 'Effective Schools' movement was directed toward the classroom, but often without taking into account important normative issues in the school. There is a clear need to bring organizational and pedagogical dimensions together (cf Miles and Kaufman 1985 and Dalin and Rolff 1993).

Miles calls the next movement 'knowledge transfer'. The idea was that knowledge from research and development should benefit the schools in a more systematic way. One of the mainstays was the idea that this required *capacity-enlarging initiatives* both with respect to individual persons (head teachers, for example) and to the entire school community (Runkel *et al.* 1978). It was just as important to build networks so that individual schools could gain 'low-energy access to information it could rely upon' (Lake and Miles 1975). Very little of this knowledge has actually been applied to school improvement in later years.

The next movement that Miles followed in the United States was *the development of completely new schools*, based on the assumption that the old schools were hopelessly outmoded and new structures and processes were needed. As much as 25 per cent of American towns and cities had 'alternative schools' and programmes during the 1970s. The most important result and experience from this work was an appreciation of the fact that traditional planning was not working, that new schools could only become true alternatives if all groups were allowed to participate. The notion of 'ownership' to changes took shape in this phase.

Toward the end of the 1970s and into the 1980s, a marked change occurred in researchers' interest in school improvement. Miles calls this *the implementation phase*. It had already become clear that schools were not adopting new solutions and that we needed to be more concerned with what took place in the implementation phase (see Smith and Keith 1971, Gross *et al.* 1971 and Dalin 1978). The perspective was focused on the *meaning* that the user attached to the school improvement process. One important lesson was that schools adapted to new practices and adapted the innovation to the organization. The perspective then changed from studying how external innovations affected the schools, to studying changes in *the system* (Fullan 1982). In this phase, qualitative methods, which stressed a new form of systematization, were applied in the study of school improvement. Understanding processes in their rightful context became a matter of importance (see Crandall *et al.* 1983, Huberman and Miles 1984). In this phase it was shown how important continuous support is for the teacher's innovation work (not just some course or two as a preliminary to a project!). The importance for the results of the teacher's mastery was also documented – a matter of fundamental importance. Much could also be learned from the fact that increased mastery also increased a teacher's commitment to innovation. This was a rich period in school improvement research; and perhaps most important of all, variables (such as 'mastery') do not exist in a vacuum but must be understood in the context of and together with a number of other variables (see Huberman and Miles 1984).

In the mid-1980s, researchers turned their attention to the management of reforms. This was a time in which the federal level cut back its investment in school improvement and left it to the states and the independent school districts to take the initiative (for which there had been very little tradition). Louis and Miles studied how 178 upper secondary schools tried to renew themselves. They also studied what the school leadership was doing to ensure the success of change (Louis and Miles 1990). More clearly than ever before, participants' relationship to the process became an important consideration, as did the legitimacy of the planning, and the manner in which this affected empowerment. Traditional planning worked poorly, but 'evolutionary planning' got people involved and created good conditions for solving problems along the way ('problem coping'). The study's conclusions, which Miles feels are a good guide to local school improvement, are illustrated in Figure 5.1.

One feature of the school improvement process that has been relevant ever since Ron Havelock's project 'Training of Change Agents' (Havelock and Havelock, 1973) is the role of consultants in school improvement. Miles discovered that there were a number of attitudes and skills that were critical to a successful school consultant relationship: good consultants were in possession of good interpersonal skills (but often completely different styles); they were competent in groups, were skilled in training adults, were themselves good teachers, and were well organized. They often took the initiative, and they were skilled in coping with key processes (e.g. conflict-

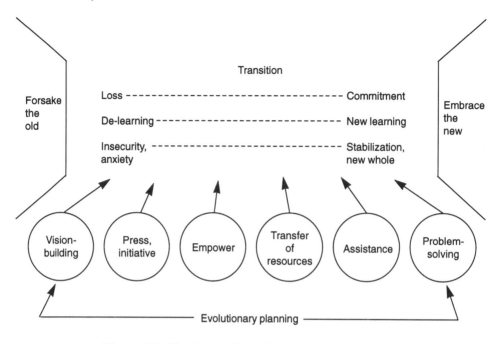

Figure 5.1 *Key dimensions in change management*

resolution, communication, etc.). The most important variables for success here, in Miles' view, are the ability to develop trust, and a relationship based on co-operation (Miles, Saxl and Lieberman 1988). Again, it became clear that *organizational diagnosis* was an important variable in school improvement.

During the 1980s, attention turned increasingly to the management of large-scale, systematic reforms. But a renewed, more intense interest in these reforms was kindled in the 1980s through, among other things, OECD's 'International School Improvement Project' (or ISIP, see e.g. Velzen *et al.* 1985). Another major project that studied national reforms in three developing countries was carried out by IMTEC on behalf of the World Bank (Dalin *et al.* 1994).

What did we learn about school improvement through these comprehensive studies? Miles calls it 'local strategic grounding'. This means that even strong centralized reforms depend completely on keeping in close touch with the grass roots – which is to say, with *all schools* and districts slated for reform. It was also clear that in those cases where reform was not working, this illustrated a vast difference in perception at the federal and the local levels. The studies also showed that there is a considerable difference between *the development* of an innovation and *the institutionalization* of it. Only when an innovation has become a natural part of everyday school life, when it works in the classroom, when it is supported and pursued, can we say that a reform has been implemented (Miles *et al.* 1987). The Swedish investigator Mats Ekholm has carried out an important project in this field, in which he followed a group of Swedish primary schools over a period of several decades. He found that, despite intensive pressure from central authorities for reform, the Swedish schools (in a number of important areas) scarcely changed at all (Ekholm *et al.* 1986).

One last movement is what the Americans call 'restructuring' – that is, the structural alteration of the entire school system – and the re-definition of content, methods and roles. A number of such projects have been initiated in the 1990s (see Chapter 8). It is not clear exactly what is meant by 'restructuring', and getting there is a complicated process (Murphy 1991 and Lieberman *et al.* 1991). It is too early to tell what we can learn from these reform efforts.

This survey, which is primarily based on Matthew B. Miles' own reflections during the 40-odd years he has been doing research on school improvement, shows that a number of perspectives have been applied and that today we have a far more detailed picture of the forces at work in school improvement.

Another researcher who, perhaps more than any other, has systematized and commented upon research in this field is the Canadian Michael Fullan. Lastly in our survey, we shall point out some of the main conclusions he arrived at. But as this cannot be done in the space of a few pages, I will deal with some of his latest and most comprehensive documentation. Fullan is a very important source for an ongoing study of school improvement (Fullan 1991 and 1993).

Fullan's perspective has consistently been one of *implementation* – that is, what actually takes place in the change process. Fullan defines implementation as

> changes from existing practice to a new practice (which potentially involves
> new material, new teaching practices, and new norms and values) in order
> to achieve better results in learning on the part of the pupils. (Fullan 1988)

As we have shown above, Fullan demonstrates that a number of factors related to the characteristics of innovation, of the school as an organization, of the local school district, and of the broader context are all crucial to implementation.

In particular, he stresses that implementation is *a process and not an event*. He shows us how important it is that the teacher is learning, that the process of change itself be a learning process, that technical assistance is essential, and that the innovation should adapt to reality in the process. He points out that most projects encounter a number of barriers along the way:

1. *Overload:* Most schools do not work with one innovation at a time; rather, they struggle to cope with a number of challenges all at once. The danger in North American schools is that the political authorities press for too many *ad hoc* 'innovations'.
2. *Complexity:* Most school reforms require new knowledge and skills. The complexity lies in the fact that a reform must be attuned to everyone in the schools. Furthermore, few know in advance what might work well.
3. *Compatibility:* Many reforms are perceived as being on a collision course with established norms and values for teaching. This is sometimes due to uncertainty about what a given reform entails, or to a lack of knowledge and skills.

4. *Mastery:* Most school reforms require new knowledge and skills. In the preliminary phase of implementation the costs are high (in terms of time, energy, psychology) and the advantages meagre (progress, effects). Unless thorough training and support can be provided along the way, reforms will easily fail.

5. *Resources:* Reforms require time, money, ideas and expertise. Most teachers and head teachers have seen neither hide nor hair of these extra resources, and the reforms usually turn out, in practice, to be quite different from what was originally planned.

6. *Strategy of change:* Many reforms are poorly planned and poorly executed. Nor do they build on lessons learned in school improvement. Getting started is the easy part; continuing is harder, and success calls for good strategy (Fullan 1991).

Michael Fullan's most important contribution to our understanding of school improvement is his book *The New Meaning of Educational Change,* from 1991 (Fullan, with Stiegelbaum 1991). This book represents a major reworking and expansion in relation to the first edition (1982). In this latest edition, as in the first, he shows how processes of change affect pupils, teachers, head teachers, parents, local communities, and governments.

Fullan demonstrates the meaning of reform processes for the individual teacher. He reminds us of Marris' conclusion that 'all genuine change entails loss, angst and battle' (Marris 1975). For the teacher the situation is often especially awkward because she does not always know what is *better.* As a rule, the teacher is left with a 'trial and error' situation and has very little opportunity for reflection (Lortie 1975, Rosenholtz 1989). Huberman points out how the *stress* of the classroom affects the teacher's attitude toward reforms. The teacher must:

- react immediately and concretely (approximately 200,000 times in the course of a school year);
- respond simultaneously to a number of challenges (fetch materials, speak with pupils, watch others, evaluate progress, etc.);
- adapt to new and unexpected challenges, because anything can happen;
- deal with pupils on a personal basis in order to build a relationship of trust (Huberman 1983).

This leads to classroom stress, which in turn forces teachers into a day-to-day mode; it isolates them from other adults; it drains them of energy; and it keeps them from abiding reflection (Crandall *et al.* 1983).

And in the midst of all this stress, there are challenges from above – yet another reform of some kind or other, all neatly wrapped in rational arguments. The problem is that it does not fit into the teacher's everyday life. Many suggestions for reform are considered unreliable; they do not address current problems. They provide no psychological rewards; they show no consideration for timetables, routines, pupils' problems, or degree of internal support. Reform suggestions fail at the outset because they ignore the school's culture (Lortie 1975, Sarason 1982).

Fullan feels that there are three reasons for this situation:

1. The teacher is bound by daily chores and by an inertia that tends to keep things the way they are.
2. There is little room for renewal, so outside pressure is strenuously resisted. Even when teachers *do* participate voluntarily in a reform process, it is usually complicated and confusing enough!
3. The tendency is to change something – preferably as little as possible – in order to survive (Fullan 1991).

Fullan sums up what he regards as important lessons:

1. It is important to evaluate every suggestion for reform with a critical eye.
2. Be aware of what some new practice will involve, and know when new practices are practised ('If I don't know I don't know, I think I know').
3. Be sure that there are clear enough guidelines for the implementation of the reform.
4. Judge whether the school's daily routine can meet the challenge of reform, and be conscious of what is required of schools.
5. Be aware that 'deep reforms' raise questions that can create angst and a feeling of inadequacy.
6. Be conscious of your own criteria for the appraisal of a given reform's values. What are the criteria for appraisal? How can we know that something is better than what it is meant to replace?

Fullan also discusses which factors are important for the instigation of a renewal process. He lists eight, and for each of these he has solid empirical references (Fullan 1991, pp. 50–64). In many ways they reflect a *technology perspective* on change. To get started, according to Fullan, there should exist 'qualitatively good innovations' somewhere 'out there', the schools must know about it, the superintendent should do some nudging, teachers should support 'the innovation', and external 'agents of change' should be able to support the process. The idea is that 'the solution' is an 'innovation' that others have developed, tested and evaluated that the schools are now about to apply. This reflects current thinking in North America – how the schools as an institution can best be renewed.

Fullan proceeds to the implementation process. As we have seen above, he recites the same factors we have found to be of such key importance in European school improvement: what characterizes the innovation itself; what characterizes the users, the schools, and the local community; and what characterizes external circumstances (e.g. government policy). When Fullan tries to show which factors affect the process in the schools – in other words, after 'the innovation' has been accepted from the outside – we find a number of similarities with lessons we have learned from other countries.

Fullan's list of 'key themes' in school improvement are well known, even outside America:

- *Development of a vision:* which he regards as a dynamic and interactive process (Bennis and Nanus 1985), and which Miles claims includes *what* the vision involves and *how* it should be carried out (Miles 1987). As we discussed in Chapter 2, Senge feels that building visions is a deeply personal process and a team process that is the *result* and not the *start* of a development process (Senge 1990).

- *Evolutionary planning:* which seeks to take into account the realities of the schools, which makes it possible to build in what we learn in the process. The message is to have a plan and to learn while working with it. Calculated risks are the name of the game. This agrees quite well with the kind of recurring open planning that characterizes IMTEC's school improvement programme (Dalin and Rolff 1993).

- *Taking initiative and sharing responsibility:* to stimulate initiative and share power and responsibility are important norms for the success of change. Louis and Miles make particular mention of project groups across departmental lines; they also point out that the trick is 'to give up power without losing control, to take initiative without getting in others' ways, and to support others without being overprotective' (Louis and Miles 1990). In IMTEC's model, developing a team and creating a culture of co-operation play an crucial role, which helps reduce teacher isolation (see also Hargreaves and Dave 1989, Little 1990). Peters and Waterman (1982) point out how important it is to feel needed, which raises expectations and the incentive to do a better job.

- *Staff development and assistance:* Fullan stresses how important it is to *learn* new attitudes and new behaviour, and that it's not all about brief, *ad hoc* seminars (often the leading edge of reform). Along with Joyce and Showers (1988), he stresses the importance of extensive ongoing help during the entire process, and the fact that *interaction* is the key to learning. This fits right in with IMTEC's model for school improvement; it also reflects what Åke Dalin considers important in Human Resource Development in work life (Å. Dalin 1993).

- *Follow-up and problem-solving:* Fullan stresses that specific information about the course of a process must lead to problem-solving and action. This applies to information about the process and (preliminary) results alike. Also, research on effective schools shows the importance of careful follow-up (Mortimore *et al.* 1988). Sooner or later, all important school improvement programmes will encounter problems, and an open problem-solving process based on the best available concrete data is a key to further development. This is also an important part of IMTEC's school improvement programme and is baked into what we call 'project management'.

Fullan's empirical findings of 'the commencement' of projects in North America, based on the fact that 'solutions are out there somewhere' which the schools need help in finding out about and utilizing, might seem somewhat strange to Europeans. Nevertheless, could it not be that this perspective has much to teach us? Isn't it so that teachers often view new curricula as 'external solutions' imposed from above and about which they have little say? Perhaps the situation isn't all that different after all.

Once a process is under way in a school, the American findings fit in quite well with our experience in Europe. In other words, there is a large measure of agreement as to what the critical factors are in the school improvement process. In Fullan's latest work (Fullan 1993), having thought about which forces are at work in this process, he gives us what he calls 'Eight Basic Lessons' in a *New Paradigm of Change* (Fullan 1993, pp. 21–2):

1. You Can't Mandate What Matters.
    (The more complex the change, the less you can force it.)
2. Change is a Journey, not a Blueprint.
    (Change is non-linear, loaded with uncertainty and excitement and sometimes perverse.)
3. Problems Are Our Friends.
    (Problems are inevitable and you can't learn without them.)
4. Vision and Strategic Planning Come Later.
    (Premature visions and planning blind.)
5. Individualism and Collectivism Must Have Equal Power.
    (There are no one-sided solutions to isolation and groupthink.)
6. Neither Centralization Nor Decentralization Works.
    (Both top-down and bottom-up strategies are necessary.)
7. Connection with the Wider Environment is Critical for Success.
    (The best organizations learn externally as well as internally.)
8. Every Person is Change Agent.
    (Change is too important to leave to the experts; personal mind-set and mastery is the ultimate protection.)

We have seen how the North American and the European empirical findings appear to coincide. What additional experience do we have from IMTEC's research and development work on school improvement?

1. We build on the assumption that an 'innovation' is not a 'solution that comes from the outside', but rather a successful result of a 'dialogue' in which external demands match up with internal needs.
2. We emphasize that important school improvement projects cannot be understood in terms of exchanging one set of practices with another, but only in terms of more thorough-going changes in the school culture and the schools as an organization.
3. As do the North American schools we have referred to, we underscore the fact that the development process is a *learning process*; but it is based on what we call the 'Real Needs' Model, which in turn is based on working seriously with the actual problems that schools encounter in the light of present and future challenges (see Dalin and Rolff 1993).

4. IMTEC's model rests on ten explicit assumptions, many of which have clear parallels in the North American findings. One of these assumptions, however, differs from North American thought – namely, the question of what constitutes 'effective practices'. Although there are general principles that can be useful in most situations, it is *the situation and conditions* in the individual school that will decide whether a specific 'innovation' will actually prove to be an improvement in a given context.

5. There are many points of similarity between what we regard as factors that support a good school improvement process and what we have learned from the North American reports – among other things, school-based in-service training, creating ownership, aspects of good leadership, and development of the schools' problem-solving capacity; but IMTEC's experiences are perhaps especially relevant where they concern the development of a *new school culture* toward *a learning organization.*

6. Schools differ in degree of maturity and in their readiness for change. We distinguish between 'the fragmented school', 'the project school', and 'the learning organization', and point out which factors are important for the developing schools' readiness for change at the various phases of development.

7. We have developed a model for the school as a learning organization which, by means of concrete school improvement data and a *dialogue* with the external environment, develops what we regard as a combined 'bottom-up' and 'top-down' process of change.

We have practically reached the end in this odyssey of school improvement research. But there is still one concern that remains: what significance does the *national culture* have for our understanding of school improvement? Can we transfer experience from one country to another? We have spent many years studying this. A recently concluded and extensive research project, *How Schools Improve* (Dalin *et al.* 1994) of reforms in Ethiopia, Columbia and Bangladesh shows that many of the same factors we have been discussing are indeed important. Nevertheless, we do find a few marked differences. In the section that follows, we will be discussing the significance of 'national culture' for our understanding of school improvement.

TOWARDS A THEORY OF SCHOOL IMPROVEMENT

School improvement cannot be viewed exclusively from one perspective. Every theory of school improvement must be a *contingency theory.*

Toward the end of the 1960s, the technological perspective completely dominated our understanding of the development process. It was taken for granted that 'school improvement' could only go in one direction: toward that which was better. The very notion of 'innovation' was associated with a benefit, and those who were against this were simply against progress!

How typically American! In time we also discovered that this was typical of many Western industrialized countries during this period. In our studies of school improvement in a number of countries and cultures, in both industrialized and developing countries, it became fairly clear that there was something we could call 'a distinctive national character', something that probably played some role or other in the processes of change. What we did not know, however, was how this distinctiveness could be described and analysed, or the manner in which it affected school improvement.

In recent years, interest in 'culture' has risen markedly. A very important contribution to our understanding of which cultural factors can play a role in processes of change has been made by Geert Hofstede in a study entitled *Cultures and Organizations* (1991). He has studied characteristics of 'national cultures' by studying a (relatively speaking) uniform company culture (IBM) in 40 countries. He found that four factors were important for whether a given culture was willing to participate in processes of change:

1. *Acceptance of power differences*, or the extent to which a culture accepts the fact that power is unevenly distributed in an organization (and in a society).
2. *Degree of individuality*, or whether it is expected that the individual or the individual school should 'take matters into their own hands' or whether the group/company/society has (collective) responsibility.
3. *Degree of masculinity*, or the extent to which the predominant features of the culture are concerned about money, prestige, a career, and things ('masculinity') as opposed to being concerned about other human beings, the quality of life, expressing emotion, etc. ('femininity').
4. *The tendency to shy away from uncertainty* by preparing for a safe career, creating a safety net of rules, monitoring conduct, and making sure that the rules are followed.

These findings may well spawn further questions. Is it, for example, reasonable that a typical individualistic culture will to any great extent rest content with the traditional school in which the individual teacher is mostly working for herself? Or can it be that a typically masculine culture that also accepts immense power differences will be more content with a hierarchical school organization? Could it be that a culture which is largely security-oriented will be cautious when it comes to major change in the schools?

The differences *within a culture* are just as pronounced as they are *between many cultures* (at any rate, when viewing the Western industrialized countries as a whole). Focusing on 'national' cultures can easily stigmatize and create superficial models. Nevertheless, Hofstede's work helps us to focus and understand more of 'the cultural variable' in school improvement.

The OECD studies, which compared school improvement projects in Europe and North America, showed clearly that 'The Characteristics of Innovation' was a crucial component in our understanding of the innovation process. The question was not whether a certain project was better than the one it replaced, but *for whom* it was 'better', who lost out in the change, and what costs (broadly defined) were associated with the development (Dalin 1973). What had previously been defined as resistance to change was, in fact, a great deal more complicated.

1. There are *conflicts of values*, since major innovations always involve changes in pedagogical, social, political or economic goals.
2. There are *power struggles*, since major innovations often involve a redistribution of power.
3. There are *practical conflicts*, either because it is unclear what the consequences of the innovation will be, or because various practical matters related to its implementation have not been clarified.
4. There can also be *psychological conflicts*, which are often based on fear of the unknown.

School improvement could, in other words, be 'political' in at least two ways: as a struggle about values and ideologies, and as a struggle for power and the distribution of resources.

This study went further, however, by pointing out that school improvement was also heavily dependent on the 'culture' the schools represent. It was not possible in this study to specify what we have called the *readiness* of the 'school culture', but it was quite clear that schools did not 'adopt' new ideas but rather 'stole' them, reformulated them, and shaped them into a form that could be used in the individual school. This was an adaptive process. In later studies by RAND, along with several other studies, this would become a major issue.

What is to be changed will largely determine *how* it should take place. Knowing what enormous challenges are facing our educational system (and our entire society) in the coming century, it is essential that we clarify which strategies are likely to be successful. We are faced not only with purely technological changes, nor merely changes in attitude and behaviour, nor structural changes, nor changes in norms and values. What we are faced with is the changing of the entire school system's role in society, its viability, its adaptability, its relationship to users and society alike, as well as internal changes in roles, content and methods. The focus is on an entirely new educational delivery system. What we mean is that the school system, like every other public institution, will have to make fundamental changes before it can master its new role in the society of the future, in close partnership with the media, industry, the church, the home, the health care system, and the local community (Dalin and Rust 1996).

A MUTUAL ADAPTATION AND DEVELOPMENT PROCESS

Even though it is clear that *one* perspective on school improvement is insufficient, and even though the significance of such crucial factors as the schools as an organization, the local community and political and economic forces of influence is becoming clearer, we still know far too little to be able to apply a contingency theory in concrete situations. In spite of this, it is possible to formulate a definition of school improvement based on *the individual school* as the unit of change.

This definition is based on the assumption that an innovation is the 'melting pot' for meeting internal as well as external needs for change and renewal. It is not something that exists in a vacuum – (i.e. apart from a concrete teaching situation). An otherwise good product, a new curriculum, or a bright idea – none of these things in themselves constitutes an innovation; but they *are* indispensable to the process. Such plans, products or ideas can help stimulate or provide direction for a process of innovation in an otherwise complicated everyday school life.

An innovation is not a new practice designed exclusively on the basis of internal needs. This internal process – or the schools' creativity – is an indispensable part of the innovation process, and can help stimulate, mobilize and qualify for the process, thus strengthening the schools' readiness. The schools do not exist, however, for their own sake. They have a very important mandate from society; and only when internal ideas and development schemes have been tested against the expectations of society (often represented through curriculum requirements, etc.) do we have the prerequisite for creating an innovation that stands a chance of lasting. Figure 5.2 illustrates schematically how we can define different kinds of schools in relationship to school improvement:

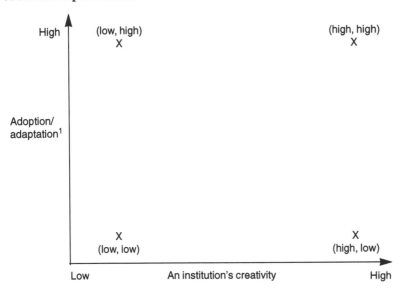

Figure 5.2 *The relationship between creativity and adaptation*
Note: [1]An institution's capacity to adjust to demands from its surroundings.

The four positions in the model are summarized as follows (Dalin 1978):

1. *Position (low, low)*
   The institution has an extremely low capacity, both for discussing new ideas, for changing internal practices, and for accepting ideas that come from 'the outside'. Changes in the institution's capacity will take a great deal of time. This position can be described as 'maximum maintenance of the *status quo*'.

2. *Position (low, high)*

   The institution has a poor (low) degree of self-awareness, a low degree of ownership to renewal, and a high degree of dependency on external help. It resorts to copying instead of thinking afresh, and there is probably a high degree of conformity between the institution's values and those of its surroundings. This position is called 'maximum adoption'.

3. *Position (high, low)*

   The institution is quite clear over its own need for renewal, but understands little about the external demands and forces that are at work. In-house motivation is high, and there is a high degree of ownership to the development work. This position is called 'maximum internal creativity'.

4. *Position (high, high)*

   The institution has a 'high' capacity for internal development and an appreciation of and use for outside ideas. The institution is able to quickly come to grips with change, work moral is high, and the institution is able to resolve conflicts and master different renewal strategies. In spite of the fact that there is a strong appreciation for outside ideas, the institution has ownership to its own practices. It is not automatically assumed that half-baked compromises are necessarily the result of negotiations. This position can be called 'mutual adaptation and development'.

Schools may be characterized at any position in this matrix, and they may well be moving slowly or rapidly in any direction. Schools differ, not only in their actual 'position', but also in their capacity to change. In earlier chapters we gave abundant examples of the many factors in the school organization that may contribute to its present functioning and its capacity for change. Understanding 'where we are' and being clear about our capacity for school improvement is a prerequisite before moving into the next section: what are promising *strategies for change* for any individual school?

This definition of school improvement presented above resembles what House calls a *cultural view* of change. However, it also takes into account *the political perspective*. We will assess this definition of innovation in terms of some of the dimensions which House (among others) has used in his analysis of strategies of change. Our conclusions will depend on *where* the school is situated on the matrix above.

Focus and values

Culture and practice in everyday school life determine the schools' attitude toward renewal. Individual schools will vary markedly with respect to their capacity and motivation for problem-solving. Every change – whether it is motivated from within or is the result of outside demands – is assessed by teachers and managers in terms of the individual school's values, the degree of conflict in values, conditions and 'need'. The schools become actively involved in renewal when the distance between actual practice and ideals becomes so great that it begins to create intolerable internal burdens. Schools also become involved *symbolically* in changes they 'don't feel a need for'. Primarily, they are subservient on the basis of formal claims. The 'culture' which the individual school represents – in terms of which all new ideas are assessed – remains 'unwritten', as a rule, and is administered by certain strong 'bearers' of this culture.

In the foregoing we have distinguished between the 'fragmented' school, the 'project' school, and the 'learning organization' (Dalin and Rolff 1993). The more fragmented an organization is – that is, the more isolatedly (or 'privately') the teachers work (usually positioned low/low or low/high), the less effort is made to create a common learning culture, and the less prepared the schools are to cope with complicated processes of change. Innovations may arise in the day-to-day classroom work of the individual teacher, primarily in the form of adjustments in content and methodology.

Values

The community called 'the school' (where all the employees and pupils are included), represents a range of values. For most schools, these are not the object of open discussion (e.g. position low/low). Practical values are characterized by a more or less unspoken compromise between teaching traditions, pupil demands and demands from the environment (for example, through the curriculum). There is a 'fellowship of values' in smaller subject groups – as well as a number of attitudes toward teaching, learning and pupils in the teacher group as a whole (typical 'project' school). Different schools differ markedly. Values of sub-groupings of teachers often conflict. Such conflicts are seldom dealt with openly; indeed, there is no need to do so, because each teacher (or subject group) can carry on unperturbed by others ('fragmented' school). The individual teachers are able to do their work in splendid isolation from their colleagues (if they wish, that is), which is exactly the case with teachers in schools that are unable to create a common 'school culture'. The pupils' values only rarely come to the fore in a *constructive* way. Pupils' contributions are often characterized by *powerlessness* (for example, protest attitudes in certain crisis situations). Their influence is strictly regulated; moreover, it is regulated on the basis of the collective interests of the teachers.

On the other hand, the more that schools have worked 'with themselves', created openness and trust, developed their own visions, and given 'their members' an opportunity for personal development and team teaching, the more the schools will be able to work constructively with both internal and external demands (position high/low and high/high, or 'The Learning Organization'). Reforms that require major adjustments, co-operation across subject and departmental boundaries, and altered roles and tasks, have a chance to succeed.

Ethics

When we think of the school system in general, 'ethics' is ultimately *relativistic*. It is seen as unfair to impose an innovation on others, because it might have unforeseen consequences, and because 'each person should assess his own work situation'. *This is particularly true of schools that do not share a common culture.* In those cases it is the individual teacher's 'practice theory' that is normative. When the internal or external demands reach 'critical mass', the teaching staff make a concerted effort to find appropriate solutions that will not affect established practice more than absolutely necessary. An attempt is made to avoid potentially threatening matters; allowances are made for individual adjustments, and *voluntariness* is a guiding principle. And if the demands for change grow strong enough, if the compromise approach does not succeed, and the principle of voluntariness can no longer be upheld, it is the schools' capacity for *problem-solving* that determines further developments (cf where the schools are placed in the matrix).

Such schools will thus react negatively to 'management', to 'production demands', to school assessment and control. Ethics is all about allowing for differences, because the multiplicity of challenges in the learning situation (as seen by the teachers) necessitates it. Thus it is difficult to be an 'entrepreneur' (or strong manager, as Mintzberg describes it). Professionality becomes a *relative* thing, partly because there is very little professional openness surrounding the individual's work, and partly because the schools largely have a 'flat organization' structure; moreover, they are 'polycentric' (leadership is spread around), or what Gomez calls a 'network' (see Chapters 2 and 3).

Total impression

Stability and cautious adjustments typify most schools. Tradition and stretching the introduction of new practices over a long period of time is the norm. Rethinking things is problematical, and innovation is not rewarded in most schools. There are, however, many schools that have 'worked with themselves' and gained an internal capacity for renewal and produced a culture amenable to learning.

In our analysis of schools as an organization we have seen that the potential for change in the individual school is relatively good, whereas the system as a whole is relatively hostile to change (cf Gomez, Chapters 2 and 3). Schools vary greatly in their internal capacity for renewal, which depends in large measure on the extent to which their problem-solving abilities and a suitable atmosphere have been developed – or, to use Gomez' terms, the extent to which the schools have moved from a techno-structure to a socio-structure and from 'alien management' (expecting someone on the outside to change the schools) toward 'self-organization' (see Chapter 2).

Fundamental principles and assumptions

It is not possible to characterize schools in broad terms. Renewal takes place by means of an inscrutible process in which the degree of interaction between independent groups is a key factor. Influencing the renewal process takes place on two planes: through the formal structure (e.g. through the school board – head teacher – teacher – pupil), and through an informal structure based on coalitions of semi-autonomous groupings. In conflicts of interest, it is usually the autonomy of the individual subject groups that rules. Where undesired changes spring from external demands, the entire teaching staff mobilizes and resists them with all their might. This happens, notwithstanding a loyal 'employee culture', by means of mechanisms that are not clear, which express themselves as demands for more resources, more time for innovation, and (in extreme cases) as a power struggle between the schools and various government departments. Power struggles are quite rare, because the culture is primarily consensus-oriented.

Most school systems are based on a classical bureaucratic view of organizations. The assumption is that decisions are rational, that the system is 'obedient', and that the individual school can be managed by means of a set of laws, directives and control mechanisms. The one force in the environment that has the strongest formal influence over individual schools is *the school administration*, whose appointed task is to protect the interests of society. But the schools are also constantly being influenced by powerful forces in their immediate environment as represented by pupils, parents, and powerful local interests. In fact, these influences can grow to such vast proportions that they outstrip the formal system in importance.

The problem is that because the schools do not have any outward pressure (a market), they are able to stave off external pressure for long periods (e.g. pressure in the form of a new curriculum). External pressure that is important might consist of such things as changes in pupils' living conditions, and various influences from the local community and the media. All these things have a marked effect on daily work, and in many cases will enjoy a higher priority than centralized directives and ordinances. Both the head teacher and the teacher must cope with a wealth of fresh challenges in their daily work, and have little time and energy to respond constructively to a steady stream of new guidelines 'from above'.

And so we return full circle to the conflict we analysed, the one between the 'rational' system bureaucracy on the one hand, and the schools' 'loosely connected' system (see Chapter 3) on the other. If the individual school is 'fragmented' and lacks those processes which Senge (1990) regards as critical for developing 'the learning organization', centralized reform initiatives (as well as 'in-house' measures') will be of no avail – provided that the vision is something more than minor adjustments to current teaching practice. The value system of the teaching staff will thus tend to set the standards in the day-to-day 'negotiations' that take place – for example between the pupils' culture and the teachers' culture.

Attention is thus re-directed toward the school as an organization. One prerequisite for school improvement is insight into what characterizes the individual school as an organization, which norms and values regulate the work day, what characterizes the teachers, the leadership and the pupils, which interpersonal relationships predominate, which structural factors govern the work day, and what kind of relationship the school has to its surroundings.

Members' role

The values of the pupils are rarely expressed openly. Their contributions are often typified by powerlessness (for example, protest attitudes in certain crisis situations), and their influence is tightly circumscribed in terms of the interests of the teaching staff. This is one of the challenges for the leadership where it concerns changes in non-profit organizations (cf Chapter 4). Internally, in the individual school, the pupils therefore become objects of the development process. 'The staff' (i.e. the teachers) steer the development work, and the pupils generally remain passive observers. The ethics of the situation are clear: teachers have a mandate (and thus a right) to alter the pupils' learning situation.

The pupil perspective is especially important where it concerns reforms meant to help us into the next century, where fundamental challenges await us. It is essential for everyone, but especially *the subject himself* – namely, the pupil – to have *lived in an active relationship to change*, having learned to live with the unknown, having coped with open problem-solving, having learned to learn in teams, and having participated in creating visions for a better future.

Part III

Strategies for School Improvement

Introduction

This part of the book is concerned with *strategic questions*. First, a word about terminology: the word 'strategy' often has an undertone of *management*. It conjures up visions of a military unit preparing for the next battle! But as used in the present context, the term is meant to include approaches and methods that are used to promote certain goals. This *can* happen by people from the outside trying to influence others, but it can also happen by a collaboration among teachers in a certain school working out an approach to promote desired goals at their own school.

Frey and Argegger (1975) define strategy as a plan that describes the interaction between people and institutions. Hameyer and Loucks-Horsley (1985) tell us that the purpose of a strategy is to 'guide activities in a purposeful, co-ordinated, consistent manner'.

In developing a strategy, Hameyer and Loucks-Horsley tell us, there are five factors that are paramount:

1. *What* is the goal of the changes?
2. *Whom* should be involved in the changes?
3. *How* do these changes work out in practice?
4. *When* are the changes expected to be implemented?
5. *Which* resources will be needed?

Many school improvement projects presuppose changes in attitudes and behaviour. As we discussed in Chapter 5, there is much to indicate that such changes assume a very close interaction between planning and execution. As a rule, such collaboration gives the parties involved in the project a sense of belonging. This raises questions other than those discussed by Hameyer and Loucks-Horsley – namely, the *process* dimensions of strategic development (Hameyer and Loucks-Horsley 1985).

In Chapter 1 we discussed the general development toward 'the new state', a development which, to a greater or lesser extent, has promoted deregulation, decentralization, streamlining, and – in part – privatization of public services (Reichard 1992). It is not possible to discuss strategies for development within the public sector without having this general development in view. Tasks which only ten years ago were regarded as being of obvious central importance have since been decentralized or privatized. We will present not only projects that have clear elements of decentralization, but also those in which the state has an even clearer (albeit different) role than before.

In Chapter 4 we described and discussed Chin's and Bennes' (1969) concept of strategy. They distinguish between *rational–empirical* strategies, *normative–re-educative* strategies, and *power strategies*. This typology is important, because it sheds light on the methods and tools that are employed in a strategy. We will make use of this typology in the practical examples that we intend to set forth in this section.

In Chapter 4 we also presented the analysis of American reform efforts that was done by Sashkin and Egermeier (1993), in which they distinguish between four distinct strategies:

1. The 'Fix the part' strategy, where an attempt is made to exchange certain 'parts' (for example, parts of a syllabus) with an 'innovation'.
2. The 'Fix the people' strategy, in which an attempt is made to change people's attitudes, knowledge and skills, for example through supplementary and continuing education.
3. The 'Fix the school' strategy, in which an attempt is made to change the individual school as an institution, for example through organizational development.
4. The 'Fix the system' strategy, in which an attempt is made to change the manner in which the entire school system functions.

In an analysis of the extensive American restructuring reforms at the federal level that have been carried out in recent years, the editors of *Education Week* show in the study entitled 'From Risk to Renewal – Charting a Course for Reform', that among the strategies which must be included if extensive reforms are to succeed are the following:

* Changes in the culture of each and every school.
* Changes in the 'rules of the game'.
* A joining of 'top-down' and 'bottom-up' reform strategies (*Education Week* 1993, pp. 187–98).

In our discussion of strategies we will make use of the typology we introduced in the first edition of *School Improvement* (Dalin 1982), in which we distinguished between:

1. *Individual strategies:* Initiatives for promoting school improvement through the individual agent (as a rule, the teacher – but such initiatives can also include the school administrator, parents, pupils, etc.). *The individual* is the unit of change. In our discussion we will consider what we know about the effects of supplementary and continuing education of teachers in relation to school improvement, and reflect on how leadership development can contribute to school improvement.

In Chin's and Bennes' strategic concept, these initiatives correspond to rational–empirical and normative–re-educative strategies. Sashkin and Egermeier discuss such schemes under the 'Fix the people' strategy.

2. *Organizational strategies:* The approaches used for promoting school improvement with *the individual school* as the unit of change. We will discuss these initiatives within the framework of *decentralization* at the municipal and the school levels. Projects we will discuss include organizational development and the development of the role of the head teacher.

   Chin and Bennes will also primarily discuss these strategies under the heading of rational–empirical or normative–re-educative strategies, while Sashkin and Egermeier call this the 'Fix the school' strategy. One prerequisite for 'the new state' is that the local administrative level and the individual operational unit (the school) prove capable of tackling their development tasks, which *Education Week* (1993) also regards as an absolute prerequisite for extensive changes in the American schools.

3. *System strategies:* The tools that are employed in promoting school improvement and which have a bearing on parts of the system or the entire school system. It is *the system* that is the unit of change.

   Primarily, Chin and Bennes would claim that system changes cannot occur without the use of *force.* Sashkin and Egermeier call this the 'Fix the system' strategy, and *Education Week* (1993) discusses this under the heading of changing the manner in which the system works and combining centralized and local initiatives.

We are faced with the following challenge: it is not easy to use *international* examples, because the concepts have different meanings. If we speak of the need for more centralized control in a country such as the United States (with more than 15,000 independent school districts), this clearly means something quite different from the need for centralized control in the [German] state of Bremen (with a total of 160 schools). That we nevertheless choose to use international examples is based on the fact that this can help us to pose basic questions about the way in which we work with educational reforms.

Chapter 6

Individual Strategies

It is widely accepted in Western cultures that the individual occupies an important place in the development of society and the development of organizations. The philosophical roots go as far back as to the days of Hellenic society; in fact, much of our Christian heritage is based on the responsibility and potential of the individual.

The United States is perhaps the country that has done the most to champion the potential of the individual. It was this relatively young nation which, more than any other, went in for education as a strategy for change in society.

Faith in the inherent power of educating individuals is crucial for the development of our entire society; indeed, it is the very foundation for worldwide endeavours in the educational sector in this century. Just what is the significance of the individual for school improvement? This chapter will primarily be concerned with the respective roles played in the development process by the individual teacher, the head teacher, and the pupil.

Without individuals there is no school improvement. However, we are so accustomed to the fact that this development takes place through the system, or institution, that we often forget the important role the single individual has played – and still plays – in school improvement. Here we are thinking first and foremost of names such as John Dewey, Rudolf Steiner, John Goodlad, and Maria Montessori. These are unique individuals who, in their own special ways, have exerted a major and long-lasting influence on school improvement in many countries.

But what about your everyday teacher, pupil, and parent? Are there ways that each of us can influence the development of the schools, or is it utopian to assume that it is possible for the individual to contribute actively toward a better school? Yes, this is possible – in the individual classroom – in fact, it takes place daily in thousands of different teaching situations. But is it possible beyond the relatively intimate, supervisable classroom situation? Will individuals be able to foster development in their schools, in their municipality, in their country?

The point of this chapter (and the two that follow) is to focus on *strategies*, i.e. the ways in which school improvement takes place. We will not be thinking so much in theoretical terms but building on the theory already presented in Chapters 1–5. To simplify matters, we will be pointing to a number of the most relevant studies as we set forth the various strategies, and the reader is invited to pursue a deeper theoretical study with the aid of our earlier discussion and the references.

THE INDIVIDUAL IN THE DEVELOPMENT PROCESS

In Chapter 4 we pointed up the significance of psychology for our understanding of change. The so-called 'normative–re-educative' strategies for change made a breakthrough with psychological researchers as diverse as Sigmund Freud, John Dewey and Kurt Lewin. They all pointed out the significance of the individual in this process, as well as the fact that changes in attitudes and behaviour are just as important as changes in the product. The philosophical foundation was subjectivism and existentialism. The counterpart to this was rationalism, which in the research- and development-oriented societies of the West enjoyed considerable favour. The empirical question came to be one of whether it was possible to prove the significance of the individual to the development process.

Everett M. Rogers showed the importance of the individual to the innovation process. He and his colleagues at Michigan State University studied the spread of innovations. They worked in the United States and other Western countries; they also did a number of studies of the dissemination of knowledge in developing countries (Rogers 1962). Among other things, they studied the following:

1. The characteristics of an innovation.
2. The spread of an innovation from one person to another.
3. The characteristics of the social systems participating in the distribution process.
4. The time dimension of the so-called 'adoption process'.

Although his was a sociological thrust, Rogers derived much of his inspiration from anthropology. At the beginning, he worked with innovations in the agricultural sector; but his field of interest spread to industry, medicine, and education. His primary focus was on such factors as:

- What characterizes those who initiate a development process?
- Do they distinguish themselves from those who follow them?
- What characterizes those organizations that tend to be the first ones to adopt new practices?
- What significance do colleagues have in the workplace?
- What rewards are essential if we want to see the rapid spread of ideas?
- How much time do we reckon it will take for a new idea to spread within a system?

Rogers felt he could show that the innovators – those who lead the way in a development process – have different personality traits than those who come after them (late adopters), who in turn distinguish themselves from those who come last (laggers). In Rogers' view, the pathbreaking 'cosmopolites' have a strong sense of self-awareness and are part of a network in which considerable social prestige is attached to trying out something new.

A number of investigators attempted to find out what characterizes development-oriented managers, who were among the first to want to put new ideas to the test.

Concepts such as 'informal managers' (Wilkening and Johnsen 1952), 'trend-setters' (Katz and Lazarsfeld 1952), 'information managers' (Sheppard 1960) and 'opinion managers' (Lewin 1952) are all examples of descriptions of key persons in the development process.

This research came to mean a great deal for the way in which the development work was organized in Western societies. In the United States something called 'Land Grant Colleges' arose; these were a network of new 'district colleges', so to speak. They represented an attempt to bring colleges and universities into a system where agriculture could be affected through a so-called 'extension service', i.e. through 'change agents' that represented new ideas developed in the university laboratories. It was the task of these change agents to convince farmers of the potential value of new agricultural methods for their own work. So it became a matter of urgency to seek out farmers who were not only willing to try something new but were in a position to influence other farmers as well (Rogers 1962).

Other workers (e.g. from organizational development – see next chapter), as well as work from group dynamics and humanistic psychology, all showed the need for an intermediate link between research and practice. Lippit, Watson and Westley showed, on the basis of these research traditions, how an 'adviser' could help individuals who were already engaged in a process of renewal (Lippit *et al.* 1958). Another sociologist who worked primarily with school improvement, Ron Havelock, sought to integrate elements from these two traditions; he set forth ideas about a change agent that could be both a process helper and an imparter of knowledge (Havelock 1969). The message was this: not only is the individual important for the start-up of the development process, but the *mediation* of ideas is a *personal* process that requires contact, support and help.

The groundwork was thus laid for what came to be known as 'social interaction theory'. Research within this tradition appears to support five generalizations about the development process:

1. The individual user – or 'adopter' – is part of a social network which exerts a major influence on his or her attitudes toward new ideas.
2. One's placement in the network is a good indication of whether he or she is willing to adopt fresh ways of thinking. (The more 'centrally' placed, the more likely he or she is to do so.)
3. Informal contacts are a vital part of the communication that is necessary for such an adoption to take place.
4. Group membership and identification with the group are important prerequisites for the personal acceptance of new ideas.
5. Speed of adoption follows a virtual 'S-curve' – i.e. it starts out very slowly, followed by a phase of rapid spread, followed in turn by a slow adoption process (i.e. when the laggers finally begin to participate).

The theory rests on the premise that, first, information in and of itself is capable of creating renewal and, second, that the individual is the kingpin in the innovation process – yet in such a way that the social system to which each one belongs retains its significance. Havelock, who further developed these theories and built models for renewal based on subsequent research results, assumed that new knowledge imparted by means of personal contacts would lead to testing and evaluation.

The studies that RAND carried out (referred to in Chapter 4) showed, however, that within the school system it is quite rare for 'testing' and 'evaluation' to be carried out. As a rule there are insufficient resources for doing a systematic trial. The RAND researchers found that educators only rarely experimented with new methods and new content in the teaching. Information from the outside also played only a minor role, unless an unspoken need for renewal already existed.

RAND also found that the interaction between teachers that is a prerequisite for social interaction is seldom found in schools. As we pointed out in Chapter 3, teachers lead a more isolated professional life than many others.

Nevertheless there is documentation to support the thesis that the way new ideas are spread in the schools can be significant for the manner in which we organize school improvement. We have already pointed to our own experiences with the spread of school improvement projects in Norway (Chapter 4), where we also mentioned the so-called 'lighthouse' effect: the first ones to adopt the ideas are those who are often geographically (and psychologically) farthest removed from a trial.

The Swedish researcher Torsten Hägerstrand sought to find out how new ideas were spread in the industrial sector in the state of Illinois. He was having a hard time finding any logic in the pattern that he found, until one day he discovered that the pattern meshed well with the system of roads and railroads in that state (Hägerstrand 1952)! Those who travel, take new ideas with them.

> In his studies, House found that personal friendship and personal contacts were both indispensable factors in the spread of new ideas within the school systems. He also feels that this spread is contingent on cultural factors: from the transportation system to membership in committees; but he still regards personal contact as being of foremost importance. In a phrase for which he is noted: ' . . . to control who meets whom is to control innovation!'

In other words, it could appear that there was a direct contradiction in the results that RAND arrived at and the experiences that 'dissemination researchers' presented. Basically, the explanation for this rests in which stages of the development process they have been studying. Rogers and the sociologists that belong to the 'dissemination tradition' have been concerned with the adoption of new ideas, i.e. with the decisions that lead to the resolute implementation of new practices. The RAND researchers, along with a number of organizational psychologists, on the other hand, have been concerned with the *implementation* of new practices, i.e. the process which follows *after* a decision has been made to introduce a new practice.

Social interaction theory can supply us with new perspectives on what takes place as new ideas spread throughout a system. And this can affect the way in which we organize school improvement. It can also supply us with ideas for strategies for school renewal (see below). There is some question, however, about how applicable these theories are in the implementation of changes in practical, everyday school life. We must take a closer look at the work situation facing each professional. What characterizes the teacher and the head teacher in their relationship to school renewal?

The teacher as a change agent

What is there to indicate that the teacher would be an effective agent of change, and what conditions must be fulfilled for this to happen?

The first question we must ask is: *Who is the teacher?* The fact is, little comparative research has been done on what characterizes those who enter the teaching profession. Their qualifications vary widely. After World War II, there was a comfortably large pool of good students in Western societies who chose teacher training (and for many years there was a steady flow from the ranks of women). In the United States, however, recruitment to the teaching profession in the last few decades has been weak. Thus it is impossible to give a common international characteristic of teachers and the teaching profession.

Brooklyn C. Derr (1986) has developed an occupational motivation theory. Groups of teachers in a number of countries have been asked, informally, what they think characterizes occupational motivation among their respective countries' teachers. Their typology provides some characteristic results for teachers:

1. 'Getting ahead', or the typical career-motivated type. We find few of these among teachers in all countries. The trend is for this type to be more predominant among teachers in developing countries. In our parents' generation, for many of us the teaching profession was a way to a better life. Today, however, those who are 'ambitious' do not choose education as their profession.

2. 'Getting secure', or the type of person who is primarily interested in a secure and stable profession, one that supplies a reasonable salary and a good pension. Such a person expects to do a good job within prescribed limits but does not reckon on expending more effort than can reasonably be expected. In our contacts with teachers, we find a very large majority of teachers in all countries who feel that this is the most important career motivation among teachers. In most descriptions of the teaching profession, the recurring complaint is the mind-numbing day-to-day routines which provide little room for reflection. The isolation of the teachers only strengthens this impression (Lortie 1975, Goodlad 1984, Fullan 1991).

3. 'Getting high' (professional motivation), or the teacher who is primarily interested in the academic challenges of his/her work. Typical of teachers in the upper secondary school is a keen interest in their *subject*, or in technology (e.g. the potential of computers). For teachers in primary school, it is usually *the pupil* that is in focus and which inspires teacher efforts. We also find here a large number of teachers who regard this occupational motivation as important to

them. They are also willing to spend large chunks of their free time for supplementary training in their areas of interest. Research in continuing and supplementary education shows that it is often those who know the most who want to know more; furthermore, they tend to want to know more about areas in which they already know a lot. If we had to make a guess, we would estimate that for at least 20 per cent of those teachers we asked, this was the most important motivation. But the numbers are just as high for those teachers for whom it was second in importance. In this category there are many motivated teachers engaged in development work, usually academically oriented persons (upper secondary school) or more pedagogically motivated (in primary school). They are often motivated, but perhaps not so much for *leadership* in school improvement. Schools often have a norm which states that 'You mustn't stick your neck out too far'. Teachers rarely characterize their own work as inherently better than that of others; perhaps this might help explain why so few teachers have the 'getting high' type of motivation.

4. 'Getting free' (ensure freedom and flexibility), or the type of teacher who chooses the teaching profession because it provides a great deal of freedom with respect to working hours and control of one's own work situation. We find many professionals with this kind of orientation in many fields. Choice of time and task is an important motivational factor for many. We also find a number of teachers within this 'career motivation' category, although many of them would probably not care to advertise the fact. For a number of reasons, the teaching profession (in some countries) has come under suspicion because the teacher does not work within a traditional '9-to-5' workday. In reality, Brook Derr's research shows that most of those of this occupational motivation in fact put in longer hours than prescribed by law; but what is important for these people is when and how the work is carried out. It is easy to find strongly motivated teachers in this category who are willing to put in extra work hours for a project, if only they can influence what they are engaged in. But the most important motivation is the freedom to choose *when* one will work.

5. 'Getting balanced', or the type of teacher who sees her profession as being only a part of her personal involvement, the type who does her job within an agreed framework but who also protects her interests in her family and her own personal development – one who regards this as crucial to being able to function as a balanced human being in relation to young, seeking people. Here too we find many teachers, especially in Scandinavia. Here we also find a number of teachers who resist 'more meetings', development work that 'robs time', and extra-contractual duties.

We have chosen to begin our discussion on the potential for teachers to be change agents in school improvement by introducing career motivation theory. We cannot speak of teachers as a *group*. Teachers are as dissimilar as other groups of professionals. But perhaps we can speak of a *configuration* of teachers with different types of motivation. In analysing the occupational motivation of teachers, it is in our opinion reasonable to suppose that there are teachers who are capable of acting as opinion leaders in a development process – but not just *any* process, and not in just any school.

The teacher's qualifications for change

Are teachers qualified to be change agents? In view of a number of reports issued during the past decade, this is a debatable proposition. Many, especially in the United States, are dubious. In fact, some claim that many teachers are downright unqualified to carry out meaningful innovations (Goodlad 1984). Many also feel that teacher training itself does not contribute positively toward qualifying teachers for innovative tasks (Goodlad 1990a, Carnegie Forum 1986, and Holmes group 1986).

Fullan (1991) points up the difficult work conditions which force the teacher into a more reactive role. He points out that evidence from a number of reports suggests that the teaching situation is becoming increasingly problematical, that the profession itself has been devalued, that the work is characterized by much routine and overwork, and that the school's 'cellular organization' complicates the process of innovation. In this difficult situation the teacher must decide whether her pupils will be well served by a given change, and whether the costs (in terms of time and worry) are worth the effort. Fullan has several bits of advice for teachers who are faced with the choice of whether to take an active role in development work.

Sarason (1982 and 1990) is concerned that we truly understand teachers' mind-set, which we must if we are to take any position on the question of the teacher's role in school improvement. He is especially critical of external reform agitators who do not take the trouble to think from the vantage point of teachers, who want the teacher to forget what she has learned; these [external troublemakers] are primarily engaged in imparting theory to teachers. Sarason feels that existing practices reflect hidden theories of what constitutes good teaching, within the set of conditions the school represents. These theories and principles are hardly ever critically evaluated and discussed. The teacher often takes them for granted. The same thing has also been shown by Lauvås and Handal (1993) and by Alexandersson and Öhlund (1986). It is important to make teachers aware of what their *theory of practice* actually is.

Sverker Lindblad has pointed out that a teacher's work is not based on a 'technological', but rather an 'ecological' rationale, where the teacher takes account of a number of circumstances in the teaching situation and where tradition and local school norms play an important role (Lindblad 1993). In my view, we are approaching the crux of the teacher's role in school improvement. The teacher works primarily alone. In time, this leads to isolation; the profession has an uncertain 'technology'; there are no clear-cut indicators of success; there is a school norm which mitigates against asserting oneself; and defeats are only mentioned in whispers. The teacher winds up in a closed role where conscious reflection and dialogue are in short supply. This ultimately serves to enormously complicate teachers' roles in development work.

It is important to understand the connection between structural conditions on the one hand and cultural norms on the other. As we mentioned, Lortie has shown how isolated the individual teacher is from other teachers and from other adults in her daily work (Lortie 1975). At the same time, a norm has taken shape which 'states' that one must rely on one's own resources, that the teaching profession is an art that nobody else is qualified to understand. Miles has pointed out that because knowledge background is weak, this leads to a fear of 'peeping'. This in turn reinforces the effects which the structure tends to create: a teacher in isolation, with little chance of acquiring new knowledge.

So it is not surprising that in studies of curriculum implementation in schools we find that it is the assessment and preferences of the individual teacher (especially her assessment of what would be suitable for the class) that determines whether the curriculum *actually* gets implemented (Leithwood *et al.* 1978). Teachers make most of the decisions relating to their teaching on their own. They are influenced to some extent by discussions with their colleagues, but less by what the head teacher feels, and are only slightly influenced by external resource personnel. Teachers are primarily concerned with how new practices will affect their own work situation and that of their pupils. It is also from their own pupils that teachers reap their greatest rewards.

Doyle and Ponder find that teachers primarily wish to pose two questions with respect to school improvement: 'Will my pupils be well served?' and 'What are the costs associated with familiarizing myself with this [new] material and making use of it?' According to Doyle and Ponder, this is quite rational and constitutes teachers' practical professional ethics.

Precisely because the teacher alone makes most of the decisions required for improving classroom teaching, it is difficult to determine to what extent she is building on others' ideas and to what extent these ideas are employed in the classroom. School development research has also tended to focus attention on the relatively larger projects that are often initiated by central authorities. So it is easy to overlook the many small but perhaps essential changes that teachers implement on a daily basis. After all, teachers are constantly being exposed to new ideas – through conferences, supplementary training, and informal conversations. Hood and Blackwell found, for example, that the sources that teachers felt had the greatest impact on their behaviour were the following:

1. The textbook.
2. Personal notes.
3. Discussions with colleagues at school.
4. Curriculum materials (Hood and Blackwell 1979).

A number of other works appear to support similar conclusions: teachers build on personal contacts (especially with other teachers), and often find new ideas in textbooks and manuals.

Clark and Yinger (1980) support the theory that far more planning goes on than was previously thought. They find that teacher planning is characterized by the following factors:

1. It is essential to the daily teaching, but is usually invisible to others.
2. It is not systematic and stepwise.
3. Teachers translate ideas from their syllabus material to their daily teaching.
4. Teachers seldom ever contemplate their own planning, but find it stimulating on the rare occasion when they do so.

Fullan (1991) feels that we can draw the following conclusions about teachers' use of new ideas and methods in their teaching. It takes place:

1. when information is relevant and specific enough to be used;
2. when the transfer of knowledge is personal and there is enough personal contact and support in the implementation phase;
3. when the school and the municipality assume a positive attitude toward school improvement and the workplace is characterized by administrative support, collegial co-operation, and problem-solving behaviour.

There are also signs that in certain situations teachers act as change agents. In the first place, it is clear from the foregoing that fellow teachers are the single most important source of help – not only because they are colleagues they associate most closely with, but also because they are colleagues they can basically trust, who can lend support over time if they should need it.

But a number of studies show that the voice of individual teachers is seldom heard in their own schools. We have previously shown that schools in the neighbourhood rarely ever copy a pioneering school in the same municipality; rather, the distribution usually takes place over large geographical areas. Sandström and Ekholm (1986), following the progress of four Swedish schools over a period of three years, found that individual teachers took a number of initiatives toward developing their own role. But these initiatives did not catch on with other teachers; they remained with the original teachers.

What we are facing here is a fundamental phenomenon of schools as organizations. There are few incentives to learn from one another. In Chapter 3 we pointed out a number of factors that could perhaps explain this, but we have yet to see any major efforts at changing the situation. We know that certain schools that make an effort to develop their climate are able to break the vicious circle – but it is not easy, and there is no clear-cut, unequivocal way to such a goal. There is also another, perhaps more serious aspect to consider: the kind of 'meta-learning' that takes place in a school in which the grown-ups are not learning from one another *can* have a negative impact on pupils' learning, both in the short term and the long term. A number of researchers have pointed out that, in later years, the hidden syllabus is more crucial to a pupil's learning than the daily teaching. Thus it is incumbent on us to discover the conditions under which adults in the schools will be willing and able to learn from one another (Dalin and Rolff 1993).

Few teachers are actively engaged in 'selling' new practices. Moreover, they are more interested in certain types of innovations. As a rule, they will be concerned with the syllabus, with respect to new content. They will be less concerned about school improvement in terms of changes in roles, interaction, methodology and management (Dalin 1973). However, we are beginning to witness a change here. As the individual schools, through decentralizing measures, begin to organize their own activities, teachers are beginning to contemplate and take a stand on questions regarding roles, interaction, methodology and management.

THE INDIVIDUAL AND THE SCHOOL CULTURE

The chance that teachers have to influence the development of the schools (and not just affect their own teaching) is closely related to what kind of school we are talking about. Schools differ in many different ways (Dalin and Rolff 1993). In an assessment of the experiences that have been gained the past ten years in the so-called 'restructuring' projects in the United States, Susan Loucks-Horsley says that what has a positive impact on a radical restructuring of schools is a culture in which the adults are always asking questions, seeking new solutions, and studying the realities of the situation. This is the same thing we expect of pupils (*Education Week* 1993, p. 118).

Today there is a solid body of research to document the fact that collegial cultures where openness and co-operation are the norm promote school improvement (Lortie 1975, Rosenholtz 1989). Fullan (1990) claims that collegiality among teachers, as well as a number of important aspects of co-operative cultures, are associated with success in the implementation of changes. He also finds that in a discussion of effective supplementary training (e.g. Stallings 1989), the organizational variables are overlooked. For Fullan it is a matter of course that supplementary training is only effective as long as it works with the schools as a whole.

Rosenholtz (1989) points out thirteen different variables which, in American schools, are associated with co-operative work cultures. Fullan (1991) has constructed a synopsis of how some of these factors work together (see Figure 6.1).

Little (1990) has also shown clearly how collegial norms influence the chance that teachers have to make an impact in their own school. She feels that there are at least four different types of collegial relationships: storytellers and a superficial quest for ideas; support and help; mutual exchange of experience; and common work. She feels that many projects which attempt to create conditions for co-operation operate on a 'benign' and superficial level. She does not necessarily mean that *co-operation* is the sole and ideal form, but that the *openness* that is necessary in co-operation is a prerequisite for growth and development.

After reviewing the literature on norms of collegiality, Rowan concludes as follows:

> Some attempts at encouraging collegiality, by the little use of time which results in limited and superficial contact, does not appear to have a major impact on teacher obligation or teaching practices. Instead, the development of a staff culture that enhances the need for continual development

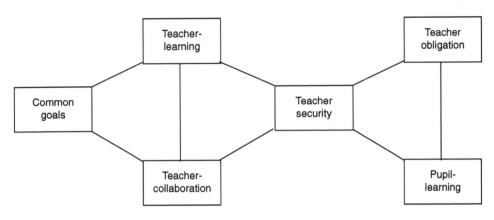

Figure 6.1 *The learning school (according to Fullan 1991)*

and maintains close collegial relations over a period of time appears to be required if collegial relations are to help improve classroom teaching and lead to increased teacher motivation. (Rowan 1990)

Hargreaves (1991) has developed a typology for school cultures that resembles the analysis we presented in our book *Changing the School Culture* (Dalin and Rolff 1993). He discusses four types: the fragmented culture, the balkanized culture, the forced co-operative culture, and the voluntary co-operative culture. He is particularly concerned that attempts at co-operation do not degenerate into a series of rule-based routines without meaning or content, but rather that organic co-operative patterns can be developed from the challenges facing teachers and the schools.

In other words, it is not only the individual teacher's motivation, career orientation or competence that will determine whether he succeeds as an agent of change in his school: the culture of the school is also crucial to the success of the effort.

Bryk and Driscoll (1988) define school culture as a common value system, a common agenda and collegial relations between the adults, coupled with a teacher's role that extends beyond the classroom. Investigators found a clear connection between culture and pupils' results in upper secondary school. The pupils were more interested in academic subjects, had a lower rate of absenteeism, and were more orderly. Fewer quit school, and pupils got better grades. Teachers were more satisfied with their jobs, they were sick less often, and morale was higher than at other schools. And there is a high degree of motivation for further school improvement.

WHAT HAPPENS WITH A TEACHER WHO ENTERS INTO A DEVELOPMENT PROCESS?

What happens to teachers who are encouraged to participate in school improvement? For the past twenty years, Gene Hall from the Research and Development Center for Teacher Training at the University of Texas has been following the progress of teachers in their pedagogical development work; he has developed a theory of 'stages of concern' which describes the kinds of reactions common to teachers in the development process (Loucks and Hall 1979):

Stage 0: AWARENESS

There is little interest for new ways of thinking and new project ideas.

Stage 1: INFORMATIONAL

The teacher is concerned about the innovation and wants to learn more about it. He or she does not appear to be particularly anxious about the project and wants to learn as much as possible about its characteristics and use.

Stage 2: PERSONAL

The expression of concern at this stage is: how will using it affect me? Attention is directed towards the changed feelings of the individuals involved as they learn about, prepare for and use new practices.

Stage 3: MANAGEMENT

Attention is now directed toward the way in which the project is carried out. Efficiency, organization, management and use of time all became important issues. As a rule, the teacher is concerned with a number of technical and practical aspects of the project and 'drowns' in copying work, organization, and daily crises.

Stage 4: CONSEQUENCE

Attention is now directed toward the consequences of the project for the pupils. Relevance, evaluation of results, and changes necessary for improving pupils' performance are usually key issues.

Stage 5: COLLABORATION

At this stage the teacher is most concerned with establishing a co-operative relationship with other teachers with respect to the use of the innovation. The teacher has now become convinced of the project's advantages and wants others to 'come aboard'.

Stage 6: REFOCUSING

The teacher can take a more relaxed view of the entire project. She is aware of weaknesses, makes suggestions for change, wants to continue the work, but also wants to make a number of important changes that would improve the project.

Gene Hall has concluded that most teachers do in fact go through the foregoing stages in development projects. However, it is not necessarily the case that the stages occur in the same order as set forth above; they usually do, but not invariably. Hall (1979a) has also found that teachers *apply* new ideas at different levels:

Level 0: NON-USE
The level at which the teacher has so little knowledge about a given innovation that she is unable to apply the innovation.

Level 1: ORIENTATION
The teacher has just received information about a given innovation, has checked into its basis of values and most important dimensions – among other things what demands the innovation would make on her.

Level 2: PREPARATION
The teacher prepares for first-time use.

Level 3: MECHANICAL USE
The teacher directs her attention to the daily problems involved in using the innovation, but has little opportunity to reflect on the consequences. Changes in the project are, as a rule, designed more to satisfy the teacher's needs than those of her pupils. The teacher is primarily concerned with mastering the basic tasks connected with her teaching.

Level 4A: ROUTINE
Application of the project becomes stabilized. Few changes are made. Little attention is given to improving the project.

Level 4B: REFINEMENTS
The teacher takes time to improve certain aspects of the project so that the pupils can get more benefit from it.

Level 5: INTEGRATION
Here the teacher tries to co-ordinate her own efforts in the project with the work that other teachers are doing, all with a view to enhancing the positive impact on the pupils.

Level 6: RENEWAL
The teacher assesses the project and comes up with modifications and important renovations for achieving better results. She is concerned with recent development trends in the field and seeks new goals for herself and for the school.

Hall and his colleagues belong to a tradition within innovation research that takes innovation for granted – that regards it as a benefit – and they are concerned with determining the extent to which teachers accept and employ a given innovation. In previous works (Dalin 1973, 1986) we have questioned this assumption. What is interesting in this context, however, is the fact that Hall and his colleagues have discovered a way of studying how the individual reacts to school improvement.

Huberman and Miles (1984) tried to find out which factors produced *practical skills* in the individual teacher. They found that in the early phase of the work, teachers felt overworked. They sought to redress this by making the procedures more efficient. Most were concerned with whether they were equal to the task. Many were worried that the project was not working in their class, but most worked through the problems. Huberman and Miles found that *previous experience* was a more important factor than the skills training associated with the project. This is probably consistent with the experience that Gene Hall refers to – namely, that *new teaching practices take years to become entrenched*. Thus we have every reason to believe that the quality of instruction in an early trial phase will be poorer than in later phases.

They found that the teachers needed from six to eighteen months to master the skills in the projects they studied. It was only when they had reached the point where they mastered the technical aspects of the project that they began to feel safe and secure. The nature of the problems changed during the course of the project, evolving from questions concerning one's own situation to questions concerning pupils, and finally to the task. In order to master the innovation, they had to learn how they could put it to use. Ironically enough, Huberman and Miles found that the future of a project was not assured merely because the teachers had mastered its implementation. More important were such organizational factors as administrative support, stability in the environment, and factors related to the 'normalization' of the project in the daily routine.

It is one thing to master the skills a project requires. But whether teachers, by virtue of the innovation work, actually change their general teaching practices is another matter altogether. Huberman and Miles sought to determine whether the following changes took place:

1. Changes in daily classroom practice.
2. Changes in technical skills (for example, participation in an information technology project might polish one's skills in word processing).
3. Changes in interpersonal relationships.
4. A greater appreciation for the schools, school policy and pedagogy.
5. Increase in self-esteem.
6. Changes in basic attitudes.
7. Changes in professional self-understanding.

There are a number of factors that affect such changes. And in the projects Huberman and Miles studied, they also found that changes did occur – especially in the following way: the project initiated project-specific changes in teaching and organizational routines. This gradually led to new understanding, different emotions and relationships, which in turn led to a raising of professional standards. Projects which inherently made heavy demands on the teachers were the ones which led to the greatest number of positive changes. These projects demanded that teachers 'take the plunge'. And with the well-qualified assistance and support of management – and despite many start-up problems – the projects led to a significant increase in capacity (Huberman and Miles 1984).

Change at the level of the individual is a learning process. Teachers go through a process in which their understanding, attitude and behaviour all undergo change. Through school improvement, the individual seeks meaning and increased work satisfaction. Learning takes time – and it takes work. Most individuals will encounter problems and experience worry and frustration. And this is why professional and personal support are so important. Through such support the individual gets the breathing room he needs to grasp what the innovation actually means to him personally, and to his class. Only then can the new situation be mastered and employed to increase the job satisfaction of pupil and teacher alike.

INDIVIDUAL STRATEGIES

By 'individual strategies' we mean initiatives whose object is to change the schools by influencing individuals. This might involve influencing attitudes, knowledge or skills, and this influence can be brought to bear both inside and outside the school. Up to now we have only discussed the teacher. In principle, the same strategies apply to the head teacher, the pupil, the parents, or other individuals who have a vital interest in the schools (see below). At this point we will discuss initial teacher training and in-service training.

Initial teacher training

Qualified teachers are the schools' most crucial resource. In all the Western countries it is the national government that has played the biggest role in teacher recruitment and has had the greatest impact on the length and content of training. Many have pointed out that criteria for admissions and the content of teacher training have little to do with present-day teacher requirements (*Educational Leadership* 1991). Torsten Husén has also showed that we know very little about the effect that teacher training has on the quality of teaching. In a study for the World Bank, he shows that there is no clear relationship between the duration of teacher training and the quality of the actual teaching in the schools – as measured in terms of pupils' results on standardized tests (Husén *et al.* 1978).

In reality, we know very little about the effect of teacher training. Quite simply, it is hard to measure, a fact that Hall, among others, has shown (Hall 1979b). In another study about teacher training done by Joyce and Showers, the authors show that most teachers' colleges fail to bring their students to a level of proficiency that could be reasonably expected to have an impact in the classroom. They distinguish between four levels of knowledge and proficiency (Joyce and Showers 1980):

1. A familiarity with new concepts.
2. An appreciation of concepts and principles.
3. Learning and practical skills.
4. Applying skills through problem-solving in the classroom.

Bolam (1981) points up the need to take a collective look at three different forms of teacher training:

1. Initial teacher training.
2. Induction.
3. In-service (supplementary and continuing).

He points out the many difficulties that teachers encounter and the need to give them special work conditions, organized aid from colleagues, and special practical courses at the teachers' colleges. The greatest strides in this form of support have been made in Great Britain, Australia and Canada.

In North America during the past decade, perhaps most in the United States, there has been a rising tide of criticism directed toward teacher training. The teaching profession, generally speaking, has a low status in the United States. Teachers' unions have never succeeded in giving teaching genuine professional status. During the next ten-year period, 50 per cent of American teachers have to be replaced because of retirement – that is, about 200,000 new teachers must be educated each year – and there is little to indicate that *quality* will noticeably improve during such a strongly quantitative expansion period.

An important study in the quest to renew American teacher training was the work of the Carnegie Forum on Education and the Economy, entitled *A Nation Prepared* (1986). A number of studies followed in rapid succession, such as *Tomorrow's Teachers*, a report for the 'Holmes group' (1986, 1990), and the report of the American organization of teachers' colleges, entitled *Task Force on Teacher Certification* (AACTE 1986).

One feature of development which is related in part to the national debate that arose in the wake of the publication of results from projects that compared standards in mathematics and natural sciences internationally has been a fortification of academic training. Up to now, however, research has not been able to confirm that a prolonged academic education leads to an improvement in pupil achievement (Wang *et al.* 1993, and Sarason *et al.* 1986).

Another feature of development has been to extend the initial training period to five years. This has not caught on; however, Goodlad points out that teacher training should be concerned with quite another set of problems (Goodlad 1990a):

1. *Lack of prestige* – owing, no doubt, to historical circumstances. The teaching profession has long been looked upon as a transitional and/or a woman's occupation – in a time when the work of career women was not highly regarded. The educational faculties of the universities are still those with perhaps the lowest academic prestige, which in turn affects recruitment.

2. *Lack of content.* Students are spread out over a number of faculties (the various educational courses are taken at different departments), the socialization process, in relation to the teaching profession, starts late (if at all), and no one is really sure who is responsible for what.

3. *Segmenting of theory and practice.* Students encounter completely different realities: one at the university, another in practice – and there is little help to be had. Goodlad feels that it is now time (once again) to develop separate 'practice schools' in the United States.

4. *Overregulation and bureaucracy.* Probably on account of the great dissatisfaction with the American schools, state authorities have tightened demands on teaching institutions. This has led to an overbureaucratization; it is hardly possible to do anything creative without running foul of some rule or other. The net result is a dreary conformity.

Goodlad has taken the initiative in a number of partnership networks in which schools, municipalities, states and universities band together in a long-term effort to develop a new form of teacher training, one that is related to the need for school improvement (Goodlad 1990b).

As with all other kinds of occupational training, teacher training is quite expensive. We are far from convinced that a prolongation of basic education – e.g. from three to four years, which has been done in Norway – is defensible. Viewed in relation to the need for development the schools are faced with, any government, as we see it, should concentrate far more on in-service (both supplementary and continuing) training of teachers, with special support for new teachers. There are several reasons for this: most students in teacher training have little experience with concrete teaching situations before they have finished teachers' college, even though there has been an increase in later years in terms of age and practical experience. Most of us need practical experience before we understand where the problem lies; we need input from both pupils and colleagues. Motivation for a serious education will increase in proportion to actual knowledge (and awareness) of the tasks facing teachers and schools. We must find the means to tackle these problems. To sum up: it would be a very healthy thing if the administrative heads of teachers' colleges would work with more experienced students and work in the schools themselves, so that the training could become more concrete and realistic, and so that they could lend support to whatever school improvement process was necessary.

A comparison of the resources available today for initial training on the one hand and in-service training on the other makes it clear that policy makers look upon the schools as a relatively stable system, one that does not need a whole lot of development resources. The classical organizational view is that tasks can be defined in advance, that 'practitioners' can be trained to function within the scope of their roles, and that this will suffice as long as the system in general is working within established guidelines. In all likelihood, many would have quite a different, more dynamic, view of the schools today. But is it not the case that the management of resources for initial training in relation to in-service training is an example of how the system, in practice, is being viewed through bureaucratic eyeglasses?

Perhaps the reason this is so is the fact that there is no conscious policy in this area. Are resources tied up by existing laws? Do institutional interests lurk in the background? Would it be more natural for institutions of higher learning to take on the job of initial training? Is the prolongation of the course of study a foregone conclusion on account of competition between the professions? In other words, is there some sort of innate growth mechanism in initial education that drains the system of resources for in-service training?

In-service training of teachers

No development strategy is more widespread than in-service training for teachers. For a decade this has been the approach the authorities have used when introducing new curricula and for other changes in the schools. In spite of this, we actually know very little about the effects of in-service training. It is still the case that a major portion of funds for supplementary education are being used for *information* about new elements in the curriculum. Sandström and Ekholm show that even in Sweden there is a long-standing tradition which holds that it should be sufficient *to inform*. Moreover, they show that a credibility gap arose when responsibility for in-service training passed from teachers' unions to national in-service training specialists (who were perceived as being representatives of the government). Only in the 1970s was the system of in-service training in Sweden changed. It became far more school-based, and there has been an attempt to create ownership to these changes through the active influence of the teachers (Sandström and Ekholm 1986).

Fullan (1991) points to conclusions he arrived at in earlier studies with respect to what characterizes the usual in-service training programme:

- One-time seminars with no follow-up, where topics are determined by someone other than the participants.
- These programmes are rarely ever geared to the needs of the individual participant, and an evaluation is seldom carried out.
- Participants come from schools and municipalities with vastly different challenges and problems, and there is no built-in plan for how to implement what is learned back in the participants' home municipalities and schools.

Pink (1989), having assessed four major in-service training programmes in the United States, comes to many of the same conclusions as Fullan. Furthermore, he points out that many of these programmes are mere passing fads. Many schemes are lacking in support and consultancy assistance, and even the good ones are prone to drown in a daily sea of diverse demands. Pink is particularly critical of the fact that none of the programmes had a well-founded conception of which problems individual schools were labouring under – e.g. the extent of teacher turnover, conflicts between the demands the courses made on teachers and the demands imposed on them by the schools, and finally the lack of clear lines of responsibility and roles between the municipalities, the schools and institutions of higher learning (which were responsible for some of the programmes).

The outspoken American labour union leader, the school reformer Albert Shanker, says that poor quality of in-service training was first and foremost due to the fact that none of the participating institutions (the municipality, the schools, the university) have given such training a high priority. Shanker claims that the other reason that supplementary training does not live up to expectations is that it is assumed that knowledge exists outside the schools, that it is merely a matter of bringing this knowledge to the teacher. One operates on the basis of a 'theory of deficit'. Furthermore, he claims that most in-service programmes bear the marks of 'somebody telling somebody else something'. Perhaps most importantly, in his view: the usual in-service model reinforces an old-fashioned 'teacher alone' tradition (Shanker 1990).

After five years of studying in-service training in the OECD countries, OECD concluded the following as early as 1981:

> Unfortunately, and distressingly, the growing interest in in-service training appears to be based more on faith than actual knowledge. Outlays for re-search in this field have been minimal, so it is not surprising that we have so little systematic knowledge about costs, the use of resources, and efficiency in terms of approaches and total investments. . . . (OECD 1981, p. 67)

The term 'in-service training' of teachers is so general in nature that it is hard to analyse. Yarger *et al.* (1980) suggest the following typology:

1. *Classroom training* (job embedded). The training takes place in the classroom and consists of practical training in working with pupils. Analysis of video tapes of one's own classroom teaching is an example.
2. *Job-related.* The training is directly related to daily problems, but does not take place during classroom hours. A group of teachers working together might, for example, take a seminar in 'team teaching'.
3. *Academic courses* (general professional). This is training whose aim is general academic competence; it is not, however, tailor made for special classroom tasks. Social science teachers, for example, might take a course in course methodology for the natural sciences.
4. *Qualifying courses* (career/credential). This is training that leads to further quali-fication (continuing education). As a rule, these improved credentials lead to higher pay and a crack at other positions.
5. *Personal.* The benefits are primarily in the form of personal growth. The training can – but need not – be related to teaching. An example of this might be a course in art history; such a course could mean something for one's personal development (also as a teacher), but it need not have this as its aim and object.

In the OECD study (1981) just referred to, the authors have sought to define in-service training for teachers. They have come up with a definition that balances *the schools'* needs with the needs of *the individual.*

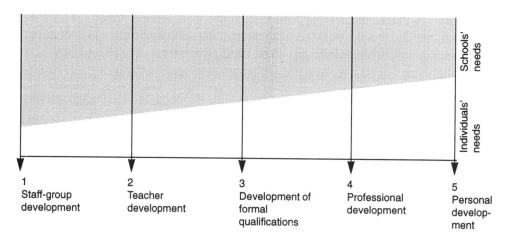

Figure 6.2 *The need of the schools and the individual for in-service training*

The five different categories in Figure 6.2 have the following meanings:

1. *Staff–group development.* The goal is to give the entire school staff practical skills.
2. *Teacher development.* The goal is to give the individual teacher practical skills (e.g. classroom teaching skills for newly appointed teachers).
3. *Formal qualifications (career development).* The goal is to give the individual teacher the potential for promotion (e.g. head teacher training).
4. *Professional development.* The goal is to provide increased academic insight (e.g. by means of more theoretically-oriented university courses).
5. *Personal development.* The goal is to provide the teacher with programmes that will result in personal growth.

Yarger *et al.* (1980), who studied in-service training in the United States (California, Michigan and Georgia) in nearly 300 schools and a total of about 7,000 teachers, tried to find out what viewpoints on in-service training of teachers were held by participants, course managers, instructors, school administrations, parents and pupils. They found that teachers were very concerned about in-service training. On the whole, they felt that there were too few schemes chasing too many needs, and that such programmes as were on offer were not very effective. They pointed out in particular that new teachers (and head teachers too, for that matter) need assistance, and that concrete training in practical skills can alleviate many problems. And here it could be useful to think in terms of different kinds of courses – from the purely motivational type (becoming familiar with new problems) to knowledge-oriented and skill-oriented courses, to courses that have school improvement itself as their aim and object.

All of the groups that were asked agreed that teachers today participate in too few in-service courses. This training should be more practically-oriented. There is a particular need for help with handicapped pupils. In-service training should be planned better with respect to timing and the administration of the courses. Teachers get most of their stimulus to fresh thinking precisely through local in-service training courses.

The OECD report (1981) points out how important it is that teachers participate actively in the shaping of their own in-service training programme, that the courses should be related to the work in a teacher's subject or class, or to the work of the school in more general terms. Actually, we know far too little about what motivates teachers for in-service training. The OECD report points out that we all have interests in our personal development, our family, free time, and occupation. These areas of interest overlap and can result in a diversity of needs with respect to in-service training.

It is also important to take an untraditional look at what 'training' really is. As a rule, we think of courses, conferences, or seminars – usually conducted off school grounds. The following ideas have been suggested in Britain:

- Two deputy directors change jobs for a couple of weeks so that they can gain a broader perspective on their work.
- A large lower secondary school plans its classroom teaching in such a way that, for one week out of the year, the entire staff can work together with the entire staff of the educational centre in order to prepare material for the next year's teaching.
- Two colleagues agree to sit in on each other's classes for a whole semester, and exchange observations after each classroom visitation (see below).
- A teacher's college offers all the local comprehensive schools in the area courses in methodology for a month. Colleagues from each school (four at a time) participate, so that most of the teachers at a given school will have undergone the same course when the 'course month' is over.
- Two course consultants in a municipality offer a methodology course. For one class hour they work with teachers in their classes and follow that up with a two-hour course in the afternoon.
- A lower secondary school arranges a 'teach-in' on the school's situation, inviting guest lecturers, getting parents, teachers and pupils involved, and carrying on from Friday morning to Saturday afternoon.

These are a few examples which illustrate the fact that in-service training does not just mean traditional courses. We know from other countries that sabbatical arrangements, job exchanges, teacher research, school improvement courses and visitation programmes at other schools are all natural elements of in-service training.

In Chapter 4 we presented a series of studies and theories about leadership in general, and about school leadership in particular. In this part we shall present three projects involving head teachers (and sometimes the leadership team) in in-service training activities. The assumptions here are generally the same as for teacher in-service training. The idea is that job-relevant knowledge and skills are learned and applied to job situations – after which, it is assumed, they will have an impact on the school as a whole. Let us take an in-depth look at these assumptions.

THE HEAD TEACHER AS THE CHANGE AGENT

LSW-Schulleiterfortbildung (LSW) – School Management Development programme

First we will consider Germany, the largest industrial state in Europe, in particular Nordrhein-Westfalen, and the large, modern research, development and in-service training institute called *Landesinstitut für Schule und Weiterbildung* (LSW) in Soest.

For about ten years at this institute quite an extensive management development programme has been running (*Schulleiterfortbildung*), under the leadership of Herbert Buchen. In 1996, the government decided that the programme should be offered to all head teachers in the state of Nordrhein-Westfalen, and an extensive period of growth is expected during the next five years.

The LSW[1] programme was designed for the new head teachers who have held their positions from six months to three years. Head teachers are gathered in groups of about 30 people who study together for a period of two years. None of the participants has any formal training that would qualify them for school management positions. The need for training is about 700 persons per year, for which LSW has been able to provide annual training for about 275 (there are about 450 applicants each year).

Until now, the programme has consisted of a series of seminars, led by a trained seminar leader. In addition, experts are brought in from a number of different areas. The goal of the programme is to provide the head teacher with the competence to act and make decisions on his or her own, 'within legal borders'. The programme consists of three basic courses and five elective courses (most choose all the seminars). The content of the training reflects the tasks of a German head teacher:

1. *School and law:* The goal here is to provide information and reduce uncertainty surrounding the legal foundation, as well as to analyse the relationships (or the lack thereof) between the legal foundation and the educational goals.
2. *Organizational development:* The goal here is to provide information about organizational development as a strategy for meeting both individual needs and organizational goals.
3. *Management style and school climate:* Here the relationship between management styles and school climate is discussed. The goal is to develop a style of management that stimulates motivation and involvement.
4. *The organization of classroom teaching:* Here the programme highlights opportunities for alternative organization of instruction and what that implies in terms of challenges to school management and instructional leadership, especially with respect to collaboration across subjects.

5. *The use of information technology:* Here the programme describes and analyses the various uses of data technology for the school administration.
6. *Evaluation of classroom teaching:* Here the programme discusses the complicated task of the head teacher, who is between a rock and a hard place when evaluating the quality of classroom teaching. The importance of common standards and a commonly accepted evaluation process is emphasized.
7. *Counselling:* The goal here is to further develop the manager's skills as the leader of the faculty. This is done by means of practical examples and role play.
8. *Meeting management:* Managers receive practical training in the planning and the management of meetings, in conflict resolution in groups, etc. The goal is a collaborative management style that breaks with the traditional hierarchy.

The programme is thoroughly implemented. It is based on extensive documentation and a well-thought-out body of instructional and learning materials, including a number of exercises that allow for practical training.

Evaluations of this programme have been carried out. And on the basis of this and a number of meetings where the programme (which has been around for many years) was discussed, fairly radical changes have been put forward. The evaluation showed that for the most part, participants, though well satisfied with the programme (especially the organizational development aspect) did, however, not feel competent to act differently on the basis of the training (Brunholz 1988).

Therefore, this past year LSW has been working with the question of how new knowledge and skills can be transferred to the practical arena (Mutzek 1988). A model has been developed for system development through a participatory development process, where continuous use is made of data on school practice, together with pupils, parents, teachers and the head teacher in an effort to create 'learning organizations'.

Tentative sketches of the new management development programme show an altogether different and binding relationship between theory and practice. From the beginning, *school reality* plays a major role, where the head teacher is responsible for 'quality development' and 'quality control'. The programme also emphasizes, at the outset, *the managerial role* in a changing school, the *school improvement process* itself, collegial counselling practised through each individual head teacher's school improvement project, and use of external consultants (if desirable). In other words, the new LSW programme, from being a relatively traditional and well-implemented management development programme, goes on to become a combined management and school improvement programme.

This is a radical change for Germany, where the head teacher has primarily been an administrator. And it requires that the head teacher can really *lead* the school improvement process at the individual school. We will take a closer look at this in the next section.

The 'Managing Productive Schools' Project

We have chosen a management-guided development project that has been in operation for about ten years. Developed by Snyder and Anderson (1986), it emerged at the height of the 'Effective Schools' movement. It is interesting because it is a very systematic attempt at changing the schools through management.

The project is based on a well-thought-out philosophy and theory. We begin briefly by describing Anderson and Snyder's vision of what they term 'quality cultures'. These are characterized by satisfied customers, strong leadership, systemic thinking (cf Peter Senge), strategic planning, continuous learning, and continuous school improvement (Snyder *et al.* 1994).

The project's *theory of change* consists of three phases:

1. *The Awareness Phase* is a dependency phase and involves staff development and support for programme development.
2. *The Translation Phase* is characterized by independence, organizational development, system design, and interaction.
3. *The Transformation Phase* is characterized by interdependence, customer satisfaction and continuous improvement.

To lead his school from the bureaucratic stage to a 'quality system', the head teacher needs additional competence. This is viewed as a continuous process, with four proficiency areas and ten types of competence:

1. *Organizational planning:* This area requires skills in setting goals for the schools in consultation with all the parties involved, being able to manage and work effectively with groups, and being able to evaluate staff work.
2. *Staff development:* This area requires skills in planning and developing effective in-service training programmes, in carrying out clinical supervision, in developing teams and in exercising quality control.
3. *Programme development:* This area's task is to develop new teaching programmes (content, methods, organization, collaboration between teachers, etc.), and make better use of the school's collective resources.
4. *Evaluating the schools' productivity:* The planning and implementation of pupil evaluations, the evaluation of teachers' work, group effectiveness, and the school's overall productivity.

The management development programme offers 25 training days during the course of one year to a group of head teachers; it is a very intense, skills-oriented programme involving a great deal of reading and practical trials in the head teachers' own schools. And since it is also a very broad programme, there is every reason to believe that the head teachers would receive thorough training, both theoretical and practical. Here theories of in-service training, the school as an organization, and leadership theories are exploited convincingly.

The intention is that the head teacher should implement changes in her own school. This is, in a sense, an individual strategy, but Anderson and Snyder make it clear that school improvement is the programme's objective. Instead of an external agent of change, the leadership of the school is provided with the knowledge and skills needed to change its own school.

Snyder and his colleagues carried out a follow-up study, during which time they interviewed 28 head teachers. 1,235 teachers evaluated the schools' culture and the process of change (Snyder *et al.* 1994). Teachers' reactions fell into three categories. The first group consisted of those who felt that positive changes had really taken place. They cite team teaching, interdisciplinary teaching, co-operative learning, participation in the decision-making process, more clearly defined goals, sympathy for teachers' concerns, and a supportive administration. Measured in terms of a 'school culture instrument', the researchers found that this indicated that a 'collaborate culture' was emerging.

There are also many teachers who feel that the schools have become *worse* places to teach in. Social factors (e.g. the pupils' home situation) and pupil discipline are mentioned, as well as a multiplicity of tasks that keep the teacher away from classroom teaching, and administrative measures that are unable to meet the needs of all the pupils. These teachers feel that their pupils no longer respect them and that the parents are no help at all in creating a better school. Moreover, they feel overworked and complain about countless new tasks and about how little support they are given to implement them. They are also sceptical about the attitudes of the administration, which sometimes condescends to give teachers a hearing, but at other times does not.

A small group of teachers feels that the schools have not changed at all. They feel that the proverbial pendulum is swinging once again, that only the underlying philosophy has changed, and not actual practice. The methods are still the same and the schools lack the necessary means to carry out the changes. In other words, it's 'business as usual'!

Researchers found that these attitudes were closely tied to the way in which the changes were implemented. One example is the way goals are defined. Where everyone (including parents) participates, and where the head teachers follow up, the goals characterize the school's activities. In less 'mature' schools, these are formulated jointly, but not with everyone participating. Therefore some feel that these goals are being shoved down their throats. What the study tells us is that a new work culture requires thorough and conscientious preparation, which takes time. Just how much time, varies greatly. In two of the schools that had existed for less than a year and where the head teacher had hired all the teachers, Snyder and his colleagues assessed the culture as a 'quality culture'.

The head teachers themselves felt that they had learned a great deal but that the application of what they had learned varied according to the particular challenges they encountered. Within those areas encompassed by the management programme, the researchers found after one year that the visions of the head teachers were as follows:

1. *Visionary leadership:* Here there was general agreement on a vision that stresses the creation of the conditions for success for all pupils, the development of school work culture, getting teachers involved in a creative development process, and creating an attitude of 'quality is everyone's responsibility'.

2. *Strategic planning:* The head teachers' visions are shared by the teachers and developed through a consensus process (e.g. the use of the Delphi-Dialogue technique, Snyder and Anderson 1986). The teachers work in study groups and a lot of preparation goes into the development of new plans. There is extensive staff development in those schools that have come the farthest.

3. *Systemic thought and action:* There is a widespread norm which requires that no one work alone but together with others. An integration of students receiving remedial instruction happens frequently, interdisciplinary studies are developed, and partnerships – both internal and between schools and local community – are usual.

4. *Information system:* Questions about how the development is progressing creates a need for exact knowledge about what the development work entails. Of major importance to the schools are such things as more relevant and improved data on pupils.

5. *Continuous development:* Giving teachers greater responsibility (empowerment) is a major aspect of a head teacher's job (as she sees it, at any rate). Approximately one-third of the teachers feel this way. There are pilot projects under way in most schools, but few of them have been developed to apply to the schools as a whole.

6. *Staff development:* The head teachers feel that this is the most important strategy. A number of workshops, 'train-the-trainer' seminars, school visits and 'co-operative training' are set in motion. Curriculum and teaching seminars were relatively rare.

How far, then, have these schools come with respect to 'quality cultures'? Snyder sees changes in the following areas in particular:

- *Programme areas:* More is done with interdisciplinary programmes and authentic learning, where the local community is also involved. Most head teachers feel that schools will gradually move from a traditional class/yearly type of organization to a more individualized one based on continuous evaluation.

- *Culture:* The head teachers feel that the schools have made great strides in moving from an 'I' culture to a 'We' culture. The local community is also better integrated, and an atmosphere that emphasizes what is positive has replaced the sense of crisis that used to prevail in the schools. In most schools there is much greater parental involvement; even several teacher 'old timers' have taken heart, and there is a growing feeling of living in an organization that is alive.

- *Customer satisfaction:* Here the head teachers single out working with pupils, which all too often in the past was not a part of the schools' agenda. By active involvement in the local community, through more authentic tasks and practical preparation, the schools do a better job for these pupils.

This is the way *head teachers* experience school improvement. True, Snyder's report is tentative and a lot of data remains to be processed. Nevertheless it is clear that the head teachers' image of reality differs from that of many teachers in the same schools. We appear to find some of the same effects that Swedish researchers found in the comprehensive Swedish management development programme for head teachers which, in existence for about twenty years, has in recent years been reorganized as part of the major reorganization of the Swedish schools (Ekholm 1992).

The Swedish in-service training programme for school leaders

Sweden was the first of the Nordic countries to initiate training for school leaders. The first design, in fact, was conceived as far back as 1972! Elsewhere we have described this programme, which lasted for nearly twenty years, as a major initiative until it was reorganized in 1993 as a regionally governed programme (for a description see Ekholm 1981, Ekholm *et al.* 1986 and Ekholm, Stegø and Olsson 1982).

One of the distinctive characteristics of the Swedish school leadership programme is that it seeks to heighten participants' awareness of the process of change in the individual school and qualify them to cope with it. There is a rather large body of work, both theoretical and practical, to impart such knowledge. The project management is aware that the way development work is carried out in different schools can vary greatly; but above all, it will take time. The first management development programme was compulsory for head teachers and lasted two years. In some of the larger municipalities, superintendents and head teachers took part in the programme for a four- to five-year period. Since leaders from the same municipality participated over time, it was possible to bring up and deal with actual present-day problems.

The Swedish school leadership training is built up hierarchically. The head teacher is supposed to safeguard national goals for the schools. School improvement initiatives are based on the head teacher's ideas on school improvement. With these as a vantage point, a development plan is worked out. The Swedish programme seeks, in reality, to educate the head teacher to become a kind of change agent. He is to be both leader and consultant for the development work at his own school.

In-service training comprised 25 course days in courses of four to five days each, spread over a two-year period. Most of the content was related to school improvement, and 'management of change' was a major theme. These seminars allowed time for reflection, allowed for a mix of several kinds of activities, and was based on the best of management training methodology.

All participants were visited by one or more resource people, three to five times during the course of the two-year period. The object was to discuss theory and practice and provide an opportunity for reflection. Much emphasis was also placed on evaluating one's own school, as well as making observations on others (e.g. how the head teachers used their time, how the school was organized, etc.). The head teachers were also given such tasks as describing and evaluating a specific example of teaching, and feeding the results back to the teachers, pupils and colleagues. The aim was to qualify the participants for school improvement; and 30 to 40 days were used to work through such issues in the school.

An unusual component in the Swedish programme was two practice periods in an organization other than a school (two weeks). During one of these periods, the head teacher was supposed to work in the municipal child and youth sector. The object was to gain a better understanding of pupils' life situations. The other period was spent in a company in the municipality. This model for the management development programme was partially modified after 1987.

Several evaluations of the Swedish programme have been carried out. Hultman did an evaluation of the project at an early stage. The head teachers had undergone basic training and had been back to work for about half a year. He found that, by and large, their reactions to the courses were positive. They stressed how well implemented the courses had been, how they had been forced to take a stand, and how they had benefited from the process-oriented parts. In other words, the head teachers came away feeling that these courses had meant something to them *as individuals* (Hultman 1981). Hultman points out that the effect in relation to the professional role of the head teachers was far less pronounced. He found that part of the reason was the way in which resources were utilized; for the most part, they were earmarked for head teachers' *courses*. This was also pointed out by Olsson, who found that the project's experts spent only 20 per cent of their time in the schools, and the working in the courses (Olsson 1980). Both Olsson and Hultman feel that the resources in the Swedish project were far too limited for the ambitious goals to be achieved.

Some of the head teachers (8 per cent) felt that they were able to observe improvements in classroom teaching in their schools. At the same time, 24 per cent reported a measure of staff irritation. This was interpreted to mean that the teachers had been irritated about the constant absences (away on course!).

Hultman points out that the Swedish project sought to find an alternative to 'the expert strategy' – that someone from the outside would 'come and change us'. In reality, as the teachers see it, the head teacher has merely replaced 'the expert', according to Hultman.

Hultman feels that a strategy more consistently geared to organizational develop-ment – that is, where development takes place from within and where management training is integrated into the process – would have prevented many of these problems. As long as this does not happen, the goals themselves, according to Hultman, should be revised in light of the fact that access to resources is likely to decrease rather than increase in the years ahead.

We should stress here that Hultman's investigation came at an early stage in the project. We know from research on organizational development that behavioural changes in the schools take a lot of time – three to five years, at least.

The earlier reports (Pettigrew 1982, Schmuck 1982, and Vormeland 1982) give us a rich and varied picture of the project. Hultman's main conclusion – namely, that the programme could not be said to have led to noticeable change in the schools – is confirmed by all the reports; and observers point out some of the reasons. Pettigrew was especially concerned with the renewal process upon which the project was based. He says:

> If the school leadership programme has an Achilles heel, it is at the very instant that the head teacher, after two years, attempts to implement changes in his school. The primary question is whether it is an effective strategy to reckon on the head teacher being the kingpin in the work of renewal. (Pettigrew 1982)

Richard Schmuck regards the Swedish development as a parallel to the development in other countries toward a 'self-developing school'. He regards it as crucial that the project management clarifies the goals of the changes and that it describes what kind of school this is – in contrast to the traditional school. Schmuck feels that it is necessary to develop clearer structures in the programme, clearer expectations, and better follow-up. He also points to measures that could mobilize the entire school for the work of renewal (Schmuck 1982).

Oddvar Vormeland points out that the 'home room' periods appear to be relatively ineffective; few teachers felt that the programme had had any impact on the school; those schools in which development work was already under way were the very ones that had benefited most from the programme; furthermore, he points out that there is little to indicate that the staff's involvement in school improvement was a consequence of the programme. He concludes: 'The development of the head teachers as human beings and administrators is itself not enough to help the schools along. The head teacher can be an organizer, but he cannot develop the school alone' (Vormeland 1982).

A more extensive and longitudinal study was carried out by Ekholm et al. (1986), who followed 35 head teachers and the work that went on in their schools. (Every head teacher in Sweden is usually responsible for more than one school.) The object of the evaluation was to determine whether the school leadership training had any impact on the head teachers' own managerial behaviour and consequently on the way the school and the teaching were conducted.

The evaluation consisted of three research visits to the 35 schools over a five-year period. The information was obtained by interviews, observations and discussions with all affected parties in the schools and their respective neighbourhoods, and the focus was on the schools' goals, organization, interaction, communication, decision-making process, interpersonal relationships, processes of change, utilization of the evaluation, and the relationship of the schools to their local communities. All of these were areas given careful attention by the school leadership programme. What, then, did the researchers find out?

1. *The head teacher's management style:* In all, eleven out of 35 head teachers had changed their management style, with a greater emphasis on collaboration. This

can be explained in part as a function of the management training programme; but during this time there was also a lot of pressure being exerted by the state and by society in the same direction.

2. *Teacher collaboration:* In 1980 only six schools could be characterized by co-operation between teachers in classroom teaching. This number had risen to nineteen (out of 35) schools by 1985. In twelve out of thirteen schools that had developed such a working style, the head teachers' management style had already become more collaborative. It was discovered that an active head teacher who takes the initiative creates the conditions for changes in the school.

3. *Pupil–teacher interaction:* The schools had in advance been classified for a 'passive/active' pupil participation dimension. Even after five years, there was still teacher-controlled instruction in 28 out of 35 principal sectors, which often made pupils passive, and the head teachers were loathe to take any initiative in the area of classroom teaching. The few changes that were noted took place in primary school.

4. *School democracy:* Here too, there was only modest change. Apart from the establishment of a student council and the participation of pupils in formal meetings, there were few signs that pupils wielded more influence.

5. *Local discussions of goals:* This was one of the main areas that the training concentrated on. With respect to the discussion of goals, there was a certain amount of development. After five years, sixteen out of 35 principal sectors were still working with discussions about goals. However, this is also an area that was given a high priority by the state during the period of time involved, and the effects can therefore only partially be explained by the management development programme.

6. *School-based planning and evaluation:* This was also an important area for the training programme. Here researchers found a big gap between plans and practice. Only three schools made active use of plan and evaluation data. Nine schools used parts of the data, and 22 schools made no use of the data whatsoever. The work of planning and evaluation remained mere paper work – in spite of the fact that the head teachers should have been eminently qualified to implement a planning and evaluation process, having received a considerable amount of in-service training in the field.

Researchers evaluate these results themselves. They particularly stress the fact that in Sweden there is little respect for local management, which has kept the head teachers from making effective use of what they have learned. There are few examples of Swedish head teachers making demands on their teachers. Many Swedish head teachers are more loyal to their teachers than they are to the politicians.

We have discussed this evaluation relatively thoroughly, not only because few programmes have been evaluated in recent years, but also because the findings are consistent with other evaluations we have mentioned.

MANAGEMENT TRAINING AND SCHOOL DEVELOPMENT

Evaluations of management training show quite clearly that, while good programmes are important for the manager's personal and professional development, their impact on the organization is limited. In our view, effective management training should be defined as a process that is a necessary – but not sufficient – prerequisite for school improvement. A number of factors need to be considered, as follows.

Basic principles

The objective for school leadership training must be to give the head teacher the capacity *to liberate resources in his own organization*. Solutions are not 'bestowed from on high', as it were (for example, with a new curriculum); the head teacher's role is *not* one of passing on a new central message. Rather, his task is to be loyal *on key issues* (goals and norms), and *experimental* in relation to methods and solutions. Problem definition and solutions take place by mobilizing the school's own forces, not by being 'an expert from the outside'.

The theoretical foundation. Eric Hoyle claims that management training should rest on six relevant theories: educational theory, policy theory, organizational theory, curriculum theory, management theory, and the theory of change. The weight given to each will largely be determined by one's goals for the programme (Hoyle 1986). The theoretical foundation is important, to be seen as a frame of reference. But above all, it must be possible to apply the theory in concrete situations.

Structure and sequencing. The traditional model, with early external management training and subsequent team development, followed by organizational development, is but *one* possible structure. We know that head teachers have different needs, and that the schools for which they are responsible are at different levels of development. This is bound to have consequences for the way the programmes are designed. In order to differentiate management training, the responsibility should probably be assigned to *school owners*, who in collaboration with the head teachers and professional expertise will then develop a plan for management and organizational development at each school. The schools' preparedness differs greatly, so the sequence will be all the more important. The point of departure must be the school's situation, and the management development programme will be only one of several strategies for school improvement.

Responsibility for training. Effective management development can be a lot of things. We agree with March that the universities *can* play an important role, because more fundamental perspectives on management and society, based on relevant research, can have great significance (March 1979). The universities should not compete in terms of who has the best 'practical' programme. Others can do that better. The universities must see their role as one of providing *alternative perspectives* that can form the basis for a reappraisal of practices. On the other hand, it is also quite clear that practical management tools have to be mastered. Here an R & D organization, an educational centre, or a consultancy firm could be just as good a choice. Again, the school owners should thoroughly familiarize themselves with existing options and request a broad list.

The learning process. Developing new attitudes and skills later in life is no easy matter. Some training institutions attempt to persuade participants, by means of relatively simple exercises, that skills can be learned quickly and effectively. There is now a wealth of programmes and other options available that are more noted for their cosmetic value than their academic content. Management development must involve the manager in the testing of new behaviour over a long period of time. Here, as for other kinds of in-service training, demonstrations, testing, feedback and coaching are all necessary. Isolated courses are *not* sufficient. There will never be sufficient resources for the the kind of close, long-term contact that a manager needs for receiving relevant support in his practices. So it is important that a 'coaching culture' be developed among the head teachers, where there is sufficient trust between teachers and head teacher.

Safety net. Any *bona fide* management development programme should have enough capacity to follow up each leader at his or her workplace. Most of them, during the course of such a programme, will be working a lot with themselves. It is important to have conversation partners and people who can provide frank and specific feedback. This must be done by professional, qualified personnel.

As we have seen, management training is of limited effectiveness where it concerns altering a leader's behaviour, let alone school improvement. What is needed today is a more experimental approach toward management development. We are only in the initial stages of what could prove to be a very interesting development. But it is vital that those with responsibility for the development work dare to tread new paths, think critically through the entire process, and seek better alternatives.

EFFECTS OF IN-SERVICE TRAINING

Can we say anything about what effects in-service training has on school improvement? Effects in relation to what? If we mean effectiveness in the sense that teachers or heads have a better mastery of those skills that are associated with processes of change in their own role, then it seems clear that so-called 'school-based' programmes are the only ones which can reasonably be said to be effective. We previously referred to Joyce and Showers, who showed that few teacher training programmes actually provide teachers with practical classroom skills. They feel that changes are unlikely to be brought about unless the following five training levels are carried out:

1. Presentation of theory and description of new skills.
2. Demonstration of skills, or 'model' teaching.
3. Practice in simulated and classroom situations.
4. Structured and open feedback situations (in which both candidate and trainer can discuss the level of skill).
5. Assistance in implementation – preferably through a two-teacher system in the classroom (Joyce and Showers 1980).

In a recent study in Richmond County, Georgia, Joyce and colleagues investigated whether systematic staff development over an eighteen-month period had an impact on pupils' learning proficiency. They found that the impact was considerable with respect to the *implementation* of new teaching methods, but the results varied from school to school. Good implementation led to sensationally positive results as far as pupil learning went (Joyce and Murphy 1990).

Showers has continued her work with trying to discover more effective educational strategies. Her work with clarifying the significance of *collegial support* (coaching) shows that teachers who enjoy such support are far better qualified to implement changes in their teaching. By 'coaching', Showers means the providing of joint activity, giving technical feedback, and the analysis of the application of new skills. For that matter, she found that teachers that were coached used about twice as much time in the classroom to work with the theoretical and conceptual aspects of their teaching compared with teachers in the control group that didn't receive any coaching. She found that teachers with collegial support felt more secure in the new teaching situation, while the others experienced insecurity and were ill at ease; and most did not overcome the difficulty of adapting new teaching methods to their classroom situation (Showers 1983).

Joyce and Showers recommend another and more thoroughgoing form of in-service training than that undertaken in Norway – or perhaps the whole of Scandinavia, for that matter. As a rule, the courses are limited to level 1, or perhaps level 2. The research carried out by Joyce (in co-operation with Yarger and Howey) shows that this form of training (levels 1 and 2) has little or no practical significance for changes in classroom teaching practices.

Stallings (1989) has carried out a comprehensive programme of evaluation for the purpose of testing various forms of in-service teacher training. The task was to improve the teaching and pupil proficiency with respect to reading skills in upper secondary school. Stallings found that teachers are more likely to make changes in their teaching when:

- they become aware of the needs through self-reflection and analysis;
- they change the course so that it fits their class and the school better;
- they personally try out ideas and assess their effects;
- they can sit in as observers in one another's classes and analyse the data together;
- they are able to report their findings to the group;
- they can discuss cases (specific pupils and situations);
- they make written commitments and learn to set new professional goals (Stallings 1989, pp. 3–4).

Stallings says that the crux of the model is *practice*, trying, adapting, trying again, relating new knowledge to past experience, learning through reflection and problem-solving in a supportive environment in which challenges can be freely discussed. His assessment of how pupils profited in terms of learning was designed to test whether it made any difference whether teachers with reading as a speciality received training, compared with *all teachers* in 'language arts' in a given school received training – compared, in turn, with all 'language arts' teachers in a given municipality received training over a three-year period. The results showed that pupils in the first group went ahead by six months (measured by standardized tests) in reading comprehension and reading skills; pupils in schools in which all the language arts teachers had received training went ahead by eight months, whereas pupils from all the schools made marked progress (here without any control group).

On the other hand, staff development trials that were not very systematic had little effect. Little (1990) shows that with the introduction of the 'mentor' system (colleague guidance), *time* for change is important, the opportunity to put them into practice is crucial, and the school's culture is important. She shows that Bird and Alspaugh (1986), in their appraisal of California's one-year mentor programme, claim that 'a lot was lost and little or nothing was gained, on account of time pressures in the implementation', because the programme spun out of control (quoted from Fullan 1990).

Sandström and Ekholm (1984) sought to clarify the effects that management development and in-service training in general have had on school improvement. They claim to have detected 'certain traces' of the courses – certain initiatives were taken that were directly inspired by the courses, for example. But programmes affecting a majority of the adults in the schools quickly died out; these schemes simply came to nothing. And Sandström and Ekholm conclude: 'In none of the schools did the plans that both head teachers and groups of teachers had worked out during their respective courses become "common property" at the schools' (p. 120). On the other hand, Sandström and Ekholt did find positive effects at the level of the individual. Their recommendations suggest that in-service training, to a much greater extent, should take place through work at the individual school, and that in-service training experts should help school personnel to take a fresh look at their own local organization, where the need for in-service training is an important element. Thus the in-service training strategy approaches what we will discuss, in the following chapter, under the subheading 'Organizational Development' (p. 184).

Effective in-service training takes place near the school, with the focus on the school's day-to-day problems. This does not mean that the courses lack theoretical content, merely that the theory must be usable. The more it is a question of skills that require interaction – whether with colleagues, head teachers, pupils, or parents, the training must be closely linked to the daily work situation. At the same time, we are faced with the following dilemma: many teachers want this kind of in-service training, and yet few of them welcome the thought of others coming into their classrooms! To the best of our knowledge, this is due to characteristics of the schools as an organization, which we have pointed out in Chapter 3. Before such attitudes can be changed, the *climate* of development work itself must change. Only then will the notion gain acceptance that co-operation with others in 'my' classroom gives me my best opportunity for self-development.

Joyce, Hersh and McKibbin (1983) have analysed teachers' motivation for participating in in-service training. They find that their basic attitude toward learning can explain many of the variations in participation and in benefit from in-service training. They describe five categories of participants:

1. *Those who are voracious* use every opportunity – both formal and informal – to learn. Books, trips, courses and museums are a major part of their life. They have found colleagues they can work together with, they make an active effort to improve the schools, and they have few complaints about resources or colleagues. Their energy is directed toward *growth*. This category includes a number of different types of teacher: the more formally oriented, who have a pronounced academic interest and who, because they often isolate themselves in the schools, are not very visible in the informal social fabric. There is also the more informal type who learns much from her colleagues and is not particularly concerned with formal qualifications. Then there is the more personally oriented type, who is most concerned with life outside of school and who learns much from whatever cultural programmes are available.

2. *The active consumers* are very active in their work and, as a rule, have some project or other in progress or in the planning stage. They participate actively in in-service training and would have no objections if more courses were made compulsory, so that 'those who need them the most can benefit the most'. Such teachers take advantage of every opportunity to 'talk shop' and discuss teaching issues.

3. *The passive consumers*, who will be present when the situation calls for it, but who never take a personal initiative. If the school starts a project, they will support it. If someone in the group suggests an activity, they loyally back it up; but they need others to take the initiative. There are those, however, who are active consumers in some areas (e.g. hobbies), while passive in others.

4. *The firmly established* are those who are well established in their jobs; they feel they are succeeding and don't want any change (in any case, none that is forced on them by others). They are not looking for courses. And if they do take any, it is within areas in which they are already successful. They seldom take a course unless it is offered during working hours, and they are attuned to any potential benefits. Courses that question current teaching practices are viewed with scepticism. Such teachers might actively oppose such schemes, or they might use the informal system to influence developments, or they might also withdraw from the project.

5. *Those who are withdrawn* seek to minimize their participation in school life, tend to steer clear of in-service courses, and work hardest for themselves in their own classroom. Some of those who tend to be the most withdrawn [at school] are the same people who are quite active in their private life. As a rule, they make it quite clear that they wish to maintain a 'minimum contract' with the school, and it would take a great deal to convince them of the use and the desirability of increased involvement. (See B. Derr's career motivation theory discussed on pages 139–40.)

WHAT CONSTITUTES GOOD IN-SERVICE TRAINING?

We take a limited – but in our view, important – perspective: we are thinking here of the kind of in-service training that promotes positive school improvement. In this chapter we have primarily focused on *the teacher*: we could just as well have discussed the head teacher's (or the superintendent's) need for in-service training and made use of many of the same arguments.

This raises the question whether it is expedient to group in-service training for different professional groups for each group individually, *if school improvement is our goal*. It goes without saying that some topics are group- and profession-related, although many are not. Would it help, for example, if the subject 'communication' or 'problem-solving' did not become a distinct part of the in-service curriculum for head teachers (in separate seminars) but rather a subject worked out in co-operation between persons and groups whose goal in their daily work is to improve communication and problem-solving? My *first concern*, therefore, is that we give careful thought to whom *the participants* are in in-service training.

My *second concern* is that a professional needs new and challenging tasks as a motivation for in-service training. This is the driving force – that the qualification requirements for the daily work situation change. If each professional does not experience such challenges – in a concrete way – then the foundation itself (the basic motivation for new occupational-related learning) is missing.

Human Resource Development (HRD) in the workplace shows in general that most practical learning takes place on the job, through self-study, through working together with colleagues, and by counselling and supervision (Å. Dalin 1993; see also Dalin and Rolff 1993). *The way in which the workplace is organized* is thus a crucial factor in the effectiveness of the practical learning. Here I am primarily thinking of the structural aspect of the question. In addition, studies we have mentioned in this chapter show that collegial co-operation – or rather, what many have termed 'an open and trusting learning culture' – is crucial to professional development.

My *third concern* is therefore the manner in which schools are organized. Albert Shanker (1990) points out that traditional in-service training reflects an outmoded form of school organization; but the question is whether most schools in fact still have a very traditional organization, one that largely insulates the individual teacher from contact with his or her colleagues.

My *fourth concern* is where the knowledge is coming from. For quite some time we have taken it for granted that the universities and other schools of higher learning are responsible for the 'production of credentials', and that in-service training is a strategy for imparting this knowledge to the teachers. During the past ten years it has been suggested by a number of experts in the field that it is the teachers themselves who know, and that it is first and foremost a question of time and place for reflecting over one's own practices and interactions with colleagues. It has become clear for most that none of these positions can be correct. The individual teacher and teachers acting jointly can surely, through critical analysis and reflection, learn important aspects of their work. The task of institutions of higher learning, in my opinion, is not 'to belabour the teacher on the subject of relevance', but to highlight the challenges as seen from new perspectives (see also Madsèn 1993). What is at issue here is a new partnership, one that develops a new form of dialogue between equal partners (see Goodlad 1990b).

My *fifth concern* is that we do not instrumentalize in-service training. That can happen, for example, when the central authorities primarily look upon this strategy as a means of mediating a curriculum, a means of getting teachers to walk in step. In-service training must not be allowed to degenerate into mere 'workshops' where people try to *solve* problems. It must also be a place where people can freely assemble and, on the basis of their own experiences, *define* problems. To make solutions our own, we ourselves must help define what kinds of problems we are facing.

My *sixth concern* is that we do not focus too narrowly on school improvement in such a way that it becomes the dominant or even the only form of in-service training. There must be scope for personal development – perhaps forms of in-service training that do not readily appear to be useful – and where we do not necessarily find any logical connection between effort expended and results gained in the classroom. What might appear to be not useful and 'just' be taken for personal development could well prove to be of fundamental significance for a teacher's own development – also as a teacher. Traditional university courses, which allow for academic preoccupation and reflection, can prove in the long term to be of inestimable value, even though the effects are not immediately discernible.

We would remind the reader of the emphasis that Peter Senge (1990) places on developing personal mastery through a lifelong personal, binding learning process as a necessary condition for understanding one's own hidden 'mental models' and for being able to experience new perspectives ('Metanoia').

My *seventh concern* is to look at the teacher's career development from an overall perspective. It is a question of more closely joining initial, supplementary and continuing training and generating a more fruitful interplay between theory and practice, between academic disciplines and pedagogy – and, not least, between the many institutions and systems with a stake in this market. As Shanker (1990) declares so well: none of the institutions that are working in the field have in-service training as a priority. How, then, can we create joint, non-competitive reward systems?

My *eighth concern* involves taking in-service training as a subject area seriously. Particularly through the work of Joyce (see, for example, Joyce and Murphy 1990) and Stallings (1989), we know much about where it pays to invest, provided we want to see practical results from in-service training. If this is to be taken seriously, then fundamental changes must be made in the way such training is conducted in most countries. And then we must also take the matter of financing seriously. Here, estimates vary from 5.7 per cent of the total school budget (Fullan 1991, p. 329), 5 per cent of the salary budget (*Education Week* 1993), to thirteen full workdays yearly, plus considerable in-service training funds (Sweden, see Ekholm 1992).

My *ninth concern* is that the kind of in-service training that aims at changes in practice in the classroom or the school ought to be based on an understanding of how new practices develop in a school. *Knowledge of the process of innovation* will be a

173

significant part of the professionalization of those who will be working with in-service training, and also for both new and experienced teachers who will bear the responsibility for its implementation.

PUPILS AND PARENTS IN SCHOOL DEVELOPMENT

The most important individual in school is *the pupil.* What could be more natural than pupils actively participating in the development of the schools – or, to put it another way, in the development of their own 'workplace'? In another context we pointed out that working with the unknown, being a part of developing one's own workplace and the institution one lives with, can be one of the most important means of preparing for the future (Dalin and Rolff 1993). So in discussing individual strategies, it is only natural that we should also discuss ways in which the individual pupil and their parents can take an active part in renewing the schools.

In Chapter 3 we pointed out that neither pupils nor parents usually play an active role in school improvement. This applies to the Scandinavian countries in general, and to most other European countries as well. The situation varies, of course, depending on what level of the educational system we are on; it also varies with the issues involved, to some extent (for example, do pupils participate more in cases where their own roles are in focus?); furthermore, it varies from country to country.

In their book entitled *Learning from Work and Community Experiences*, the authors pointed out the significance of actively involving pupils in school improvement (IMTEC 1983). In studies that have been carried out for over a decade, the American foundation National Center for Resources for Youth (NCRY) pointed out the value that 'learning by participating' can have (Dollar 1981). Conrad and Hedin, researchers at Minnesota University, have shown that pupils who play an active part in the planning and implementation of their own learning also learn more than other pupils (Conrad and Hedin 1981). IMTEC arrived at the same result in its evaluation of reforms in Norwegian nurses training (Dalin 1979, Dalin and Skard 1986). Goodlad comes to the same conclusion in his nation-wide study entitled *A Place Called School* (Goodlad 1984).

We have seen that pupils seldom participate in decisions that concern their own learning. Rather, they are treated as immature and unmotivated, as unskilled labour that cannot take responsibility for their own learning. Arends *et al.* (1980) have shown how a systematic exclusion of pupils from the decision-making process led the schools into a vicious circle.

Usually we regard pupils as objects to be *treated*, as entities who ultimately stand to benefit from our projects. Pupils are looked upon as *products* of the school system. They are to be offered services, be protected, monitored, punished, or in some other way 'brought up' by adults. They are rarely ever regarded as rightful members of school society, members who can participate in planning, problem-solving and the implementation of change.

Sarason shows that the rules for communication in the classroom are usually laid down by the teacher. This is based on the assumption that 'the teacher knows best', that pupils are incapable of taking an active part in the development of rules, and that they aren't interested in doing so anyway – moreover, that rules are for the pupils, and not for the teachers (Sarason 1982). I hope and believe that this is a distorted image – even of an American classroom – but Sarason claims more generally that pupils know little about how teachers think. How teachers think about what they think (which is never made public) is the very thing that pupils are most interested in. What Sarason is trying to show us is that a lack of openness and reciprocity effectively hinders pupils from participating actively.

It is a dangerous thing to regard pupils as mere objects. In the first place, pupils have first-hand knowledge of the schools. If anyone knows where the shoe pinches, surely it is the pupils? They are in possession of valuable information. In the second place, participants with little influence in an organization tend to react counter-productively in a development process. They are not consulted beforehand, they are often fearful that changes will only make things worse for them, and they have been known to react by lodging protests. Is it so unreasonable to assume that pupils, just like teachers, undergo 'fluctuations of concern'?

Arends *et al.* point up a number of areas where pupils have shown great interest in taking an active part in decision-making processes, areas where development projects would have a direct bearing on pupils' interests. Pupils are concerned with the principle of fairness, with how they can give vent to their feelings (including anger), and with what is specifically expected of them. When can pupils disagree with their teacher, and what are the consequences? How are tests marked, and how can pupils participate in discussing the criteria?

Pupils are also taken up with school issues of a more general nature. They want to have a say in determining which electives are offered. They also wish to play an active part in the shaping of a school's profile. Furthermore, they are concerned with creating better forms of co-operation and a better school atmosphere in general.

Fullan (1991) would have us understand that pupils (not just teachers) must change if school improvement is to become a reality. And pupils are just as irked as teachers at merely being informed of what is going to happen. They should be allowed to participate, as far as this is feasible. In reality, they are never even asked! That is why they often react with bewilderment; they might even ignore what is happening (nothing will change anyway, they think), or they might regard it as a respite from all the tedium. Fullan points out several studies that all show the same thing: many attempts at renewal have no effect on pupils' learning or work situation. In fact, they go altogether unnoticed by the pupils. And in those cases where change actually does occur, it takes the pupils by surprise. One particular pupil whom Fullan refers to put it like this: '. . . Suddenly [the teachers] tell us that they are going to start teaching us as though we were adults . . . after having taught us like babies for years' (Fullan 1991, p. 183).

Where to draw the line is a matter that concerns most pupils. It is not necessarily a question of 'How far can we stretch the rules?', but 'Which rules are fair?', and 'Where do we draw the line when it comes to providing us with optimum learning and fellowship?' Pupils are also very concerned about which teachers they get. Are they given any say in choosing? How can they enter into a dialogue with teachers who are doing a poor job so that the situation can improve? When renewing the schools, why not make use of pupils' experiences?

One of the most difficult questions we face in the evaluation of pupil participation in school improvement is the degree of influence pupils should be allowed to have on the schooling of next year's class. In a three-year school the turnover rate is at least 33 per cent each year. Experience from schools which make use of pupil evaluations as a basis for changes in classroom teaching show that a given class can have quite special opinions about both the teaching itself and the teaching environment. To what extent should a teacher take into account the assessment of an individual class? (Dalin and Skard 1986).

While teachers comprise 'the stable core' of a school, pupils change schools regularly. We also know that certain classes can be very different to work with. Just how 'tenable', then, are these pupils' evaluation? (We will disregard, for the sake of argument, the issue of their maturity.) Provided they participate actively, over a long period of time, and provided a dialogue is arranged between teachers and pupils, in our opinion there is no reason to cast aspersion on pupils' evaluations. The reason these can be pronounced from one class to another with respect to very similar teaching situations is *vital information*. We know that classroom atmosphere is an important factor in learning and a sense of well-being. We should therefore expect that what from the outside might be seen as an identical teaching programme will, in fact, not necessarily be identical at all.

We know little about active pupil participation in school improvement. The trend in Scandinavia has been to go in for a representative pupil democracy and elect one or two pupils to committees that have dealt with school improvement. It is highly unlikely that this way of involving pupils is regarded as important by the individual pupil; nor is it likely that the resulting contribution will have any major impact on the outcome.

We have pointed out approximately 70 practical examples from Scandinavia, the Netherlands, Great Britain and North America, all of which show that pupils can have altogether different roles in the schools than those we are accustomed to. Pupils can take responsibility for their own learning, for that of others, and for various tasks both inside and outside school. And through such *learning by participation* we found that pupils learned more and had a greater sense of well-being (Dalin and Skrindo 1983).

Other studies performed over a period of a decade have shown that 'co-operative learning' can point to clear and positive results both with respect to the individual's learning, social development, work and teaching atmosphere and personal growth. More than anyone else, Robert E. Slavin from Johns Hopkins University has systematized this research; today he can point to significant positive learning effects from *making active use of pupils as a resource* in the classroom and in the schools (Slavin 1990).

All co-operative learning shares the notion that the individual is responsible for his or her own learning as well as for that of the others in the group. As opposed to usual group work, *co-operative learning is the primary form of organization for teaching*. It is assumed that:

- the individual learning group (as a rule, together with the teacher) sets clear and realistic goals against which the group is assessed and for which it is rewarded;
- *every pupil's learning growth* is a part of the evaluation of the group's productivity. Thus it is important that the pupils help one another so that each of them can master whatever trials *the individual pupil* might have;
- every single pupil *should have the same opportunity to contribute to the group's productivity* because individual effort is systematically assessed in relation to the individual's qualifications.

Most forms of co-operative learning are based on learning groups of about four pupils. There are a number of methods, techniques and materials that can help individual pupils and groups to reach their goal, as well as help the individual teacher in providing critically important assistance to those pupils and groups that need it the most. Co-operative learning is not the same as group work – which is often a rather unsystematic supplement to the usual teaching. Rather, *co-operating learning is the actual form of teaching* – or the primary production unit in the classroom – and the work is prepared systematically and with great care.

Today there are over 60 comprehensive studies of the effects of co-operative learning. There has never been any doubt that pupils develop socially, that they learn co-operation and joint problem-solving, and that co-operative learning stimulates personal growth. There are also clear parallels between co-operative learning and the form of learning that is typical of society in general. Outside school, learning together with others is rewarded. Companies are concerned with developing their own system of knowledge. Learning tasks are often goal-oriented, context-sensitive, and related to specific tasks.

The arguments against co-operative learning have focused on how it vitiates the academic level. This is just not true. Co-operative learning has been systematically evaluated in thousands of classrooms for a number of years, and as gauged in terms of traditional tests, the results are quite plain. Pupils who work with material on the basis of a co-operative learning model learn more – in some cases a whole lot more – than pupils exposed to traditional classroom teaching.

These results have begun to attract the interest of economists, as well as others who are not particularly concerned with educational methods. As the result of a joint project with Stanford University, the University of Arizona and the development organization Research for Better Schools (Philadelphia), comparing four 'innovations' (increased hours for instruction, reduction in class size, use of computer-assisted instruction, and co-operative learning), found the latter (using pupils as a resource) to be – by far – the most cost-effective innovation.

I have deliberately referred to studies that use pupils' academic results as their criteria, for the simple reason that the argument against changing the role of pupils in the schools has been that this would weaken them academically. This is nonsense. If pupils are used systematically as a resource, both they and those they work with will learn more than they would with traditional classroom instruction. And this applies to bright pupils and weaker ones alike.

The Norwegian schools have a long-standing tradition of using pupils in advisory and decision-making bodies. On the other hand, apart from certain special schools (such as 'The Oslo Experimental Gymnasium', for example), we have little experience with using pupils as a resource *in classroom teaching* (that is, unless we go back a number of years to the schools in country villages, where it was and still is necessary to use whatever resources they pupils had). Co-operative learning is nothing other than a more advanced form of using pupils as a resource, where both teacher and pupils have the means and facilities at their disposal. When this is clearly possible, when it can be done with existing resources, and when it leads to *markedly* improved results, then what is there to wait for?

Parents have played a very modest role in school improvement. This also applies to primary school. In certain major projects, the central authorities have elected a parental representative to various committees and boards. As a rule, they have had very little opportunity to work effectively. Unlike teacher representatives, who serve while on the job, parent representatives, as a rule, must use their leisure time. As opposed to those who work within the system, parents are usually cut off from any systematic work with parents from other schools where school issues are concerned.

There is ample documentation to indicate that the closer parents and schools work together, the better the development of the learning situation for pupils will be, which shows up in general well-being and improved academic achievement (Fullan 1991). Epstein has carried out systematic empirical research on parent–school co-operation; he finds that it has clear ramifications for the individual pupil. As for the well-known television programme 'Head Start' for pre-schoolers, Berlin and Berlin find no long-term effects of the programmes, with the exception of children whose parents were directly involved in the classroom (Fantini 1980, p. 14).

Most teachers would agree that a constructive dialogue with the homes is a prerequisite for good school work. Rutter and his colleagues have shown, for example, that common norms for homework are an important condition for learning (Rutter *et al.* 1979). A number of schools have made efforts to get parents actively involved, but with little success. There are a number of questions to be resolved:

- What responsibility and what role do we want parents to have in the schools?
- What are the structural and financial conditions for active parent work?
- How can we ensure the participation of parents from less well-to-do homes?
- When does parental responsibility for their children's schooling begin, and at what age level does it end?
- What practical conditions must be fulfilled before teachers can work together with parents in a constructive way?

Several attempts have been made to draw parents into school improvement at the classroom level. Parents appear to be actively interested in their own children's class, and in the work that goes on to improve the classroom environment and create norms for being together and for learning. Though parents may feel powerless with respect to the system, perhaps they can find meaning in having an impact on their local environment? At any rate, this is an area worth working with if we want parents, pupils and teachers to develop the schools together. Parents are represented on the school board (also in the majority) and share responsibility for all school operations in a number of countries. This does *not* mean, however, that parents in general participate in the schools.

What will it take for parents as individuals to make a contribution to school improvement? We will return to the question of what they can do *as a group* in the chapter that follows. As far as we can tell, parents as individuals have a choice between two strategies:

1. Choose *against* a particular school alternative in favour of another school. Freedom to choose schools is beginning to become a reality in several areas both in Europe and North America. Indirectly this could lead to renewal; however, it represents a reactive, and not a proactive, strategy.
2. Get involved in working with the individual teacher and class. This can be done in most countries, but is harder to achieve in countries that have no tradition for active parental participation. In any case, it will be the first cultural change that must take place.

Note
1. Information about the LWS programme was taken from a note written by Klaus Isselburg, LSW.

Chapter 7

Organizational Strategies

Organizational strategies affect every aspect of the schools. The process can be *political*, because it affects the interests of individual people and groups. It can be viewed from a *humanistic* perspective, because it largely affects the relationship between human beings and the motivation and needs of individuals. Organizational strategies require, as a rule, a rational division of roles and tasks; thus a *structural* perspective is probably also a prerequisite. As organizational strategies gain ground, we also see examples of how a symbolical perspective can prove fruitful. What we are faced with, then, are strategies that cannot be easily confined to a single perspective. Only when we begin to look at the specific strategy can we analyse which organizational perspective and which perspective of change the strategy is based on (see Chapter 5).

Organizational development processes, which we will be dealing with in particular in this chapter, were originally based on a *humanistic* perspective in the view of Bolman and Deal (see Chapter 2). But as the practice of organizational development grew, it increasingly came to deal with all aspects of the organization – and therefore also represented a *structural* perspective as well (see below). Practices in recent years have shown, however, that organizational development as a process can cope with political and symbolical problems – albeit in terms of a basic vision which considers both human beings and organizations to be essentially *rational*. Often it does not appear that way, but that's only because our view of rationality is too restricted (see below).

System strategies and individual strategies represent a long tradition in the schools. Organizational strategies, on the other hand, have a very short history. The first tentative steps were taken about 30 years ago; but even today, such strategies are not widely used. In other organizations – companies, for example – organization-based strategies are commonplace. In decentralized school systems – such as the American and British systems, for example – organizational strategies have gradually gained acceptance, and in recent years we have seen examples, also in Scandinavia, of changes originating with the individual school. Then what is our justification for regarding the individual school as a starting-point for change? Before we answer that, we would like to give an example that we believe would ring a bell with most teachers and pupils. We know that classes vary greatly. A teacher can dread the prospect of a certain class hour, and yet be full of courage to press forward at the prospect of another one. And both cases can even involve the same subject and grade level. Pupils are well aware that there is such a thing as 'class climate'. Most of us have attended a number of classes and know that what we got out of it varied widely. There is something indefinable that we might call 'climate', with unwritten rules and laws, and which is full of significance for both the teaching and the learning processes.

The same thing is true of schools. Where we once had very little empirical knowledge about the difference between schools, today we have a much more dependable grasp of the factors that make schools different (see, for example, Rutter *et al.* 1979, Arfwedson and Lundman 1983, Fullan 1991, Mortimore *et al.* 1988, Reynolds and Cuttance 1992). A school is a social system. The particular culture represented by the individual school is the point of departure for the strategies that we will be discussing.

THE SCHOOL AS THE UNIT OF CHANGE

Organizational strategies assume that *the school* is the unit of change. This means, in other words, that all schools must be developed from within, that it is pointless to come up with something in certain schools and try to carry that over to all the other schools. Each school must implement and institutionalize its own development process. Only then can we be assured that good educational and organizational solutions will be developed.

Counter-arguments are legion. We know what 'good teaching' is. The arguments go like this: the change agenda is merely *informing* or providing *in-service training* to teachers who need it as a basis for renewal. If all teachers are equipped with up-to-date knowledge, change will follow! Unfortunately, our well of knowledge in pedagogy is extremely limited, and even if we knew what was right, it would still be the specific teaching situation that determined what good teaching is. Moreover, to *know* what is right does not mean that we change our individual and organizational behaviour accordingly.

A number of attempts have been made to ascertain what research can tell us about good teaching and effective schools. Wang *et al.* (1993) consulted 61 leading learning and teaching experts; they went through 179 of the most extensive educational research reports, ran 91 so-called meta-analyses, and discovered 11,000 potential variables that could have an impact on pupils' learning! They found 228 specific variables they felt were worthy of closer examination. The results of this gigantic analysis were both typical and disappointing.

Researchers found that those factors which were most closely related to the teaching situation – the psychological factors (metacognitive, cognitive, motivation and emotional variables) had the greatest impact on the results, together with what they termed *instructional variables*. What counted here were such factors as the quality of the interaction between teacher and pupil, the way in which questions were asked, the quality of the social interaction, class 'culture', and co-operation. What they call 'distal' variables, such as curriculum, guidelines, appointments (with teachers' unions, for example) have very little impact on pupils' learning.

Certain questions can be raised about this type of research, about whether the results are tenable, etc., but we will not delve into that now (see *Review of Educational Research* 1993). If for a moment we were to conclude that these results were tenable, then what would they tell us? Probably not much more than we already know – and maybe much less. And if *this* is our storehouse of knowledge, then we are in a heap of trouble!

This research is based on the so-called 'production' paradigm. It seeks to find relationships, either between input and result (for example, see Hanushek 1989), or between process and result. Now if this research could tell us that there was a strong connection between a specific form of teaching and a given result (such as we wish to define it), then this would help us somewhat. But what really counts is how the teacher applies this interpretively in a concrete situation.

Qualitative research in the classroom shows that the teacher must usually resolve dilemmas; she must choose between many options, none of which is ideal. And precisely because the teacher's choice is *context-sensitive*, we must take a critical look at the kind of research that seeks to find valid answers to situationally-sensitive problems.

For the last fifteen years, extensive research has been carried out which has sought to determine what characterizes effective schools. In the present context we will merely mention that even this type of research, at best, can only point out variables that we know to be important (good management, for example); but such checklists of variables are virtually meaningless in concrete situations. Is good management, for example, the same in the Canadian schools (where there has traditionally been a certain distance between management and staff) and in Norway (where there has been a widespread egaliltarian tradition)? And is good management in one Norwegian school the same as in another? Surely not.

The first argument for the individual school being the unit of change is the fact that we don't have an external generalizable storehouse of knowledge that can be applied *to the individual school*. Each individual school, with general knowledge as a starting point, must develop its own storehouse of knowledge.

The second argument is that strategies which ultimately do not change the schools' culture do not get at the crux of all school activity – the learning process. It is important to reach the individual teacher and understand how he or she thinks and teaches (see Onosko 1992); that is why *individual strategies*, which we discussed in the previous chapter, are important. But if the development stops at the individual teacher, the schools will remain unable to resolve the formidable joint tasks facing them in the transition to a new century (Dalin and Rust 1996).

The main strategy in this chapter is called *organizational development* (OD). As we have seen in Chapter 5, this is a strategy that seeks to maximize the rewarding of both the individual and the organization itself. OD is the very foundation for a number of other 'schools' that have appeared on the scene during the past twenty years. Strategies such as decentralized management: Management by Objectives (MBO), Total Quality Management (TQM) – not to mention Human Resource Development (HRD) – spring from the OD strategy. Also a number of more individual-oriented strategies such as 'personal growth', counselling, coaching, and group dynamics has grown out of the OD philosophy. A variety of techniques, such as problem-solving, conflict resolution, internal assessment, and survey feedback have their origins in OD (Gray 1993).

In their qualitative study of five upper secondary schools in major American cities, and a follow-up study (telephone interview) of 178 head teachers in major upper secondary schools, Louis and Miles (1990) sought to clarify how processes of change take place under very difficult conditions. Many have given descriptions of what characterizes good schools, but the question is *how do we get there?*

The lessons that Louis and Miles learned are strongly reminiscent of OD strategies! According to these authors, if a school hopes to make significant progress, the following five factors must come into play:

1. *Clarity:* New knowledge must be comprehensible and clear, not vague and confusing.
2. *Relevance:* New knowledge must be seen as meaningful for everyday school life and not irrelevant, inapplicable or impracticable.
3. *Workable:* It must be possible to illustrate the knowledge in terms of specific acts. Teachers must know what they are doing to get there.
4. *Will:* There must be a motivation, an interest, and a will to do something with new knowledge.
5. *Skills:* Each individual teacher (or administrator) must have the necessary skills to implement new practices.

When we discuss these five main factors, which closely resemble what, in Chapter 5, is called the 'Real Needs Model' of change, the following advice is given by Louis and Miles:

- Focus with the aid of OD, school-based evaluations or effective school programmes.
- Provide training in negotiating tactics and conflict resolution.
- Request participants to look 'back to the future' as if it had just happened (a well-known planning technique in OD).
- Take time for team building, for problem-solving in groups, and for decision-making processes.
- Make the work processes a matter of routine; use creative techniques such as brainstorming, and follow up decisions.

The interesting thing about this list, taken from an extensive study of complex problems in large upper secondary schools in urban areas in the USA, is that the solution (with few exceptions) nearly always consists of established techniques in organizational development (Miles and Louis 1990).

We feel that it is important to understand the foundation of the OD strategy, and so we will analyse OD as a strategy from an *historical* perspective. We want to grasp the basic elements in the development and also account for much of the criticism that has been directed toward OD as a strategy. Further, we will illustrate the OD strategy with two major school projects, involving several hundred schools, that have been in progress for a number of years. These are Hank Levin's 'Accelerated Schools Project' (Standford), and IMTEC's 'Institutional Development Programme' (DP), which began in 1976 (see below).

ORGANIZATIONAL DEVELOPMENT – DEFINITIONS

There are a number of definitions of what OD is. To understand the various nuances that exist, we must first look back at the development of OD in the schools over the past 30 years.

OD grew out of a human relations orientation; at the outset it was undoubtedly strongly inspired by individual- and small groups-oriented programmes. In the 1950s OD projects were started up in industry (ESSO was quite active, for example). As for the schools, the first project commenced in 1963 at Columbia University; it was led by Matthew Miles (Miles 1967). This was rapidly followed by the renowned COPED project, which was financed by the federal authorities and was also led by Miles. After that, a number of OD projects were built up at the Center for Advanced Study in Educational Administration at the University of Oregon (starting in 1968). In the 1960s, there were also projects at the University of Michigan (Institute for Social Research); the so-called Educational Change Team (1967–70) was especially important.

The development bore the stamp of social psychologists, with an emphasis at the outset on group dynamics and organizational psychology. The projects were financed externally (federal funding) and assigned to university (or independent) institutes; these were then made responsible for contracts with schools.

In 1968 the so-called SAMS Project got under way in Norway. Developed by Arne Ebeltoft and marketed by the Institute for Organizational Development, this was a 50-hour collaborate course geared to a school faculty, with chief emphasis on communication and group dynamics. It closely resembled COPED's group courses and had close parallels to several American projects. SAMS was financed in part by the National Council for Innovation in Education, which wanted to find alternative ways of initiating school improvement.

The first definitions of organizational development were, naturally enough, heavily influenced by the initial projects. We can say that they were process-oriented:

> Organizational development is a theory, a method, and a value system (often hidden) for improving the human aspects of an organization's life, thus improving productivity (task–goal accomplishment) in those same organizations. (Derr 1974a)

> OD is a systematic attempt to transform an entire organization in the direction of a more effective development of human resources by applying behavioural-scientific methods. (Gorpe 1974)

Gradually, these definitions came to have a more consistent aim, in which human and structural factors were more balanced:

> OD is . . . activities that provide all the members of an organization with satisfactory conditions for participating in a correct and all-round way. This optimization should take place simultaneously in the social and technical systems, i.e. as a total (if gradual) improvement of the functional, structural, ideological and collaborative aspects of the operations – and, naturally, in such a way that the necessary interaction with the environment is maintained. (Ebeltoft 1974)

Certain definitions gradually became more general in nature and stressed the need to give the organizations a 'self-renewing ability':

> Organizational development can be defined as a planned and continual activity in the application of scientific methods to improve a system, especially by means of reflective, self-analytical methods. (Miles 1971)

> Organizational development is a long-term attempt at improving an organization's problem-solving capacity. (French and Bell 1973)

> The schools institutionalize a problem-solving school improvement process as a regular, continual function with maximum participation. (Bassin and Gross 1978)

After an investigation of a number of OD projects, an evaluation of research and literature in the field, and based on their own experience, Miles, Fullan and Taylor came up with the following revised definition:

> Organizational development in schools is an interrelated, systematically planned, supportive effort for achieving self-analysis and renewal. The various schemes direct their attention in particular to changes in formal and informal procedures, processes, norms and structures by the application of behaviour-developing concepts and methods. The goal of organizational development is two-fold: meeting the needs of the individual ('quality of life') *and* improving the way an organization functions and the subsequent results. (Fullan *et al.* 1980)

A number of OD theoreticians have critically questioned the use of OD in the schools. One of these is Brooke Derr, who in a critical article attempts to compare OD qualifications with what he regards as chracteristics of the schools as an organization.

School organization and organizational development (Derr 1976):

Organization of the schools	Organizational development
A) The schools lack commonly accepted standards for their activities.	A) Preparedness: the need for renewal a prerequisite. The client must suspect that he/she has problems before effort can be expended in working with them.
B) The relationship of the schools to their environment: survival guaranteed. Crisis-oriented.	B) Renewal orientation: renewal is worth the time, the money and the effort. Learning from experience is crucial (self-development). Development takes time.
C) Few demands on interdependence: no need to collaborate. The advantages of collaboration do not exceed the disadvantages.	C) Systemic orientation: genuine advantages (with the use of rewards) for promoting collaboration (and the costs of non-collaboration.
D) Functionary mentality: goal displacement. Safety important. Inbreeding. Terms of hiring in conflict with educational objectives.	D) External and internal capacity: hiring the most qualified OD consultant internally (regardless of formal ranking). Using both internal and external OD consultants. Roles and structures are flexible and dynamic. Choosing the best person for the job. Risk-taking and trying out new methods is rewarded.
E) Few resources.	E) Adequate resources.

Matthew B. Miles – who also took part in the same seminar where Brooke Derr first made his criticisms – gives the following response:

- OD is not necessarily based on the co-operation and participation of everyone; rather, it is based on a persistent and reflective use of behaviour-scientific methods for improving the way in which organizations function.
- Personal variables such as 'functionary mentality' are less important than structural variables.
- OD often arises on account of lacks, stress or difficulties, not necessarily on account of the documented weaknesses of goal realization.
- Certain personal traits do not necessarily exclude OD (Derr 1976).

The OD debate gradually took on a more marked political profile. In industry, OD soon came to be known as a strategy that management financed and exploited for its own purposes. A number of employee's organizations grew sceptical (Berg 1986). This was part of a broader criticism of OD as consensus-oriented, apolitical and relativistic.

Friedlander and Brown claim that, as a rule, OD is used to promote the objectives of organizations at the expense of those of the individual (Friedlander and Brown 1974). Forbes feels that many OD consultants are not working with renewal at all, but with 'restabilizing' – i.e. they are attempting to free the organization from crises and conflicts in order to create a new equilibrium (Forbes 1977). Crockett claims that OD often seeks to lure the parties into a 'state of bliss', as it were, while the goal is actually the *status quo* (Crockett 1978). Lundberg, who argued more in Marxist terms, claims that OD has uncritically accepted capitalistic values, adapted to economic and technological growth quite uncritically, and shamelessly accepted the social standing of the participants (Lundberg 1976). Gunnar Berg echoes many of the same critical viewpoints:

- The tendency to constantly disregard an organizational–historical perspective.
- To carry on the work of change without evaluating the general terms that were drawn up by the employer or principal party.
- That no discussions be held concerning the paradox that lies, on the one hand, in the humanitarian view of humanity and, on the other hand, in a situationally-adapted work ideology.
- That no discussion be held concerning the power of a 'change agent'. Where does the boundary go between 'process supporter' and systematic influence in certain directions? (Berg 1986)

In our view, this criticism is well taken. The first OD projects in industry were unequivocally governed, financed and run on management's terms. This was particularly the case during the 1960s. The past fifteen years have seen altogether different types of OD projects – organized, in part, on 'the shop floor'. Later in this chapter we shall return to a more detailed discussion of these questions in relation to the schools' situation.

Another type of criticism is directed at OD as a theory:

Organizational development is not a concept in the strict scientific sense of the term. It has not been precisely defined. It cannot be reduced to specific, clear, observable behaviour. Nor does it have a prescribed and confirmed place in a network of logically related concepts – a theory. (Kahn 1974)

Friedlander, having taken a look at the potential conflicts that are latent in the OD tradition, claims that there are three distinct philosophical traditions in OD practice: rationalism, pragmatism, and existentialism (Friedlander 1978; see Figure 7.1). Friedlander sees the conflicting definitions and disparate practice as a result of these three competing philosophical traditions.

Rationalism attempts to make OD more scientific, more theoretical and concept-oriented, more logical and mathematical. Activities are often geared toward creating models and understanding the underlying forces in the organization. *Pragmatism* seeks to make OD more serviceable by making the organization more effective, productive and economical. *Existentialism* seeks to move OD in the direction of a humanistic way of thinking, toward greater self-awareness – to make it more experiential and personally growth-oriented.

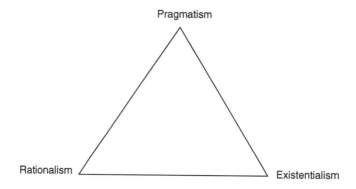

Figure 7.1 *Friedlander's OD analysis*

It often happens that the rationalist fears that the pragmatist will choose activities solely on the basis of the criteria that 'they seem to work'. By the same token, existentialism fears that the pragmatist will tend to choose activities that result in a manipulation of the individual. The rationalist is often regarded as abstract, irrelevant and having little concern for either the organization or the participants. The existentialist is looked upon with scepticism because his or her 'work with human beings' is regarded as irrelevant for the organization, characterized by lots of loose talking – unproductive and 'mystical'!

Friedlander, perhaps better than anyone else, has pointed out the considerable tension latent in OD practices. We shall now take a closer look at these as they are expressed in a number of projects.

EXPERIENCE IN ORGANIZATIONAL DEVELOPMENT

After 30 years of experience, many are still wondering what OD really is and how the work is organized. Part of the reason for this is not just that OD has meant different things to different people at different times, but also because no one can seem to agree on a steady, step-by-step development model – such as the R, D & D model, for example.

In fact, we have here one of the most fundamental differences in the overall view of development work. While the R, D & D model and other related planning and development models are based on a plan in which the goals are given and the methods chosen according to a logically constructed sequence, OD is seldom based on a fixed plan. The work is planned, instead, step by step according to an open problem-solving model that makes it possible to intervene at regular intervals and adjust both goals, methods, and thus the results. The road takes shape as we walk it. An OD process is synonymous with *living with the incomplete*, never being completely sure of the goals or the plan, and never being sure whether the goal has been reached.

Motivation for OD

Most OD programmes come about because the superintendent or head teacher feels that they represent a promising approach. This resembles the situation in the business community, where it is no secret that 'support from the top' is crucial for OD's success. What kinds of problems, then, does the school leader feel it is important to find a solution to? In the study that Fullan, Miles and Taylor carried out, 'communication problems' were listed most frequently (25 per cent), followed by such tasks as 'reorganization' (11 per cent), 'value clarifications' (10 per cent), and 'effectivization of the decision-making process' (8 per cent). Only in 5 per cent of the cases were 'pupil problems' given as a basis for entry (Fullan *et al.* 1980).

It goes to show that most projects that are initiated have enjoyed support from the top. Most people claim that support from the top was the most important reason why these projects came into being at all (41 per cent). Other important reasons were extra resources (21 per cent), or one or more capable consultants (18 per cent).

Even though these results are from North America, there is good reason to believe that we will find similar results in Europe. The management development programmes in the Norwegian schools are deliberately based on the acceptance of the superintendent and head teacher. No doubt, this is also the case with the management training in Sweden. True, we could ask whether support from the top is a distinctive requirement of OD projects. Aren't the schools so hierarchical that any significant development projects would have to enjoy support from the top anyway, both at the national and municipal levels, or in the schools?

The IDP project and the 'Accelerated Schools' project, which we will discuss later in this chapter, have consciously sought to discover a process in which *all parties* participate in the decision-making process with respect to the project's entry. Organizational development can definitely have an impact on individual pupils and teachers. A development, however, in which OD only gets started with the head teacher's blessing spells nothing but danger. In the quest to democratize the schools, it is essential that all parties should be involved from the outset.

Questions of values

Weisbord claims that starting up with OD at all is primarily a *question of values* (Weisbord 1978). Moreover, OD calls for a way of thinking that is unlike the traditional philosophy behind development work. It also calls for a way of thinking about schools and development that is rather rare. We are convinced that the values of OD, the fundamental understanding of the process of change that follows in its wake, and the way of thinking about the schools that is implicit in OD are all far more important than OD techniques and work methods. A number of reports on entry problems in OD indicate that the presentation has been diffuse. It has not been clear what OD has stood for, and this has created uncertainty about what the project might lead to. It is essential to clarify from the outset the value premises the project rests on. The problem here is that OD represents a way of working that is foreign to most. OD has to be *experienced* to be understood. Therefore, many researchers introduce OD by using simulation, or by utilizing proven OD work methods in their presentation.

IMTEC's experiences from the Netherlands and Germany (with the same project and a uniform arrangement) tell us that the need for a plan and a structure varies greatly and is probably culturally conditioned (cf Hofstede 1991). In the Netherlands we found that participants (teachers, head teachers and consultants) were used to working with 'open agendas', that they were highly tolerant of changes in plans, and that they lived and *thrived* with the unfinished. Our experiences in Germany are not unambiguous. Germans, of course, are just as different as Norwegians, but in our experience, partners much prefer firm plans, agreements, and clear expectations. Inductive methods are relatively unknown, and more 'didactic' arrangements, where the course of the teaching material has been explained beforehand, appear to be familiar. When our partners have to work with a number of unknown factors at the same time, this often leads to frustration.

Several observers point out that the values of the OD project must be reasonably in keeping with those of the organization. Runkel and Bell put it this way:

> Our experience shows that organizational development that aims at structural changes is strongly influenced by the psychological preparedness of those who will be affected by the change. Preparedness, as a rule, is greatest where there is an appreciation of open lines of communication, where skills are developed jointly, where there is a widespread desire for collaboration, where the administration lends support – or, at the very least, is not negative to change – where there is agreement at the outset on the educational goals one hopes to achieve by a restructuring, and where the staff has a history of 'trials' that have not failed to produce good results. (Runkel and Bell 1976)

Actually, this tells us nothing more than what we pointed out in Chapter 5 in our discussion of the RAND study on changes in schools. The RAND researchers found, as we know, that the greater the differences in values between the organization and the project, the harder the project was to carry out. Runkel *et al.* (1978) point out that 'the organization' ought to appreciate open lines of communication, collaboration and clarity of purpose – and that it should preferably not have a 'negative trial history'! That is all well and good. But does this not leave us with a selection that is in no need of an OD project?

One important question is whether schools that are not in a satisfactory 'state of preparedness' can or should get started with OD. For us, the crucial point is what we mean by the term 'organization'. If it 'only' means management, or certain leaders among the teachers, then this will not suffice. It could well be that other teachers, pupils or parents are more favourable to the idea of starting OD work, but perhaps on other terms. This raises the question of whom the OD consultant is serving (and who is serving him or her). If we accept a 'No thanks, not now' answer from the head teacher as evidence of lack of preparedness, we could well end up making an untenable situation intractable.

The question of entry is also a question of whether the schools are subject to a sufficient degree of internal or external pressure. Our definition of change (see Chapter 5) assumes an accommodation of *both* internal and external needs. Most of IMTEC's projects are concerned nearly exclusively with the head teacher and teachers. In those projects (and the number is rising) in which pupils and parents (or institutions in the local community) participate, the external demands are more apparent.

The external demands can also be encountered in the form of a new curriculum, new guidelines, or a new set of rules. Often this is perceived as a *technical* matter: replacing parts of a syllabus or substituting one method for another. Schools seldom understand that many new curricula require cultural and organizational changes before they can be implemented with the expected results (Dalin and Rolff 1993).

Defining the problem

A number of OD projects run into trouble from the outset because they are not specific enough and do not focus on a problem area where the parties feel a clear-cut need (Franklin 1976). There could appear to be a built-in weakness in the OD strategy – namely, that the parties themselves usually wind up defining the process on an *ad hoc* basis, as they go along. This also changes the objectives, which often become process goals rather than product goals. Precisely because those responsible for the project know that it is difficult to make hard and fast promises at the outset, they tend to promise too little. But experience shows that all parties need to see a concrete goal at the very beginning, and that it is important to *achieve* something concrete not very far along in the process, either in the form of concrete decisions that are made, or that the parties enjoy a better co-operative relationship, or that desirable changes take place (e.g. in the schedule), or that pupils become involved in the school's development (Bassin and Gross 1978).

Being able to see concrete results early in the process can be important for the *motivation* to continue the long-term work. That being the case, it is nevertheless inadvisable in the entry phase to formulate goals that are too concrete. One of the main results of the OD process is that we become far more aware of where we are and where we wish to go. Visions are something we discover and learn about along the way.

Actually, schools do not necessarily enter into an OD process in order to solve 'a problem'; it can just as well be a *challenge* that's at stake. Our experience at IMTEC is that it is often the stronger schools, with lots of experience in development work, that become involved in the OD process. The challenge could be anything from a new curriculum to new tasks. Some schools enter the process simply because they want a review of the school's work; they also wish to create an overall assessment and a process which, in turn, can unite the school on important goals.

Contract

OD is different from many other types of activities that the head teachers and teachers are involved in daily. A recurring feature in all these projects is that the process takes more time than the parties anticipated (see below). Derr and Demb claim, for example, that it is highly unlikely that an ordinary OD project would stand much of a chance in larger city schools (Derr and Demb 1974). They claim that pressing duties, continual crises, financial pressures, a lack of internal dependence, and general scepticism and lack of trust render OD inappropriate. Conway (1978) and Milestein (1977) concur with Derr and Demb and feel that alternative models will be necessary if OD is to stand a chance of ever getting off the ground in larger city schools. Programmes of this nature have in fact been developed, one of the first being a New York project led by Bassin and Gross (1978). They claim that one of the keys to a 'contract' is that the participants should be able to see the practicality of the project:

> To succeed in a complicated city school, organizational development must first and foremost be practically oriented. Those who work in such schools simply have no tolerance for school improvement that is unable to show tangible, practical results within a short time (six months) and with a minimum use of money.

So here we see what is virtually an unequivocally *pragmatic* orientation in OD (Friedlander, see above). They also take up another point that keeps cropping up in various discussions on entry – namely, money; the project must not be expensive. Perhaps this is because of the generally poor financial situation that schools are in, but it is also likely to have to do with the fact that OD has so few concrete results to point to. It is no easy task to make a convincing case for the usefulness of an OD project.

Every development project must be 'sold', whether to the school superintendent, the head teacher, the teachers, the pupils, or to those who hold the purse strings. In other words, 'political negotiations' are required. People tend to tie their hopes to the project in such negotiations; by the same token, the project's limitations are also determined here, limitations that could later prove to be difficult to circumvent.

Many have found that a kind of 'mini OD entry' can be quite effective. Precisely because it is so difficult to get a handle on what OD actually is, a presentation could consist of involving the group that will be taking a standpoint in an existential activity that promotes their understanding of what OD might involve. For example, this could be a systematic problem-solving sequence, a clarification of values to see what each individual and each group wanted, a communication exercise that yields process experience, or a minor 'survey feedback trial' that puts concrete data on the table.

Courses of action

The fundamental values toward which we have agreed to work, the tasks which the client feels to be of primary importance, and the contractual terms that have been agreed upon all define, to a large extent, how the OD project gets started. Nevertheless, where a course of action is concerned, we are faced with a range of options.

There is no clear answer to how a project should be initiated. A number of observers have pointed out that 'survey-feedback' has proven to be a good entry method. We will discuss the use of survey feedback below. Others stress that the schools' readiness to confront and modify factors that arise through the use of good questionnaires is decisive for whether 'data feedback' is an appropriate entry procedure or not.

Our choice of procedure is also dependent on the client and the human and material resources the project has at its disposal. The most important thing is to find a good mix of approaches, not getting bogged down in the idea that there can only be *one* right way to do things, but recognizing that what's needed is to pursue those approaches which best satisfy the needs the schools are faced with. A purely training programme – for example, an arrangement for providing the project team with communication training – might be appropriate. It can be that the leadership ought to be given training in problem-solving. Or it can also be that the consultant should approach a conflict situation with the aim of finding a solution jointly, together with the other parties.

Even though we should remain flexible, I still feel that it is important to retain certain fundamental guidelines:

- OD works with *the school* as the unit (in the long term, at any rate).
- OD requires maximum *participation* in the process.
- OD requires the use of new work methods.
- OD has open problem-solving processes as its model for planning.
- OD works with individuals, groups, and the entire school.
- OD is based on a self-correcting process.

Work methods

Most projects make use of a number of work methods during the course of the project. According to Porras and Berg, a development toward more comprehensive types of OD projects has been under way, employing a variety of techniques. This is consistent with what Alderer found – namely, that on the whole, OD works with the *entire* organization (Alderer 1977). Derr makes a clear-cut distinction between organizational training (OT) and organizational development (OD). He does not discount the value of training individuals in interpersonal skills, but it is only when the participants in an organization jointly enter into a binding collaboration toward a common goal that such training can be regarded as OD (Derr 1976).

Developments in the past few years show that many organizations (and schools are no exception) become involved in the development of specific techniques. These can be exercises in context-sensitive management, work with conflict-resolution or collaborative training, or a reorganization in favour of decentralized management or total quality management, to mention some popular (and often useful) techniques. In a broader strategy, in which such techniques and skills have their natural place, they can be useful. But seen in isolation, it tends to result in frustration, because the use of the new techniques, to be effective, requires restructuring and the development of a new culture.

OD consultants

From the very beginnings of OD, OD consultants have traditionally played a major role in these projects in the United States and Canada – due in large measure to the National Training Laboratory, which conducted systematic training of OD consultants as far back as 1965. This organization alone, over a 30-year period, has offered several hundred courses for OD consultants each year. In addition, there are a number of colleges and universities with both theory-oriented and skill-oriented courses.

In the OD philosophy itself, one of the essential norms is that schools should be 'self-developing'. This being the case, is it not, then, in conflict with OD values to bring an external consultant into the process? Before we attempt to answer this question, allow us to define what we mean by an OD consultant:

1. *Internal consultant*

   This concept is often used about a person who belongs to the organization, often one who is responsible for the OD process internally and who has received a certain amount of training in OD work. We have already seen that these consultants are put to extensive use (on average, for about 200 days over a three-year period). Fullan, Miles and Taylor found that a typical internal consultant was an administrator (about 80 per cent of the municipalities listed administrators, 58 per cent listed teachers, 56 per cent educational 'experts', 33 per cent listed parents, and 15 per cent listed pupils among their consultants). Only about half of them had any formal training (from university or similar background), but this training was short term; furthermore, they had little professional support.

2. *External consultant*

   This is a person who does not belong to the organization but who is called in to help with the process. His or her role can vary greatly. Fullan, Miles and Taylor found that the number of days for each project varied from between two and 990 – fifteen days being the most usual (over a three-year period). This means that most external consultants limit their work to seminars, planning sessions, etc. However, many of them also work directly within the organization. As a rule, external consultants have formal training and are part of a network of professional colleagues.

What kind of role can an internal or external consultant play? That depends, of course, on the project and on the qualifications of the consultant in question. In a training programme developed by the North West Educational Laboratory, twelve distinct roles have been identified:

1. *Expert:* Reports research results and offers advice.
2. *Teacher:* Teaches and explains concepts.
3. *Trainer:* Diagnoses training needs, chooses skill areas and organizes training.
4. *Data collector:* Devises procedures for the collection of data, gathers data, and seeks to find a better basis of knowledge.
5. *Mediator:* Recommends resources and resource persons, organizes meetings, and joins people and groups together.
6. *Model:* Mediates concepts through experimental actions and is a personal example.
7. *Advocate:* Advocates certain opinions and values and recommends specific solutions for the schools.
8. *One who confronts:* Uses conflict situations as a point of departure for changes, and uses non-coercive methods to encourage the client to think through problems.
9. *Observer:* Observes behaviour and provides feedback.
10. *Analyst:* Studies data, identifies potential interpretations and explains alternatives.
11. *Planner:* Plans the project, organizes activities, finds the resources and personnel for the work, writes up reports, etc.
12. *Evaluator:* Carries out formative or summative evaluation.

There will be a need for one or more of these roles – and often a combination of them – in every OD project. The question of *who* at any particular phase ought to take on a particular role is partly a question of *goals* (for example, 'When shall we be able to do things ourselves?'); of resources ('Can we afford to pay a good external consultant?'); and of qualifications. Most projects settle on a combination of roles between four different persons and groups:

1. The participants.
2. The internal project committee.
3. The internal consultant (often the leader or secretary of the project pommittee).
4. The external consultant (often someone from the municipality or from a college or a university).

Most researchers who have studied organizational development agree that such inter-action is essential. It is vital to understand how the external consultant should be used. The important thing is to use him or her in such a way that internal capacity is enhanced, not so that the schools make themselves dependent on the consultant. The most effective way to exploit the relationship is probably to let the external consultant regard the internal consultant primarily as his/her client and help him to build up his competence.

Data collection and survey feedback (SF)

This has been a key approach in many OD projects. As we have seen, the use of this technique has increased dramatically the past few years. One of the first to point out the effect of survey feedback (SF) was Bowers (Bowers 1973). He compared the effect of four types of OD techniques: survey feedback, interpersonal consultation, task-oriented consultation, and external training. He also had two control groups – namely, data feedback without explanation, and a group that received no help. His study included 23 organizations, with over 14,000 participating in the process.

Bowers investigated the effect of the programmes over a period of time in areas such as communication, the decision-making process, leadership, goal-orientation, relationships with colleagues, and job satisfaction. He found that SF had the greatest effect, followed by interpersonal consultation. Task-oriented consultation had a neutral effect, while external training and data feedback without explanations had a negative effect.

Although this is an extensive study, we should view the results in terms of what we have reported above: survey feedback is an important and effective strategy; but we also know that it must be carried out by trained consultants (which was also the case in Bowers' study). Fullan, Miles and Taylor are sceptical of Bowers' assessment of task-oriented consultation where schools are concerned. Other results reported above show that such consultation is desirable and that it does have an impact. In particular, they point out how schools must have immediate results – which is often associated with a 'task' orientation.

As we see it, the greatest value of survey feedback is that it provides participants with a good basis for dialogue. It gives everyone, regardless of their verbal skills, a chance to express their opinion. Bringing up problems for discussion is made easier, because they are already 'on the table', as it were, and good questionnaires provide an overview that other methods cannot match. But the technique also has a number of questionable aspects: questionnaires tend to alienate, oversimplify, even confuse what is already complicated enough. To use the technique, one needs trained consultants and questionnaires that are professionally up to par.

At the end of this chapter we shall discuss school evaluation as a strategy for school improvement. In this context we will remind the reader what Bowers found to be a prerequisite for the positive effects of evaluation with feedback. School evaluation is in itself no guarantee for school improvement.

WHAT DO WE KNOW ABOUT THE RESULTS OF ORGANIZATIONAL DEVELOPMENT?

Apart from the effect study carried about by Fullan *et al.* (1980), there have only been isolated evaluations of the effects of OD in the schools. We have explained these earlier in Dalin (1986). We will sum up the most important results.

The three researchers found that OD had positive effects in terms of concrete results (in the form of improved teaching practices, and 70 per cent of the projects had a positive impact on the pupils), in terms of attitudes (the municipalities were satisfied with the projects, by and large; 60 per cent related their experiences to others), and in terms of institutionalized practice (88 per cent of the municipalities continued the work).

What could account for these results?

According to Fullan, Miles and Taylor, positive effects can best be accounted for in terms of the following:

- Larger and more comprehensive projects.
- Strong professional and technical support throughout the entire project period (the use of external and internal consultants, materials, etc.).
- Continual task-orientation with clarity about what one wishes to achieve, and a pursuit of the goal. Positive effects are less likely in municipalities with a not altogether positive trial history, where changes are obligatory, and where a major share of the funds are used for trips and meetings outside the school. In-service training alone, or the training of individual participants (e.g. the head teacher) are related to school improvement (institutionalizing) in a negative way.

Positive attitudes can be explained in terms of the following factors:

- Technical and professional support. Here, however, the internal consultant and planning group are more important than external support.
- Task orientation. Here, *pedagogical* task orientation is important – that is to say, those pedagogical tasks which the schools themselves regard as important.
- The fact that the municipality is in the process of implementing significant changes in the schools (in other words, that there is a positive climate for change).

As for what could explain the continuation of OD in the schools – institutionalization – the following factors are important:

- Large, costly projects were *less* likely to continue, partly because financing in the project phase originated from the outside and the municipality could not afford to keep going.
- Poorer municipalities tend to continue OD, probably because, on general principles, they do not initiate costly projects.
- More 'classical OD', projects that involve interpersonal relationships, norms and values, structural questions and management, have the greatest chance of continuing. Again, individual training, seen in isolation, is negatively related.
- External support should be reduced during the project period if OD is to continue, perhaps because ownership may have a better chance of developing, perhaps because it will be cheaper.
- Technical support, especially good handbooks and materials, are important for the continuation.

- The motivation of superintendents who are in control of district resources will largely determine the continuation.

In conclusion, if we look at those OD programmes that appear to have the greatest impact, produce the most positive attitudes and guarantee institutionalization, the following picture emerges:

- Classical OD, i.e. OD which focuses on the entire school, uses data feedback (or, at the very least, self-analytical methods), which is structured with external and internal resources, and which lasts at least three years, clearly yields the most positive results.
- Personal development, i.e. in-service training, management training (isolated), and the training of other individuals without it happening *together* with colleagues, was least likely to succeed.

These results fully support a number of other studies which show that 'a little OD' or partly practised OD has minimal effect; in fact, it can even harm a school. Runkel and Schmuck show that building up a good OD project takes time, resources, and well-trained consultants (Runkel and Schmuck 1976). Those projects which are able to build up a strong internal capacity and enjoy the added help of qualified and varied external support (e.g. consultants, consultant training, materials, evaluation etc.) are those most likely to succeed.

RECENT CRITICISM OF ORGANIZATIONAL DEVELOPMENT

Some of the criticism of OD in recent years is based in part on the conflict which some see developing when the individual school tries to define its own problem while the school authorities, in reality, have established the schools' goals. Gunnar Berg from Sweden claims, for example, that the aim of 'development of the organization' (OD) is to bring the school more into line with official goals, and that the problem is the gulf between school practice and society's goals for the schools. Thus a consultant should be a *spokesperson* for specific curricular options. At the same time, Berg attempts to use American OD practice to support his assertion that OD is an unrealistic strategy for Swedish schools (Berg 1986).

For Berg, the term 'environment' is problematical, because it reminds him of a market model. Equally problematical is each school being allowed to interpret the demands of its environment. In the first place, every school improvement strategy will be practised differently in different cultures. OD in American schools reflects American culture. There are a number of European OD projects which differ – sometimes greatly – from the models that were developed by Schmuck and his colleagues, and which Berg discusses.

In centrally governed countries (e.g. Germany) the most important determining factors in the environment will be *the school owner* and *the state*, who – by means of laws, curricula and regulations – attempt to govern the schools. But even in these countries this is only one of several important factors of influence which every head teacher and teacher must take into account. Other major factors are represented by the teachers' unions, the parents, the youth environment, the media, and by colleagues. The curriculum is like a map: it is a useful thing to have. But when, as occasionally happens, the map does not equate with the terrain, it is usually best to assume that it is the terrain that is correct!

Earlier in this chapter we explained why it is crucial for the development of good teaching that each school be viewed as the unit of change. It is only when problems of implementation are considered to be the important *professional* problems, and not just technical adjustments to 'orders from above' that the quality of the teaching can be assured. We can only see the importance of organizational development when we understand that the answer does not lie outside the school, but must be developed *in* the school in an open atmosphere of trust between pupils, parents, teachers and the school leadership.

Berg claims (on the basis of an example from Oregon, where the central authorities sought to implement a certain curricular reform) that OD thus became impossible to practice. The reason was supposed to be that OD demands that the schools themselves decide what they want to do. It is possible that some organizational development consultants in Oregon define this as a problem. In the European tradition (as well as in several American traditions) this would hardly be regarded as a problem. The consultants' task is at all times to help the schools define and solve their critical problems. In the situation that Berg describes, it could well be that a conflict of values exists between the school personnel and the school authorities. If that is indeed the case, then this conflict must be clarified and solved. Perhaps there is also a conflict of values between the staff and the parents? Or between the staff and the pupils? One of the most important tasks an OD consultant has is to work with conflicts of value. The problem, however, could just as well prove to be something altogether different. 'The problem' is *always* defined by the client in terms of the demands and influences she encounters in her work. The nature of an OD consultant's work does not change just because the school authorities happen to limit the school's freedom of action.

However, in his criticism of OD, Berg also appears to assume that the goals of society are clear and set. The task is 'merely' one of narrowing the gap between practice and objectives. In reality, the goals are quite diffuse. It is up to each school and each teacher to interpret the school's goals in their own particular situation. Schools are marketplaces where negotiations take place and deals are struck. One of society's most important tasks is to regulate 'the trade', so that the weakest end up better off than they would have been without the control that is present today. In our experience, if the schools are to take this goal (which is but one of many) seriously, they will need *knowledge about themselves* – e.g. how the weak function – before they can renew their practice. And this is the essence of organizational development.

During the last ten years of decentralization efforts, organizational development (often not recognized as such) has become vital as a change strategy. Before we discuss some practical projects, we shall give an overview of the decentralization movement known in North America as 'Site-based management'.

Site-based management

First we would remind the reader that the basis for the new and increased interest in organizational development as a strategy for change must be viewed in light of the decentralization that we discussed in Chapter 1. Especially important to bear in mind as we consider a broader project in this tradition is the American restructuring movement, with its emphasis on site-based management, where the head teacher is given a new and broader mandate to manage development projects. Our case, developed by Robert H. Anderson and Karolyn J. Snyder at the University of South Florida (Snyder 1988), is called 'Managing Productive Schools'.

In North America there is an acceptance of a far greater distance between management and staff than is the case in Scandinavia. A strong leader is regarded as a positive factor in school improvement (which we have seen from the 'Effective Schools' research).

In the early phase of the 'Restructuring Movement', the usual conception was that if only we could modify *the structure* (thinking here primarily in terms of roles and responsibility), then school improvement would virtually follow automatically as a result. In any case, major hindrances of a bureaucratic nature would be swept out of the way. But it soon became apparent that giving the head teacher greater responsibility changed very little. So it became clear that not only formal restructuring, but *modifications in school culture*, of the way the school functioned as an organization, was also necessary before significant changes could be brought about (cf Dalin and Rolff 1993). In an interview with editor Ron Brandt, Phil Schlechty, a well-known American manager trainer, defined restructuring as follows: 'Restructuring means changes in the system of norms: the usual, tried and trusted way of doing things, the way power is distributed, the way decisions are made, the way education is achieved' (Brandt 1992).

'Restructuring' in the 1990s in the United States takes a critical look at rules, roles, and relationships that govern the way that time, people, place, knowledge and technology are used. The work ranges from the classroom, the learning process, the curriculum, organization and management to the new role that both district and central authorities can play in a 'restructured school'. We are approaching what Peter Senge calls a systematic perspective and a 'learning organization' (Senge 1990). A number of recent projects, based on the world of the pupils, seek to redefine both instructional content and processes. If we take a serious look at the life situation of many young people (Dalin and Rust 1996), we will see that the school of today is inherently ill-suited to the learning process that young people need (Gardner 1991). Several recent projects, such as Ted Sizer's 'Coalition of Essential Schools', or Hank Levin's 'Accelerated School Project' (see below) or 'Charter' schools are basically 'restructuring projects'.

Even in a number of these grandiose projects it has not been possible to create new school organizations, as the instigators had hoped. Fullan (1993) discusses a well-known example, 'New Futures Initiative', financed by the Anne E. Casey Foundation, whose purpose is to restructure American city schools. Forty million dollars was spent over a five-year period in four medium-sized American cities to give children in slum areas hope for a brighter future. The schools were asked to establish collaborative groups in which families, schools, companies, and representatives of the welfare office and the city government participated. Each school carried out a needs assessment, and they all received ample technical support, in-service training, etc. (Wehlage *et al.* 1992).

The project was intended to give the schools more independence in relation to the municipality, give teachers more flexibility, pupils more individual options and follow-up, and individual teachers tailor-made training. Every school was given the opportunity to link up with other schools and resources (networks). In spite of this sweeping support, the authors found that the schools did not change in any fundamental way, that they (merely) added new elements to existing practices; the basic organization of the schools remained the same. Neither did the changes lead to any qualitative differences in the way teachers related to each other; most were accustomed to working alone and were unsure of how to work together with other teachers.

Even this sweeping example of restructuring shows that fundamental change *in the schools' organization* is not easy, even with ample resources. Standard teaching practices could not be changed in these four schools; *the learning culture* remained unchanged. Similar results have been obtained in other studies of restructuring projects (see, for example, Taylor and Teddlie 1992, Fullan and Miles 1992, Fullan 1993).

In several European countries, the development of 'annual plans', or 'development plans' is a must. Wallace (1991) shows what can often result from such measures, based on the introduction of development plans in British schools. The aim of these plans was relatively clear: to help the schools develop plans in line with the new curricula and guidelines, which would clarify the need for in-service training and provide a framework for external support. What Wallace discovered was that these development plans came to be regarded as extra work; furthermore, they were of little value as management devices for the schools, and the school administration continued to follow their usual short-sighted management routines that left them to react to the unexpected – a recurring phenomenon in the schools. Attempts, therefore, to change a 'simple' thing like a single procedure (how planning is done) had very little effect on school improvement.

Fortunately, some restructuring efforts met with at least partial success. Fullan refers to several trials reported by Cox and deFrees (1991). Ten schools in the state of Main have made giant strides in areas such as changes in pupils' learning experiences, changes in the teaching processes, and the 'redesign' of the schools, as well as improving the relationships between the schools and surrounding institutions. Fullan sums up what Cox and deFrees believe to be the essential lesson from this trial: to clearly focus on what is expected (from pupil to the head teacher), be aware that the changes have to do with relationships and power, and that the process *must be learned by all parties*; and finally, that it costs extra!

One of the most important lessons of these restructuring projects (and here we are at the crux of the strategy we shall soon be describing) is that the head teacher is presented with a new slate of challenges. A new organization must be developed – all the way from the pupil to the head teacher. New relationships and new roles must be assumed. Experience from Scandinavian industry (Dalin 1993) and from IMTEC's IDP-project (see below) shows that most of this new learning takes place *when we are given challenging tasks*; it takes place as practical learning. And as a rule, there is a change of *culture* before there are changes in *structure*.

The task of the head teacher is to steer a cohesive development process whose ultimate objective is to make the school *a learning organization* (Dalin and Rolff 1993, Senge 1990, Fullan 1993). We discussed the elements of such an organization in Chapter 2. Senge emphasizes the fact that the leader is both a *designer* and an *organizer*.

In our view, Scandinavian head teachers are better equipped in this regard than their North American counterparts. Scandinavia has an egalitarian tradition, one that stresses consensus and joint effort. Even if the head teacher takes an initiative (or, as we see it, helps foster creative resources in the schools), he or she, at the earliest possible moment, must transfer responsibility and create a situation in which everyone feels they have a genuine responsibility for developing a vision (Dalin and Rolff 1993). Christensen (1992), who studied head teachers in the project entitled 'Accelerated Schools Project' in the USA (see below), found that head teachers had to learn to focus on the pupils' situation, to share power, take chances, develop a critically inquisitive environment, and take time to deal with pupils, teachers and parents alike – while keeping a clear vision in debates, actions and evaluations.

The Accelerated Schools Project

This project was developed by Professor Hank Levin at Stanford University in California. In 1994 it had approximately 600 'member schools' throughout the United States. Levin's point of departure was his concern for pupils at risk, pupils who for one reason or another fell outside the scope of what the schools had to offer. Many of these pupils also grow up in big city slums and attend schools which in most respects fail woefully in their ability to provide their pupils with a worthy range of school programmes.

Hank Levin and his colleagues, having analysed the situation in these schools, found that many of the pupils who had been relegated to remedial teaching would have benefited from the same programmes that were offered to the brightest pupils. And this brought his vision into focus: all pupils can learn, even academic subjects, provided they receive the challenges and the right teaching in a new 'learning culture'. He discovered that the way in which teachers worked with their pupils depended in large measure on the way they intuitively categorized them in their subconscious mind.

The secret lay in building on pupils' strong points. These were not easy to discover! Many teachers defined these pupils solely as 'problem cases', and quickly found out what they could *not* do. Levin also discovered that in order to motivate the teachers for a new learning culture, he had to work with the teachers' strong points. He found that their assets were not being used in a creative way. The schools could never become a good place in which to be and a good place in which to learn for the pupils until this became true for the teachers as well.

Levin also found that parents' resources were not being used. Parental attendance at PTA meetings could be as paltry as 5–10 per cent. After several years of project work, 95 per cent of the parents are participating today!

The project is developed according to the following norm:

1. Interested schools are sent reading material and a twenty-minute video explaining the ideological foundation and practice. If the school wants more information, a co-worker is sent (usually one of the project's teachers or head teachers) to a meeting at school.
2. The project requires full participation: not only must the head teacher be interested, but all the teachers, parents and pupils must be included in the discussion. And at least 80 per cent must commit themselves to creating their 'dream school', one that will be good enough for their own children.
3. A contract is made by the project administration and the school (signed by all who are participating).
4. The school chooses a representative project team, where all the interests of the teachers, pupils and parents are represented.
5. All teachers are first given a five-day intensive course, followed by five half-day courses for a period of a year, followed in turn by seminars and courses as needed. It is assumed that it will take five to six years to 'transform the school's culture'.
6. The process begins with an internal evaluation of the strong and weak aspects of the school. As a rule, this takes place in small groups, with varying methods being applied.
7. A school improvement consultant (process consultant) is hired and visits the school on a weekly basis (later, every other week) to help with problem-solving, coaching, etc. The contract clearly states that the consultant is merely a process consultant and that the responsibility lies with the school, which is the driving force in the development work.
8. Starting with the evaluation, a very creative period begins that can last for weeks or months, a period in which a new vision for the school emerges. And here there is no room for compromise! What's at stake is no less than the designing of a dream school – for 'my child'. From this work a vision emerges that becomes the common property of the participants, a vision that is the product of a long learning process and not just a 'mission statement' on paper.
9. Not everything can be done at once. A prioritized development plan must be worked out where a maximum of three to four important tasks are involved at any one time. Work groups for each important task are set up, which report to the project team, which in turn meets, on average, once a week.
10. The entire school comes together for an evaluation of the development process at least once each quarter. It is the school that has the responsibility and must make the decisions concerning potential changes.

It will soon become evident that the school needs external support. This can best be given by a 'reformed administration'. Expert assistance, staff development, evaluations and much else is needed. While the school itself is responsible, it needs support.

Perhaps the most important aspect of this project, as an example of organizational development, is the marked emphasis placed on *creating new and positive expectations* which, because they are shared, are reinforced. Levin does not start by changing attitudes, but rather by *changing behaviour*, by asking the teachers to try something new (after they have received instruction and training in use). The teachers themselves must further develop what they start. The consultant does not tell them what they should do, but tries to highlight the general principles. When the teachers and the school begin to taste success, this strengthens the learning process (Brandt 1992).

This is a project developed from a vision that is created *outside the school*, and from the application of OD as a strategy for change with the aid of external consultants. The project goes into some of the most difficult schools in the United States and focuses directly on the pupils' situation. While the schools, on their part, must commit themselves to the broad vision, in the process they will further develop it so that it becomes a vision for each school. The project is also based on a number of clear principles, such as: joint goals, mutual trust and joint power to the teachers (empowerment), and rests on strength. Relatively stable strategies and methods have been developed for creating new organizational forms that give pupils at risk a real chance.

Such a radical strategy requires new leadership. Christensen (1992) found that the head teacher had to learn to put pupils first, to share power, to take chances, to develop an open atmosphere, and to take time to mingle with pupils, teachers, parents and others in the local community – and always to focus on the vision.

The Institutional Development Programme (IDP)

The philosophical foundation for the project is given in the information IMTEC provides would-be participants:

> The goal of IDP is to help each school to carry out a process of self-evaluation and self-renewal. We regard the individual school – not the school system (nor the individual, for that matter) – as the unit of change. This does not mean, of course, that we disregard the significance of the system, or that of the individual's attitudes, behaviour and capacity. Our experience tells us that school changes must be an integral part of the 'school culture' that each school and the local community represent. The changes must be rooted in a need on the part of pupils, teachers, the school leadership, and the local community, and the solutions must be those of the ones who will be carrying out the innovations.

In the book *Changing the School Culture* (Dalin and Rolff 1993) there is a description of the assumptions upon which the project rests:

1. The school is the unit of change.
2. The school is *the driving force* and must lead the processes of change itself.
3. Each person's subjective and objective sense of reality is the basis for the project's development.
4. Collaboration is a prerequisite for development.
5. Conflicts breed possibilities.
6. The project is based on *process values*, which in their own way regulate the interaction; but it is the school itself that develops the project's *goals*. Goals and visions develop along the way, on the basis of an open learning process.
7. 'Effectiveness' must be understood in the specific context in which a remedy will be employed (contingency theory).
8. The project assumes that the school has the necessary 'breathing room' to be able to act independently.
9. Planning and implementation constitute a single process.
10. Schools can learn.

Is IDP organizational development or something else? Is it perhaps action learning or action research? Is it system learning (Senge 1990)? IDP draws heavily on theory and practice within many development traditions, but the programme has developed a unique set of principles and practices that highlight school improvement.

IMTEC gives potential users a thorough introduction to the methods used:

> For schools to develop from within, those who work in them must know themselves and their own organization. Our experience has been that teachers often know little about each other. Teachers seldom speak out about what they stand for; teachers and pupils rarely have such a good dialogue among them that they can constructively improve the climate and the teaching. Once again, we must bear in mind that schools differ. At some, an open, deliberate process is already under way to clarify practices and what one wants with the school. Sometimes there is an open and constructive dialogue between colleagues, but seldom with the pupils. In other institutions there is only whispering in the corridors. We assume that schools have different points of departure, and that this is an important factor when the self-evaluation and development process gets under way.

Since the school is the unit of change, school culture plays a critical role both with respect to work strategy and methods. In another context we have distinguished between *fragmented* schools, *project* schools and *learning organizations*. In the first case, the IDP consultant might need to work with *individuals*; in the second case, with a *group* or *department*; and in the last case, with *the entire school* from the very outset.

Entry

Some schools contact a consultant because they wish to solve what for them is a tangible problem. Others do so because they are facing a specific new challenge and would like help getting started. Still others want to work with their entire organization to develop a good school. In this contact phase, the consultant will be working with three different tasks:

- *Understanding the different needs* for change and conducting a dialogue with the school on tangible problems.
- *Building relationships* with one's partner (often the head teacher or project team), investigating potential roles and anticipated tasks, and clarifying the extent to which there is internal preparedness for entering into a development process.
- *Establishing a contract* with the school that can describe the general objectives, who the partners are, what the respective roles of the school and the consultants are, how much time and resources are available, and what each party's obligations are in the process.

Joint analysis and diagnosis

IDP is based on collaboration and collegiality. It is not possible to find good, tenable information – let alone make a joint diagnosis – unless there is a climate of trust in the school. That is why the collection, analysis and diagnosis of data is not just a technical question; it is primarily a question of creating a genuine dialogue in an atmosphere of mutual trust. In this phase, the processes 'recycle', and one constantly discovers new aspects of a problem – and one learns to appreciate goals. In this phase, the consultant will be occupied with the following tasks in particular:

- *Priority tasks:* By brainstorming, thorough discussions, and 'confrontations', the school (usually the project team in this phase) seeks to formulate those tasks which should be prioritized.
- *Data collection:* In addition to the information the school already has, the project team will usually want to gather new information. This can take place by means of very informal methods or by the use of more structured tools (e.g. standardized questionnaires).
- *Data analysis:* This is always a responsibility for the project team (or the one who is defined as partner). The consultant tries to support and organize the process.
- *Data feedback and dialogue:* In which all the participants (e.g. all teachers) help each other to understand the information and to analyse its significance for them. Data alone tells us very little. What really counts is how the participants relate to the information.

Vision and goals

The school's ability to formulate its own intentions and visions and establish alternatives is the most important part of this phase of the process. The data analysis usually makes it clear that there are a number of challenges and options. Thus it is important to marshal a creative process that will help the school to formulate its goals and visions. A number of activities are involved here:

- *Formulating prioritized goals* among many alternatives. This is difficult. The consultant helps the school to do this by formulating so-called *problem formulations*, and by utilizing these to sort out the implications of the data for the participants.
- *Value clarification* is a process that lasts for the entire school improvement programme. At this stage, however, it is particularly important, since the school must now decide what it wants to do. IDP does not aim at a consensus. Values must be negotiated; at times there will be agreement on what should be done, and at other times the school will have to live with a multiplicity of values – and perhaps even with a vast range of disparate action programmes.
- *Action planning* – transforming intentions into concrete plans that can be realized in the school. A number of project planning techniques, as well as a delegation of work to work groups, is the normal pattern in this phase.

Testing and evaluation
Before schools can turn plans into reality, they must usually test some of the project ideas on a small scale and give some teachers and pupils the chance to try out new practices. In other cases the concept of change involved is itself so comprehensive that it entails the need for everyone at the school to change more or less simultaneously (for example, when changing the way the work is organized). In this phase, the role of the consultant may be altered, and the following activities can take on major importance:

- *Training* and consultation – areas such as project management, development of project models, evaluation and management of groups (e.g. team building) are all important activities. There might also be a need for offering training in content-specific areas (e.g. the use of computers in mathematical simulations, for example). Such training is customarily given by other IDP consultants, who no doubt see it as their task to connect the school to the requisite external resources.
- *Follow-up and evaluation* of the implementation of new projects is essential ('formative' evaluation). This is important not only because the impact of a project can be unclear, but also because only a small number of teachers usually participate in the first phase. So there is a need for providing information to others as well as information feedback to those participating in the process. As a rule, the consultant participates in the development and the evaluation design, as well as in collecting data and feeding it back throughout the duration of the project.

Generalization and institutionalization
As a rule, pilot programmes pass through several phases, with increasing numbers of teachers and pupils becoming involved in each successive phase. This means more

staff training, and often more material development and other types of support. At some stage the school will have to phase in the work of change to the normal life of the school. A number of activities are important during this phase:

- *Some form of summarizing the experiences*, which attempts to appreciate new practices, must take place. This evaluation must be done in a warrantable way, especially if there is initial disagreement about a project. Discussing the evaluation data can lead to a deeper understanding of the needs and form the basis for modified programmes or new pilot programmes.
- *Structural modifications*, or changes in the way the schools are organized, in the way they work (procedures), and in the modification of norms and rules, are important at this stage.
- *Allocation of resources*, or at a minimum a new distribution of existing resources, is often one of the keys to making new practices part of the normal routine. As schools are rarely in possession of a great many unallocated resources, it is often a question of using time in some other way.
- *Staff development*, or assisting teachers who are not yet involved in new practices to gain the necessary knowledge and skills so that the new practices to be introduced generally can be used by everyone, is often a major key to school improvement. Schools should be able to use their own experienced teachers in this process, since they will have gained a lot of experience during the project.
- *The withdrawal of the consultant* can take place before, but at this stage it is important to conclude the partner relationship. Issues such as the following must be addressed: Has the school achieved what it set out to achieve? Has it gained the necessary experience, and is it now capable of rising to new challenges? If not, in which areas will it be wanting help in the future?

It is important to understand that these activities do not take place in a linear manner. They arise at different points in the process. They can crop up more than once, and they can also occur on different levels and with differing degrees of understanding. The process is essentially cyclical. While data collection and analysis of data is going on, there is plenty of opportunity for team development. Staff development should be made a priority in different phases of a project; and an evaluation can provide a fresh opportunity to pose questions. School development is a complex learning process in which changes in the school's culture feature prominently.

The school as a learning organization
IDP's goal is to develop schools as 'learning organizations'. This is important for the school itself, for its ability to cope with a constant stream of new challenges; but it is equally important for the pupils who, through their own experience of a changing school, learn to cope with institutional changes. It is a matter of course that the pupils are fully-fledged partners in the process.

In our work in Germany, we have seen that many schools wish to depart from a form of organization in which the teacher is autonomous, in favour of a model in which *the schools* are autonomous – or perhaps have greater freedom to manage their own resources. On the basis of the IDP project in Germany, models have been developed for how the schools themselves can gradually become learning organizations (Horster 1994, and Rolff 1993, 1994b).

In this process it is also important to keep the individual clearly in view. Organizational development, as we have defined the term in this chapter, aims to secure the maximum benefit for both the organization and the individual. Peter Senge (1990) reminds us that development begins with the individual, that personal growth is an important condition for change – indeed, that personal visions are necessary. Perhaps this is more important than anything in the teaching profession. If we neglect this aspect, IDP can easily degenerate into a programme that only works with the organization (Mietz 1994). As Peter Senge puts it, it is when we understand our hidden mental models that we discover new perspectives. As with all development work, IDP requires time for reflection.

Strategies for school improvement that take the individual school as their point of departure have great potential – but they also have their limitations. We will conclude our description of the IDP project by mentioning some of the dilemmas we are facing:

- *Consensus – conflict.* OD is not necessarily consensus-oriented, nor is it 'value-neutral'. Based on specific process values, it aims to create agreement where this is possible, but does not shrink back from highlighting or resolving conflicts.
- *Restabilization – renewal.* OD's objective is an organization that is in a constant state of renewal. Toward that end, it aims to give schools the capacity for self-awareness and self-renewal. The goal is *not* to 'cool things down', i.e. to get the schools to settle into a new stabilization. Such rest can only come about through a deliberate policy of growth; it is through joint efforts for a better school that our expectations for the future can be met.
- *The leader's or the schools' premises.* OD has long been known for being an 'errand boy' for management. In this discussion we have also seen that the head teacher's support is important. But this does not mean that OD is obliged to work on the head teacher's terms. In Scandinavia in particular, where the head teacher's influence is relatively limited and where teachers and pupils are gaining influence, OD – when put to proper use – can encompass the (often conflicting) interests of the entire school community.
- *The individual – the organization.* OD – again, when put to proper use – takes aim at the whole school as an organization; but it does so in such a way that individuals can benefit from the programme in terms of their own development. The overall objective, however, is to provide the individual with a development in his or her particular daily work situation. Individual training, apart from the daily work context, may well be an effective form of training for the individual, but it is not organizational development. Precisely because management plays such a major role in development work, all good OD programmes must provide for good leadership support throughout the project period.

- *Process and content.* An OD programme is process-oriented because it aims to give the schools the capacity for self-awareness and self-development. At the same time, it must be concrete and practically oriented toward goals that are not only attainable but desirable from the standpoint of the parties involved. To achieve both these objectives, external assistance must limit itself to providing process help (of different kinds) and to helping the schools themselves (through the project teams, for example) to organize a process in such a way that concrete objectives can be promoted.
- *Self-development – equality of educational opportunity.* With the school as the starting-point for change, schools with ample human resources *can* go farther than those where such resources are scarce. In fact, this is already happening. It is simply an illusion to believe that we have equality of educational opportunity just because we have a relatively equal distribution of resources and relatively equal access to education. Rutter has just pointed out the disparities that exist today *without OD* (Rutter *et al.* 1979). Surely it is an important task for the authorities to pave the way for OD in those schools that need it most.
- *Self-interest – ownership.* OD rests on the philosophy that the individual school – that is, all parties in the development work – should be able to perceive it as something of which they are an integral part. Herein lies OD's greatest potential – and also its most important limitation. There are important development goals which could well conflict with the wishes of individual schools, or conflict with strong interest groups at these schools. In such situations, it is necessary to resort to alternative strategies for change.

Organizational development works when the process is qualified and when it is voluntary. But herein lie the OD strategy's major limitations. What happens when the process is not implemented in a professional way? And what happens to those schools that do not wish to become involved in a development process, whether by OD or any other method? We shall first take a look at *evaluation* as a potential development strategy; in the next chapter we will discuss system strategies.

EVALUATION AS A STRATEGY OF CHANGE

The purpose of this presentation is not to provide a methodical introduction to school-based evaluation or external quality assurance; rather, our purpose is to assess evaluation as a strategy for school improvement. In the present chapter we will focus on *internal school evaluation* (External Quality Assurance, see Chapter 8).

Our knowledge of the processes of change in the schools, particularly from the standpoint of organizational development, has shown that under a given set of conditions, the collection, systemization and feedback of data can all contribute to school improvement. What conditions must be fulfilled before an evaluation process can lead to *renewal* and not to stagnation?

Let us first look once again at a couple of examples that clearly illustrate how complicated the introduction of internal school evaluation can be. In Sweden,

Ekholm (1992) reports that those head teachers who had received training (both theoretical and practical) in school improvement over a period of two years were finding it very difficult to introduce these practices in their own schools. After five years of work, only three out of 35 schools were using school evaluation as it was intended to be used. The reason for this, Ekholm feels, is the fact that evaluation (apart from pupil evaluations) is not a part of the Swedish schools' work culture; moreover, the position of Swedish head teachers is such that they dare not cross their own teachers. This situation is probably not peculiar to Sweden.

Our experiences with other countries, such as Germany, for example, confirm the above. In Chapter 3, we pointed out a number of typical characteristics of school culture that might help explain the difficulties:

- The divided decision-making authority, where the head teacher does not get involved in pedagogical decisions.
- Limited pupil or parental influence – and thus lack of user control.
- Insulated teachers who prefer to work with their own class and their own subject and who are not accustomed to discussing their classroom practices with colleagues.
- Loosely connected units, where what takes place in a math class appears to have no relevance to what happens in gym class, which follows.
- Lack of tradition for quality control (with the exception of strong pupil control).
- Informal evaluation from the surroundings that have no specific consequences for the school.
- The difficulty of evaluating so complex and complicated a thing as a school.

We could probably add to this list. What happens in the process that emerges in response to an *external demand* for school evaluation? We have discussed what we know about school improvement processes, and we would now like to remind the reader of some of the key aspects here.

1. *Genuine need?* What interest does an experienced teacher have in spending a lot of time and energy on a school evaluation process, and suffering the hardship involved? It is much easier to see a less experienced teacher's need for coaching, or a pupil's need for greater influence in the daily teaching, or a head teacher's need to understand what goes on in the classroom. And what do we do with those (the many?) who see no need for this at all?
2. *Complexity and compatibility:* Evaluating a school's operations in the face of a multiplicity of complex and diffuse goals is a difficult job indeed! Furthermore, when some are of the opinion that the evaluation is on a collision course with established norms and values, problems can arise.
3. *Competence:* Like other professionals, teachers want to master new tasks. During the first phase, the costs are high (in terms of time, energy, psychology), and the advantages few (progress, impact). This is particularly true of the school's internal evaluation, which is often not tangible enough. Even more so than with

other reforms, it is important here that reforms and follow-up take place over an extended period of time.

4. *Resources:* The teacher is bound by her day-to-day duties, and by forces which conspire to maintain the *status quo.* Thus, for something as complicated as school evaluation to be successful, it takes a willingness, making time, and enough energy. The tendency is to change *something* – preferably as little as possible – to survive (see Ekholm 1992).

5. *The school leadership:* School evaluation is dependent on a leadership that represents the whole, and that can vigorously champion the idea behind school evaluation: an open, learning organization. By the same token, the head teacher must be a supporter – both with respect to creating enough room and time, offering concrete in-service training, supplying the school with the necessary resources, and (above all) providing for a personal follow-up over a period of time.

Here it might be appropriate to recall Michael Fullan's advice for schools that are on the verge of introducing a reform (Chapter 5):

1. It is important to evaluate every suggestion for reform with a critical eye.
2. Be aware of what a renewal in practice entails, and know when new practices are actually being applied ('If I don't know I don't know, I think I know').
3. Check to be sure that there are clear enough guidelines for the implementation of the reform.
4. Decide whether the school's daily situation can bear up under the challenge of a given reform, and know what is required of the school.
5. Acknowledge the fact that thoroughgoing reforms raise questions that might breed anxiety and a feeling of inadequacy.
6. Be aware of your own criteria for evaluating the values of a reform. What are the criteria for evaluation – how do we know that something is better than what it is replacing?

The school – not the system – is the unit of change. Each school has its own culture. We know of schools that have been practising school evaluation since the 1960s. And there are examples of schools in which pupils participate daily in an open evaluation of the teaching. There are several hundred examples of how school evaluation – in some form or another – can make an effective contribution to school improvement. Since the mid-1980s, many countries have had a policy of institutionalizing certain aspects of internal evaluation of school practices – e.g. evaluating teachers' work (Teacher Appraisal) in Great Britain, employee interviews (the Netherlands), peer appraisal (a number of States in the United States), and broader internal school evaluations (often as part of an internal/external quality assurance system such as in the Netherlands, New Zealand, and elsewhere). School evaluation is, without a doubt, most widespread in the Anglo-American community.

Experience points to mixed results. In some cases there are a lot of 'drawing board' exercises. Annual planning, which is often associated with school evaluation, can easily become a drudgery involving only a few people. The work might have some symbolic value, but it has little or no impact on the daily teaching. What we often see is that the 'higher-ups' often become impatient and acquiesce in superficial solutions (for example, the submission of a written annual plan).

The prerequisite for success is an acknowledgement that a reform such as school evaluation *must be practised differently* at the various schools and in varying phases. Processes of change are learning processes, and change is a trip, so to speak, and not a decision. On this trip we must take opposition seriously, and realize that when we try to change an important aspect of culture, *the entire culture* changes. That is why such changes are systemic in nature, not a kind of 'add-on' structure that merely supplements what is already established.

Consequently, school evaluation becomes a link in *the modification of the work culture*, which in most cases cannot take place without long-term organizational development. Viewed in isolation, school evaluation – as a new 'component' to be added to an established set of practices – has little chance of success, if school improvement is our goal.

Chapter 8

System Strategies

In the previous chapter we argued that the individual school is the unit for change. Does that mean that the system does not count? As we shall see in this chapter, the system has a major influence on the process of schooling. Moreover, all schools need system linkages, unless we want a 'village policy' for schools. The local environment, parents and organizations do, as we have seen in earlier chapters, have a major influence on schools. Also at the system level there is a need to influence schools, e.g. to secure stable and equal financing, to implement certain educational and social policies and to secure quality (to mention a few system needs). Moreover, as we have seen, individual schools need assistance in various forms. The challenge is to create a responsive system to meet school development needs.

FROM ADMINISTRATION TO DEVELOPMENT

In this chapter we will present and discuss strategies that have *the system* as the unit of change. We will exemplify this with the trend in many countries toward the 'new state', or the state moving from a maintenance function toward a developing function. In particular, we are concerned with the consequences of decentralized management for the role of central administration.

In Chapter 1 we explored the new balance that must exist between the centre and the periphery when important decisions are being decentralized. In part, the process consists of a task displacement, from the centre to the periphery; and in part, new tasks arise at the centre as a consequence of decentralization; and in part, task-solving must be varied in its approach, in accordance with a new paradigm.

The rationale for the role of the state has previously been a paternalistic one: the state was alone in its ability to produce *a society of equal opportunity*; moreover, *the state knows better* – i.e. much of its role is based on the attitude that people don't really know what's good for them. In considering most OECD countries, we would have to say that this policy, which is based on a strong role for the central government, has led to positive results – e.g. universal education at a fairly high level.

The national government can no longer sustain this paternalistic role. In the first place, change is taking place so rapidly, especially at the workplace, that strategies for change have to be developed more swiftly. In Dalin and Rust 1996 we illustrated the

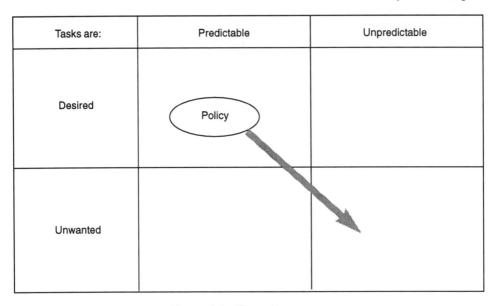

Tasks are:	Predictable	Unpredictable
Desired	Policy	
Unwanted		

Figure 8.1 *The policy arena*

dilemmas confronting us with a continued traditional process of central planning. Furthermore, the school as an organization must become more efficient, and this cannot be brought about through external means. And last, but not least, resources are scarce.

Perhaps more fundamentally, every political function that aims to set goals and guidelines today is faced with a mounting problem, which we have illustrated in Figure 8.1. The political function has traditionally been associated with tasks that are *predictable and desirable*. Politics, to a far greater degree, must address itself to tasks of ever-increasing complexity and *unpredictability*; the result is often *unwanted* consequences.

The typical reaction from central authorities, when plans cannot be implemented, is 'more of the same', with more detailed norms and rules and more stringent control. Without question, this leads to a growing problem with implementation. Central authorities often interpret this as sabotage, evasion, and resistance to change. After this process repeats itself a number of times, we end up with a decision-making process that no longer functions, because the trust from which authority derives its legitimacy no longer exists.

In every political system the government is faced with hard choices with respect to its centralized role. The education authorities, as we have previously discussed in this book, must first and foremost consider *the distinctive character of teaching*. As we have seen, we are faced with two different organizational designs, which Rowan (1990) describes as the difference between a 'control organization' and a 'mutually binding organization'.

In organizations that work chiefly with routines, research shows that a mechanistic control strategy can be effective (see Chapter 2). The solutions, since they call for a minimal amount of adjustment and creativity at the operational level, can thus be arrived at elsewhere and applied at the local level. The role of the evaluation becomes that of seeing to it that the system works.

In organizations where tasks are complex and the consequences unpredictable, *professionalism* is called for, which can best be developed in a mutually binding strategy. Here it is assumed that the local challenges are the important ones and that an answer must be found locally. The task of the 'centre' is to set the stage for a creative local process.

In the OECD countries, we are gradually moving away from a bureaucratic model in which it was assumed that all important decisions of strategic significance were made at the top of the pyramid (and where the grass roots merely carried out routine work) to *an organic model*, where all important professional decisions are made at the lowest possible level and where the 'centre' supports this process.

The means that decision-makers have at their disposal are, respectively, *rules* (new curricula, guidelines and regulations), *resources* (most often in the form of funds, job positions, materials), or *persuasion* (as, for example, through in-service training, research and evaluation, etc.). Figure 8.2 shows the dimension of tools, but also two other important dimensions in the choice of strategy – namely, the various levels at which one can intervene, and the particular phase in which intervention can occur:

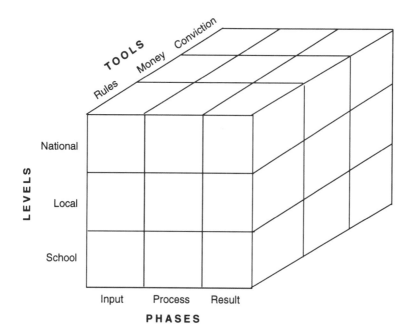

Figure 8.2 *The decision-making cube*
Note: This presentation was inspired by a lecture and a discussion with
Roel Int'd Veldt, the Netherlands.

We have already said that with respect to means, a logical consequence would be to use 'persuasion' as a tool. But does this exclude, for example, the use of 'control' as a tool? Certainly not; but it does call into question *the objective*, and it makes demands on how this control is carried out (see below). In particular, we shall consider evaluation as control and the new role we envisage for the inspectorate (in those countries that still have one).

Up to now we have only mentioned the one axis of our decision-making cube. The state – or, more commonly, the external role – must also evaluate which phase of the process a given tool is to be applied to. In the traditional bureaucracies, one was primarily concerned with input – or, more commonly, the presuppositions a given decision rested upon. Approval of textbooks, rules for school buildings or credential criteria for teachers are all examples of this. Both rules and funding were used as tools. Today, input factors are chiefly left to the users to define, and the state primarily enters the picture as a regulative organ in the form of financing.

Process factors (or what takes place in the teaching and learning process), as we discussed in Chapter 3, have proven to be difficult to change from the outside. In any case, the 'central' role in relation to the process of teaching and learning is quite complicated. We shall discuss this role in areas such as curriculum development and research and development work. A number of tools, chiefly rational–empirical, have been employed in these areas. Increasingly, the central authority applies management by objectives, which in principle does not intervene through rules and regulations (see below).

Up to now, *the result* of school activity has primarily been assessed in terms of pupil learning. With decentralized management and decentralization, renewed demand is generated for a far more comprehensive control of school activity by central authorities. In principle, this is a question of building up a comprehensive informational and control system as a tool for management, as illustrated by the work of Malik (1981). So 'control' becomes much more than a mere question of achievement data. The task becomes one of knowing how all parts of the educational system function.

The third axis in our decision-making cube comprises the *levels* at which decisions can be made – in principle, from the pupil on up to the central political authority – and, in turn, which tools and rules of the game are to apply to the system as a whole, and for which decision levels.

The development we now see unfolding (through decentralization) could indicate that the state's *authority* is being weakened. If that is in fact the case, it would endanger democracy and spell disaster for the schools. The danger is that if coercion always follows in the wake of authority, then authority itself is undermined. As I see it, the state, to a much greater degree, has become caught up in a vicious circle, precisely because coercive means are used (in a 'control paradigm'), instead of preparing strategies in a 'mutually binding paradigm'.

CENTRALIZED MANAGEMENT IN 'DECENTRALIZED' SYSTEMS

We shall take a closer look at *the central role* in some of the countries we have previously discussed in this book. Let us begin with the country that made an early start and has developed the system the most extensively – namely, New Zealand. We will subsequently make comparisons with developments in a number of European countries.

New Zealand

This country has a long-standing tradition of ensuring equality of educational opportunity for all its citizens, including the Maori folk and other minorities. The management challenge was therefore great when, in 1989, the country made a successful transition from rule-based management to management by objectives. In principle, this process of change should have improved quality, but the question was whether it also just as successfully safeguarded *the ideal* of equality. We have already discussed, in Chapter 1, some of the consequences at the school level after four years of reform implementation. We will be taking a look at the reform's ideological basis and its systemic aspects.

This reform not only involves a change of management structure for the individual school, but a redefinition of the role of the state as well. One distinguishes between the state as owner, as buyer and as regulator. Great emphasis is placed on the fact that these roles vary and must consequently have different structural and organizational consequences.

This reform has based a number of its ideological arguments on 'Public Choice' theory (Boston *et al.* 1991), which in turn is based on a rational understanding of humankind. The goal is to provide each user with the greatest possible freedom of choice. In New Zealand, the many 'layers' of administration between the Minister and the school was, quite simply, dispensed with in 1989. The charter between the individual school and the Minister regulates the relationship. At the same time, negotiations on teachers' salaries are discussed all the way up to the State Services Commission – in other words, this meant *increased centralization.*

The reform also derived many of its ideological underpinnings from management theory. Terms such as decentralization, deregulation, and delegation are expressions for how managers should lead, and no one knows better where the shoe pinches than the one who is wearing it. But even though a major decentralization has taken place, control remains at 'the centre' (Rae 1994).

Centrally, a number of changes have taken place:

1. The Ministry, once organized as a bureaucracy with a number of directorates, three regional offices and thirteen inspectorates, has been shut down. It was described by Picot (1988), who led the reform committee, as far too complex and overcentralized. There was a lack of information and electives; the Ministry was

based on outmoded leadership principles, and gave most people a feeling of helplessness.

2. The Ministry was radically downsized. The Ministry now has three main tasks: policy development, funding, and the administration of state property.

3. A special independent central organization has been established which is responsible for quality assurance (Educational Review Office). Its main task is to evaluate each local school at regular intervals (every other year). Below we shall discuss the strategy that this office is pursuing.

4. In addition, a body called the New Zealand Qualification Authority (NZQA) has been established which, being curriculum-based, defines (in operational terms) what one can expect to be produced in each local school. A bank of 'unit standards' is created, which is intended to be binding on the schools. A number of tools, which present the criteria, define quality management and what it means to set and follow up standards, is distributed to all schools; and the training of head teachers also takes place. The Ministry and NZQA concur in developing 26 national curricula standards within seven essential teaching areas (cf Curriculum framework, discussed in Dalin and Rust 1996). This is a controversial process, involving strong central control of the schools' teaching programme.

5. There is yet another agency that is exclusively concerned with financial control, or an audit of the school's accounts, which is carried out on an annual basis.

6. All the usual central tasks, which were often programmes made available to the schools (e.g. curriculum plan development and consulting) have been taken out of the hands of the Ministry and organized into separate institutes that work under contract for the Ministry.

Then what does this new central structure mean with respect to the state's ability to develop quality and ensure equality of choice in those options that are made available? We have already discussed some of the tentative effects at the school level. We will be taking a closer look at the state's choice of intervention strategies.

Policy development takes place first and foremost through long-term projects which focus on future needs, e.g. the basic document *Education for the 21st Century* (Ministry of Education 1993a). It is formulated as a discussion document that invites all interested parties to contribute. As a result of a process characterized by dialogue and discussion, a declaration of principles has been developed that is binding on everyone: 'The New Zealand Curriculum Framework'. This document provides curriculum guidelines for all kinds of schools.

Even though the document opens the door to developing a tailor-made curriculum at each local school, the central curriculum is very clear about which courses pupils are expected to take, which facets of knowledge, skills and attitudes one hopes will result. Emphasis is on how the school's curriculum can be precise enough for evaluation by the independent Education Review Office (ERO).

So far, no precise formulations or indicators have been developed to guide the head teacher in her management task. Therefore the schools are in the midst of a process in which they must move from relatively general academic goals to precise areas of learning in which the results should be measurable. In any case, in the next two to three years, a large degree of flexibility must be accepted, which will most likely create problems for those who will be doing the evaluation work (Rae 1994).

To get at a more precise definition of the curriculum, the National Educational Guidelines were developed; these set forth ten national pedagogical goals and six administrative guidelines. These guidelines deal with areas such as curriculum, personnel policies, funding and property matters, health and safety, and legal demands (e.g. pupils' attendance), as well as the length of the school day and the school year. The local school board for each school is given wide latitude within this framework.

The next step in the national management strategy is the New Zealand Qualification Authority (NZQA). This is the most ambitious national project of any under way today for managing quality development in an educational system. It is difficult, in the space of a few lines, to describe this work (which, after all, is quite well documented in a number of publications). Here we shall deal with some of the key aspects as seen from a system perspective.

NZQA has aimed to create a 'National Qualification Framework' – a binding operational description of all the knowledge and skills that are required within defined educational pathways. NZQA's tasks are as follows:

1. To develop (and further develop) a comprehensive, flexible and accessible description of all defined knowledge and skills within registered educational pathways, from upper secondary school, colleges and universities to industrial training, in-service training, and 'on-the-job' training.
2. To regulate and quality-ensure all who provide services in the system, as well as those who develop standards and study units, and suppliers of educational services (public and private schools and colleges, institutions, communication companies, and a variety of firms in the business community).
3. To ensure that New Zealand's qualifications are recognized abroad and that foreign qualifications are recognized in New Zealand.
4. To administer secondary and tertiary exams.

The goal of this grandiose effort is to provide a choice for those who are studying, ensure quality in every course offered, ensure a flexible transition between dissimilar units of study, and regulate competition between everyone who wishes to provide educational services. Hopefully, many will want to participate in in-service training by creating a number of equally viable alternatives, develop teaching programmes that are more relevant for the individual's life situation, simplify the exam and qualification structure, and create a more just system.

The chief strategy here is to reckon that all course units should be able to document knowledge and skills (performance-based learning). For this to happen, each unit of study must be defined in detail; at the very least, the end product must be defined in such a way that it can be measured.

Subsequently, each and every institution must be quality-ensured. This takes place when each school or institution (whether public or private) is accredited for implementing a specific course of study (each unit of study is quality-ensured). There are not only requirements as to the professional qualifications each institution sets, but also as to the way that institution ensures quality through its organization and management (Total Quality Management).

To illustrate how complex and comprehensive this reform is, we shall take a brief look at the process for which the central NZQA is responsible. Up to now, over 1,500 'standards' have been defined within different fields of study and professions. The entire process sparked over 1,600 comments from various groups and institutions, and the Ministry arranged over 300 meetings ('Learning to Learn', NZQA 1992).

The process of developing a *standard* is left to a national board of standards, composed of people from all interest groups (e.g. educational institutions, the business community, pupils, etc.) The following goals are adhered to:

1. The point of departure for every standard is a *needs assessment* within a given field. On the basis of this analysis, a 'unit' is developed.
2. It defines, in operational terms, what can be expected of a pupil who has completed the study unit, or what standard can be expected for passing a final exam.
3. Having completed certain technical analyses, the unit is registered and an evaluation of the relations between this and other units that have been developed is carried out. This unit then becomes a part of the National Qualifications Framework, and is placed within a hierarchy of units on eight levels which represent three separate exams (National Certificate deals with the first four levels, National Diploma the next three, and Degrees and Higher Certificates and Diplomas the last level).
4. 'Suppliers' of courses of study must all complete a process of accreditation before they can provide training in a specific 'unit'. As mentioned earlier, the institutions are accredited both with respect to their professional capacity, as well as their organization and management. If the institution lacks certain academic prerequisites for being able to provide a given course of study, NZQA tries to arrange a collaboration with another supplier. The institutions are 're-accredited' at regular intervals.
5. Once an institution is accredited, it has wide latitude in putting together a course of study, in choosing materials, textbooks, methods, and the use of defined resources. It is not necessary for a pupil to follow the teaching in a given period of time. Both shorter and longer periods of study are regarded as normal.
6. Evaluation of a pupil's learning takes place by internal assessment and by an external examiner, who must be officially approved. Great emphasis is placed on the evaluation being predictable (based on a described standard that both teachers and pupils are familiar with), that it is fair, valid and consistent. The pupil is not competing with other pupils, but with a standard!
7. The entire system goes through what is called 'moderation', i.e., a comparative understanding and application of standards is aimed for. Here NZQA takes the initiative, but all accredited institutions have a continuing responsibility.

This system represents no less than a revolution within the educational system. This can be first seen when it is tried out in practice and is about to become reality at several thousand established schools and colleges. It is easy to succumb to the temptation to write this off as a traditional 'behaviouristic model', but that would be too facile. The programme is at least as concerned with *the processes* as it is with *the product*. The following has been written about quality:

> The product is the new skills and knowledge acquired by the educated or trained person. . . . The process of learning is also very significant. Therefore the quality is also sought in the service that is the provision of an environment that enables the new skills and knowledge to be acquired. . . . (NZQA 1993a, p. 6)

In the same booklet, we read the following concerning quality:

> Quality is likely to occur where overall there is interactive participation in quality management by all partners. Quality is unlikely to occur where one partner acts unilaterally. . . . (NZQA 1993b, p. 11)

In our context, NZQA represents perhaps the strongest central strategy for influencing the teaching process that we have witnessed so far in practice. Even while in New Zealand each institution is given a lot of leeway to prepare the way for local self-government, the reins are tightened significantly inasmuch as 'the product' is defined so unambiguously and as clearly as possible. The aim is first and foremost to give each pupil *freedom of choice*, and above all create equality of opportunity for all and (perhaps) weaken the educational monopoly that public schools have enjoyed.

Education Review Office (ERO) is the last central strategy we shall briefly mention from New Zealand. This body represents what is called in Europe 'the inspectorate'. ERO is a completely independent, central agency whose task is to monitor school activity. In an addendum to the School Act of 1989, the different roles of the Ministry on the one hand and ERO on the other were clarified in 1993. ERO carries out 'reviews' of schools, either on their own initiative or on that of the Ministry.

There is a focus on the school boards' ability to manage the schools according to central guidelines and local needs that are set forth in the school's charter. ERO visits the schools on a regular basis (at least every other year), and its report is public and accessible. A distinction is made between three kinds of evaluation:

1. 'Assurance audits', or some form of report in which ERO investigates whether the board and the school administration are managing the school in accordance with the intentions of the charter and whether they meet the standards of quality that are defined. Such an audit report is based on internal school documents, the inspectors' own investigations during their school visits, and the schools' feedback on the first draft of the report. Where special problems arise, the first audit is followed later by more specialized investigations (see *Accountability in Action*, Education Review Office, undated).

2. 'Effectiveness review' is yet another form of evaluation that is carried out at each school. Here the main emphasis is on the teaching situation and on analysing pupils' learning – information that is aimed at the public as well as the Ministry and the local school. Each school's culture is taken into account, what the board stresses with respect to results, and what the national curriculum plan says. Also in this form of inspection, emphasis is on internal school information. The school is asked: 'What do you regard as *results* of the school's activities?' This sets in motion an internal evaluation process, which in turn forms the basis for the external inspection. Marks are stressed, but emphasis is also placed on what can 'help the pupils in this school to learn' (see 'Evaluation Towards Effective Education', Education Review Office, undated). Otherwise, the process follows the traditional internal/external evaluation process. To date, over 1,000 such external school evaluations have been carried out, all amply documented.

3. 'Evaluation services' is the third form of evaluation work carried out by ERO. This is what we have termed elsewhere 'meta-evaluation'. It is based on school evaluations and other data for investigating a specific subject (e.g. how is the quality of teaching in English for Maori pupils?). ERO also carries out special institutional studies that are not covered by the regular evaluations; and it takes on evaluation assignments.

As if this were not enough, each year the schools must also undergo a financial audit, carried out by the national auditing service. This could also include school visits and the preparation of a great deal of documentation. In view of all this, it should come as no surprise to anyone that head teachers feel overworked and that some of them choose early retirement. The total pressure from the centre toward the periphery is quite great and is keenly felt by all those who will be in charge of the actual teaching.

We have examined the systematic aspects of a reform that redefines the balance between the centre and the periphery. It gives considerable power to the local level (both parents and school administration), to the individual pupil (freedom of choice and flexibility), and to the centre, by means of a far more powerful management strategy. We see the transition from a 'loosely connected system' to a *tightly connected* one. In what follows we shall compare this reform with similar schemes in some of the countries we mentioned in Chapter 1. Even though a significant body of documentation from New Zealand already exists, it will take several years before we begin to have an overview of all the consequences of this ambitious educational reform.

The Netherlands

In Chapter 1 we described the radical decentralization in favour of the individual school that has been going on in the Netherlands in recent years. As is the case in New Zealand, each school has a local school board (there are 6,300 at present). In some cases, the board for one or more schools is situated in the municipality itself. All schools (including the public schools, which account for 30 per cent of all schools in the Netherlands) are organized as foundations. Private and public schools are treated alike; all are 100 per cent financed by public funds (Fuchs 1992).

We will take a look at some of the changes that have taken place at the central level. Most conspicuously, a deregulation has taken place; the means of management have changed. The reform is strongly characterized by 'public choice' theory. The local community and the parents have new rights (e.g. freedom to choose schools), while the schools themselves are developing like companies, often in head-on competition. Gradually each school is assigned the entire budget as a framework appropriation; they have wide latitude in administrating what is allocated. This has ramifications at the central level.

To begin with, the rules of the game were decided at the central level. A heated debate has been raging the past three to four years in the Netherlands over the terms of a transition to self-administration. The rights of pupils and personnel have figured prominently, as well as the ensuring of a global financial guarantee. And in large measure, this has succeeded, even though the effects at the school level have not yet been charted.

As we have seen in New Zealand, evaluation is a vital tool for the national government in its management system. The Netherlands has a long-standing tradition of using centralized tests to gauge pupils' knowledge and skills. These tests are prepared by the central test institute (CITO). Approximately 60 per cent of all pupils after comprehensive school are tested, and all pupils who complete upper secondary school take central tests. CITO prepares school statistics – primarily aggregated test results that are used by the comprehensive schools to guide parents in the choice of upper secondary school. Unlike the practice in Great Britain, the test results are not made public; they are accessible internally, however (Weeren *et al.* 1992). As in Sweden, a national spot check of the level of knowledge and skills is regularly carried out for various subjects, with a selection of 200–300 schools participating.

As in several European countries, a rule was introduced during the mid-1980s which stipulated that each school should devise a binding plan of operations. This plan, which in the Netherlands is drafted every other year and forwarded to the school inspectorate, contains the school's 'philosophy' goals, a selection of teaching materials (seen in relation to the school profile), the organizing of classroom teaching, criteria for evaluation, and a personnel plan. This plan, in turn, forms the basis for discussion and consultation, and only in rare, special circumstances (on account of legal circumstances) will the schools be asked to change their plans.

In the third place, the Netherlands now has a new, independent school inspectorate, with approximately 500 employees (Bik *et al.* 1991). These new inspectorates have four main tasks:

1. To guarantee that laws and regulations are respected.
2. To chart the situation in the school system by means of regular inspections.
3. To improve schools through a dialogue with the school boards and the management.
4. To write reports and forward recommendations to the Ministry.

The main work takes place by means of school visits from an external team, a process we have described for New Zealand, and one that is familiar in a number of countries. Greater and greater emphasis is being placed on self-evaluation as the basis for the external evaluation. Stress is also placed on a dialogue as the basis for counselling. In any case, it is the local school board that has the final say on any potential changes to be implemented after an inspection.

Theo Liket, who was a key figure in the development of an evaluation system for universities and other institutions of higher learning in the Netherlands, describes what he calls 'Qualitätssorge' (1992a) as a process with five phases:

1. The school's own self-evaluation.
2. Dialogue with the external assessor(s) to determine result indicators.
3. Visit by external evaluation team where relevant topics are discussed and investigated.
4. Presentation of the results to a representative group at the school.
5. An official report on the school's strong and weak points.

This process has just begun; there are examples of both process and tools (Hanboek Kwaliteitszorg 1993).

Even in the Netherlands, the trend is toward making the external reports public. Compared with New Zealand, there is far less binding management from central authorities with respect to specific result indicators. There is also a greater degree of liberality and less concern than there is in New Zealand that the system may gender inequality.

Denmark

As we discussed in Chapter 1, Denmark has a long-standing tradition of decentralization. It is also the country in Scandinavia that has come farthest in the development of self-governed schools with strong user participation. What, then, are the consequences for the central authorities?

To begin with, the Danish inspectors enjoy the status of national advisers in educational matters, and their position in the Danish school system is well entrenched. These inspectors, who are experienced teachers, usually serve for only three years. They are familiar with the work of teachers and command their confidence. Basically, their job is to hold the system together, as it were, making sure that there are open lines of communication from top to bottom.

The inspectors participate in the formulation of curricula, including goals and content, and they serve as advisers both to the Minister of Education and to the schools. Although they make school visits only once a year, they maintain contact in other ways. For example, they receive reports from each teacher in March of each year (before exams), check what has been studied, point out any weak spots (which are then addressed), and evaluate both oral and written exams. In general, the primary concern of the inspectorate in Denmark is the relationship between curriculum, classroom teaching and exams. In this respect, communication at every level and between all parties becomes a paramount concern.

In addition, they receive complaints lodged by pupils and parents against teachers; they are seated on a number of committees whose goal is to improve classroom teaching; and they serve as advisers to the head teacher and the teachers. The Danish inspectorate probably has an even more important position today, now that the schools enjoy greater independence, and it enjoys a large measure of trust, both at the school and ministerial levels.

In 1988 a centrally-run quality assurance project was initiated whose goal was to develop a new evaluation practice, one that would be better able to document the quality of Danish schools. Led by the Ministry, this project encompasses various forms of internal and external evaluation of schools. This project assists schools that wish to implement internal school evaluation; it also carries out certain external evaluations of schools – so far, only two school evaluations per year. However, these are comprehensive and thorough, and are based on a voluntary internal evaluation and a four-day intensive visit, as well as a visit approximately one year later for discussing whatever initiatives the schools may have developed for improving the work (at present, this project applies only to the upper secondary level).

This project has given rise to various forms of assistance for schools that are eager to join the school evaluation process. One of the most important of these, which is also a *standard* that the Ministry wishes to use in school evaluation, is the document 'Signs of Quality' (*Gymnasieafdeling* 1993). This is an important management document for the external school evaluation. Discussing what constitutes a 'good school' goes far beyond what is characterized in international literature on the subject as 'effective schools' (see Chapter 5). Moreover, many admirable attempts have been made to describe these characteristics in measurable terms ('signs'). Considerations such as the following are discussed:

- The school's climate, what is encompassed by the term 'open climate', the significance of social activities in the school and the significance of team spirit, and – above all – what is encompassed by the term 'good pedagogical climate'.
- The school's self-awareness and 'profile', what it 'thinks of itself', and what is required for a dynamic development – all of these factors are discussed and defined.
- What is meant by the term 'good teacher' and a 'good faculty', where the teacher's need for in-service training is also defined and discussed.
- The meaning of the terms 'good class', 'good pupil' and 'good class hour' are defined and discussed.
- What is needed for a good pupil evaluation and the significance of differentiation and specific programmes directed toward individuals are discussed.
- The requirements for co-ordination, management and collaboration, and resources, are all thoroughly defined and discussed.

This is perhaps the clearest definition we have yet found of what a 'good school' really is; it is also the most concise. As such, it will also serve as a vital tool in school evaluation. Thus the Ministry has taken the initiative, which is important in management of any kind.

The Ministry also contributes by supporting the schools in their school evaluation work, e.g. through a 'Theme series' (for example, see Theme 32 (1992): 'A Catalogue of Ideas on Quality Development and Self-evaluation'). The Ministry has also begun to publish its school evaluation reports (see, for example, 'Report from a Visit to N. Zahle's *Gymnasieskole*', The Ministry of Education 1993).

Unlike New Zealand, in Denmark there has not been a total reorganization at the central level; nor is such a reorganization thought to be necessary, since the decentralization process in Denmark must be regarded as quiet and evolutionary. Nor has there been any effort to define results in the form of result indicators or standards; this would represent a marked break with Danish pedagogy.

Sweden

We have already described the Swedish decentralization as a kind of 'municipalization' and discussed the ramifications at the local level, especially in relation to the local school (see Chapter 1). Here we will give a brief description of the ramifications of the reform for the more central levels.

To begin with, the powerful National Board of Education *(Skolöverstyrelsen)*, has been shut down. This institution was particularly powerful in a very centralized Sweden, but the government proposal for legislation entitled 'Responsibility for the Schools' (1990/91) heralded a new era.

A new national governmental body, *Skoleverket*, was established. This was an institution with a much clearer profile of government by objectives and with far less bureaucracy. In the government's proposal (1990/91, p. 20) it states, among other things:

... Parliament and the national government shall govern school activities by means of national goals. Basic objectives shall be established by law. Other goals and guidelines for teaching that have general validity are to be specified in the curricula.

The national government shall make a contribution to school activity; it should take the form of financial support, and not serve as a regulator.

The municipality or other parties responsible for the schools (Hovudmann) are to be responsible for ensuring that all activity is carried out within the bounds set by Parliament and the national government.

The schools' activities are to be monitored and evaluated. A follow-up of the evaluations shall serve as a basis for determining whether specific measures should be taken, or whether adjustments need to be made, in order that national goals and guidelines can be maintained and results can be improved...

The prerequisite for the implementation of these principles is that lower levels be given responsibility for tasks for which the state was once responsible. The most important changes in the municipal management of the schools are the following:

1. The Swedish schools now have a new state support system, one that is based on the principle of lump sum funding. State allocations are based on the number of pupils and are calculated by weighing the various factors that have an impact on classroom teaching. These funds go to the municipalities, not to the individual schools. This makes it possible for the municipalities to see the schools' activities in a broader context, in which the library system, youth work etc. are an integral part.

2. Nowadays, teachers are municipal employees, and the municipalities have bargaining rights with respect to the teachers' unions. A series of contracts exists which, in large measure, safeguards the rights of teachers.

3. Through the new management system the schools are no longer automatically assured of 'contracts'. The municipalities (in many cases) 'place an order' for teaching; the schools 'submit an offer', and – in theory, at least – the best bid wins the contract. In other words, to all intents and purposes, a market system has been established internally between the municipalities and the schools.

4. The municipalities are to work out a school plan and evaluate it at regular intervals; this plan will serve as part of the foundation for national inspection of the municipalities.

The national administration has undergone significant change. This is a consequence of the transition from rule-based management to management by objectives. The state, represented by the Ministry and *Skoleverket*, has two tasks:

1. To follow up, evaluate and keep tabs on the Swedish school system. *Skoleverket* is responsible for a nationally co-ordinated evaluation of the public schools. It also has a supervisory function.

2. To further develop the schools. This applies to the general guidelines for the Swedish schools and may also include the state's means of control. This policy assignment is closely related to the evaluation and supervisory function described in point 1.

Of particular interest to us in this context is how the relationship between state – municipality – school is regulated. In Sweden the state does not intervene directly in local school affairs. *Skoleverket* addresses itself to the municipalities, and collects a wealth of information about the schools' development from municipal statistics and routine visits to the municipalities. The Swedish inspectorate stops, so to speak, at the municipal limits.

The comprehensive, nationally governed evaluation project which, with a structured sample of 101 comprehensive schools, has investigated various aspects of school activity (pupil results, school climate, etc.) was carried out for the first time in the spring of 1992 (Öquist 1993). This project is so extensive that no overall report has yet been made, and a new national evaluation project was implemented in 1995. This project has three goals:

1. To evaluate the quality of the Swedish comprehensive schools.
2. To give the national government and the public an idea of the extent to which national goals for the schools have been carried out.
3. To use the national goals as a frame of reference for the schools' own self-evaluation.

Sweden has also aimed at integrating self-evaluation into the schools' work culture. At present, we have very little experience. Ekholm (1993) and Franke-Wikberg (1992), who have been working with such processes for many years, have experience with internal evaluation that is coupled with an external peer evaluation. Not much connectivity to the national evaluation project, however, appears to have taken place.

Sweden has carried out a careful decentralization, and has taken advantage of this process to do some housecleaning in the central bureaucracy. The tools, which are based on a positivistic philosophy, have not been abandoned, however; in fact, the centralized evaluation project is a good example of this. It remains to be seen to what extent each school experiences greater freedom with respect to school development, or if the new system spells centralization and more control.

Great Britain

Under the Conservative government, the trend was towards introducing a 'public choice' and 'management' philosophy within education; but the practical consequences have varied from those in other countries we have discussed so far.

Great Britain has had a tradition of great independence for its local schools, a system in which the head teacher is a key figure. The nation had no common curriculum, and choice of subjects and courses was largely left to the individual school. The British system has also had well-established, strong municipalities (local educational authorities), which have had major support functions *vis-à-vis* the schools, and a powerful central inspectorate (Her Majesty's Inspectorate, HMI), which has evaluated school activity.

These fundamental circumstances were modified in the new system that was introduced in the late 1980s. The following changes in particular have proved significant:

1. A centralized curriculum and a set of national examinations was introduced (ages 7, 11 and 14, Dearing 1993), which provoked strong reactions. It must be said that the British curriculum, as viewed with Scandinavian eyes, is a general framework plan, but of course it also represents a marked centralization in relation to previous practice; it is also a narrowing of the individual school's, the teacher's, and the head teacher's responsibility.
2. Since 1986, compulsory, annual evaluations of every teacher have been introduced, for which the head teacher is responsible. This aroused considerable scepticism and opposition.
3. The reforms also gave the local schools an opportunity to break loose from local education authorities and establish direct links with the Department of Education (Grant Maintained Schools). This was regarded as a strategy for weakening the

229

influence of local politicians and local administration and for enhancing state control of the schools.

4. An effort was made to improve parents' range of options by making exam results public and publishing them as 'lists of rankings' (of schools) in the daily newspapers. This serves to give the schools a high profile and leads to a concentration of exam-related work.

5. One of the most important changes is that a completely new structure for inspecting schools has been devised. A new, centralized, independent body – Office of Standards in Education (OFSTED) – emerged. This body does not itself carry out internal school evaluations; rather, it determines the criteria, standards and procedures. Independent teams (both public and private) then submit bids for inspection assignments. The team leader must be qualified and accredited. The reports are discussed with the schools and made public. (For an evaluation of the new inspection form in England, see Ofsted 1994 and Dean 1994.)

These developments in England and Wales have led to a new balance, primarily in the direction of more centralization, or – more to the point – a weakening of the intermediate level (local education authority) in British education. The system seeks to improve the quality of classroom teaching and provide parents with more and better options. One consequence of the system is that it weakens the teacher's authority and further strengthens the head teacher's role.

Norway

Finally in this context, we will consider the development that has taken place in Norway and assess it from an international perspective. We will give a brief account of the main principles behind the government's efforts to change the management structure (Parliament Bill 37, 1990–91).

We can recognize some of the management principles we discussed above. These are:

*   Decentralized management as a general management principle, but with several reservations here.
*   An unequivocally hierarchical organizational pattern in which the state, at the *central* level, deals with matters of principle; in which the state, at the *regional* level, deals with planning and follow-up of the state's interests; and in which tasks of less overall importance (for the state) are decentralized to the school owner (the municipality or the county).
*   A structure that appears logical and useful for co-ordination of education across sectors, and a system that is justified on the basis of better utilization of resources.

The parliamentary bill describes *why* changes are needed. It is claimed that the role of the Ministry is unclear; and the mandates of the central advisory bodies are especially worriesome. (Norway had several professional educational advisory bodies to the Ministry which also worked directly with the schools.) Conflicting 'management signals' are sent out; the distinction between 'purely professional and political decisions is ambiguous', and these ambiguities 'contribute to a growing disrespect for what the central authorities decide'.

It is claimed that this sectorization makes it harder to carry out a comprehensive educational policy. It is also claimed that current policy is too demanding in terms of resources, and users of the educational system have trouble finding their way in the complex administration maze.

The advisory councils for lower comprehensive and upper secondary schools were terminated. The regional arms of the state – state offices in each region – were closed down and a new national educational office (which is responsible for the interests of the state for the entire educational system) was established in nineteen locations nationwide.

Prior to that, the EMIL project was initiated; its task was to pave the way for a comprehensive evaluation of the Norwegian schools (Granheim and Lundgren 1990). One proposal for a comprehensive evaluation system has recently been published (see below). A set of guidelines for internal school evaluation has also been prepared.

During the past two years a great deal of planning work has taken place in the Ministry, aimed at the introduction of a reform that is primarily aimed at the upper secondary school level (Reform 94). One basis for this reform is a general curriculum for the entire school system, which we described in Dalin and Rust 1996. The goals of this reform are ambitious and call for an extensive overhaul – both as to subject matter, organization, and structure.

At the same time, Reform 94 also introduced a highly significant change in school administration (Parliament bill 37, 1990–91). From a purely practical standpoint, this meant that the Ministry was to relocate several hundred people in record time, create nineteen operational educational administrations on the regional level, re-write 350 new curricula, and implement the extensive review process that is so typical of Norwegian public administration. A comprehensive curriculum reform, to include the 6-year age group for the first time, was introduced in 1997.

The extent of this work can perhaps be illustrated by the following numbers: approximately 30,000 pupils who fail each year to be admitted to an upper secondary course of study (and who do not receive any qualifying training) were to be guaranteed admission until such time as they met the formal qualifications. In order to provide a more relevant initial training in their respective subject areas, the basic courses were cut back from 110 electives to thirteen, which meant a radical change in syllabus and teacher in-service training. Another aspect that is new is that all teachers must undergo an in-service training programme (primarily to update subject areas and didactics). In addition, there is now a teacher's guide for each subject area in the basic courses (in addition to the curriculum and textbooks).

The Ministry has had these reform proposals under review (before hundreds of review bodies) for a period of two years. And several hundred work groups are currently (1994) involved in planning of various kinds, led by a special 'Reform 94' project organization in the Ministry.

The strategy thus far can be described as follows:

1. *External pressure:* Reform, according to the Ministry, was long overdue; and it was no longer acceptable to leave almost 30,000 young people with no options, or allow several thousand pupils to wander aimlessly between basic courses – all because there was no room for them in upper secondary level courses. So this reform did in fact meet *a genuine need.*

2. *Shock therapy:* Instead of the plodding, cautious trial strategy with small, well-defined steps, evaluation and gradual enlargement (in accord with the R & D & D tradition), it was decided to implement the reform *without* any foregoing trials. All upper secondary schools were to implement the reform at the same time. It would not be unfair to claim that this was a deliberate power strategy.

3. *Broad participation:* Plans – curricula in particular – were developed with broad participation on the part of teachers, head teachers and others, and the hearing drafts were distributed more broadly than had ever been the case before. In so doing, the Ministry was building upon a Norwegian and Scandinavian tradition of full openness and participation when important decisions are in the making.

4. *Clarity of goals and premises:* Parliamentary Bill 33 (1992–93) was exceptionally brief, clear and concise. Parliament knows what it has had before it to consider, and it knows what has been decided. So does the Ministry, and this has served as 'an agent of control' in the process.

5. *In-service training:* the past two years, more than 180 million Norwegian kroner have been spent on in-service training of teachers and head teachers of the comprehensive schools. Such training is a requirement for teachers in upper secondary courses. This is an exceptional sum for a country that has made only modest appropriations in this sector. This commitment corresponds to a month's salary for every teacher in upper secondary school.

6. *Development of the regional educational offices:* Reform 94 has given the new offices – the departments for upper secondary school, in particular – special tasks. As a result, these offices now have a wealth of development tasks that will stand them in good stead, and from which the reform itself stands to gain.

7. *Continual evaluation:* Although the reform implementation does not include a trial phase, continual evaluation has been built into the process and – in principle, at any rate – changes can be made along the way.

How, then, has this strategy been working? Up to now, nearly everything has fallen into place in the planning phase (curricula, in-service training, most textbooks, school leader training, information). The Ministry has good reason to be satisfied with what it has accomplished.

Not everything has been painless, however. Strong criticism has been directed at what has been termed 'a rush job'. There are many who still would have preferred a trial model. And since negotiations for a new teachers' contract came right in the middle of the in-service training phase, some courses were boycotted. But perhaps the greatest weakness has been the Ministry's failure to win over public opinion. Whatever the case, relations with the media have proven to be a relatively weak aspect of the strategy.

On the other hand, the Ministry enjoys the full support of the unions and organizations in business and industry; moreover, the teachers' unions have generally been positive. Perhaps it was a lucky thing that the teachers' unions merged at the same time the reform was introduced, which perhaps put a damper on the criticism that one might have expected from that quarter.

The form of management that was introduced means that the Ministry's work with the Reform will soon be over. Implementing the reforms in the schools is the responsibility of the counties. In principle, neither the Ministry nor the educational offices are to work directly with the schools; their task is to lend impetus and support to the counties. In this way, the Norwegian and Swedish management models are similar.

The form of management was designed to give the schools more breathing room; in spite of this, pressure from the centre has never been greater. And (within upper secondary education) the state has never been physically present at the nineteen offices throughout the country. Could one result of this be that the schools feel that their toes have been stepped on and that they are under greater control than before?

One peculiarity of the Norwegian schools is that they do not have a quality assurance system. For example, Norwegian schools have no inspectorate, as is customary in a number of European countries. And apart from final exams, there is no way of obtaining systematic knowledge of the individual school or the school system as a whole. The new national programme for evaluation of schools was meant to go a long way towards making amends. One example of this is given in the pamphlet entitled 'National Programme for the Evaluation of the Comprehensive School' (KUF, undated), which emphasizes that all school levels have a responsibility and a role to play in school evaluation. Evaluating school activity is purportedly demanding, because the goals are so manifold and complex. For this reason, a conscious attempt is made to find means of evaluation that will satisfactorily address the breadth and complexity of the schools' objectives. Further, an attempt is made to make the work of evaluation meaningful for pupils, teachers and head teachers.

The programme is based on the principle that an evaluation is to be a *dialogue* between people and groups and between various levels in the system. Thus, communication and an emphasis on good evaluation methods is important. By the same token, the evaluation is meant to help promote a unified information system whose task is to improve practice, so that all the goals for the schools can be better realized. The programme is illustrated in Figure 8.3. This shows that the Ministry envisions a comprehensive programme that calls for extensive co-ordination. The information from the various components is meant to promote learning and to aid in the development of the system as a whole. The various components are the following:

1. *Exams and tests:* This includes the traditional national tests and will ultimately include a number of diagnostic tests.
2. *Learning benefit:* The primary focus is on diagnostic tests that help the individual teacher to determine whether a given pupil needs remedial aid. Teacher experience with this work will provide increased insight into pupils' learning benefit.

3. *General conditions for learning:* While the Ministry does not feel that there is any obvious connection between general conditions and learning, it wants to learn more about how the two are related. To begin with, matters related to management, co-operation between home and school, and the organization of the school and of classroom teaching will all be analysed.

4. *School-based evaluation:* At issue here is not only the individual teacher's (and the team teachers') evaluation of their own teaching, but also a general evaluation of school activity, where both pupils and parents participate.

5. *Statistics provide an overview of the most important quantitative factors.* At present, school statistics provide us with information about classroom resources, pupil statistics, personnel statistics, and exam results. This body of data will become more broad-based in the years to come.

6. *Area evaluations:* We have previously referred to this as 'meta-evaluation'. It involves the investigation of areas of particular interest. The Ministry would like to begin by investigating matters such as the teaching of pupils with special needs, equality of opportunity, and the restructuring of the state-run schools for students with special needs.

Little is said about the kind of analyses to be done, what weight is to be given to their various components, and who should carry them out. It is complicated enough to make effective use of information based on school evaluation within a municipality, especially because it is not clear who 'owns' the information. The Norwegian schools are a long way off from having a quality assurance system; moreover, it is not yet clear what roles the centre and the periphery will play.

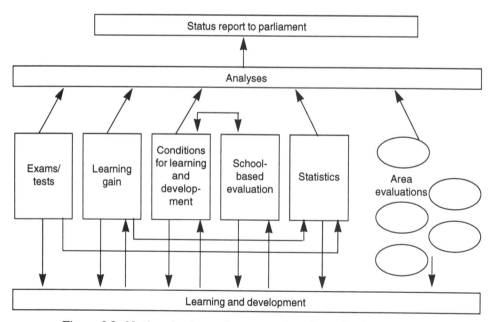

Figure 8.3 *National scheme for comprehensive school evaluation*

In an overall evaluation of the past few years of development in Norway, we would probably be justified in claiming that the 'new balance' between centre and periphery has led to increased centralization. The nineteen educational offices are major players in highlighting the interests of the state in the various regions. Whether this will lead to better co-ordination than under the old system, and whether it will result in better quality – not to mention better school development – remains to be seen.

The strategy that has been pursued in planning and executing Reform 94 is a classical example of the 'central role' and of a system of management by objectives. The centre provides the direction, is clear, and instructs the next link; and the reform will stand or fall on this ensuing link – the counties. It will be the Ministry's responsibility to evaluate each county's professional, administrative and financial capacity for management, support and follow-up in each school. Finally, success depends on the school and on the individual teacher.

Other countries

We have experience with changes within central management systems, but where general principles of management remain unchanged. What comes to mind here are the school inspectorates in France and (in part) Germany (Burkard and Rolff 1994). In France, a relatively cautious decentralization has taken place between the three levels of inspection. The trend has been away from individual teacher inspection toward an assessment of the school as a whole; among other things, this calls for teamwork (Lafond 1993).

Relatively speaking, the pace of development in Germany has been slower. The traditional inspection (*Schulaufsicht*) has been occupied with a number of questions related to quality assurance, such as evaluating individual teachers (as a rule, at the time of promotion), organizing important exams, and a type of ombudsman role for parents and as 'communicator' between the schools on the one hand and the Ministry on the other. In Germany, a relatively clear-cut distinction is made between *Fachaussicht* (academic inspectors), *Dienstaufsicht* (inspection in relation to teachers' tasks and duties), and *Rechtaufsicht*, which relates to the monitoring of the school owner's role.

There is an ongoing critical debate in most of the German states as to the role of the inspectorate. Changes are planned in all three areas of the inspectorates' fields of work. The trend is toward distinguishing between legal tasks on the one hand and academic-pedagogical tasks on the other. The trend in certain states is also away from evaluating individual teachers and toward a more broad-based evaluation of the individual school (Burkard and Rolff 1994).

In other countries there are a number of examples of central initiative – in part, very radical attempts at creating a new balance between the centre and the periphery. We could have chosen Australia as an example, because developments in that country closely reflect those in New Zealand. In North America, a number of states and school districts have developed performance-based systems. Some of the most advanced models are in the state of Oregon (Oregon Dept. of Education 1992) and the state of Kentucky (Foster 1991). Both states are working towards a radical restructuring of their educational systems. They are attempting to invest the local level with considerable power and responsibility and to increase user options – heightening the benefits of systematically managed quality assurance in the process.

The Charter school movement

Since 1988, 16 states in the USA have passed 'school choice' laws granting students admission to attend schools beyond the geographic borders of their local school districts where tuition fees are paid. More than 4000 'magnet schools' allow students to select specialized teaching or curriculum themes within their school systems. The first Charter school opened in Minnesota in 1992, and there are now nearly 800 such independent public schools educating more than 165,000 students (Toch 1998).

Charter schools provide for private initiative, and provide public resources for such initiatives. A great variety of initiatives have been taken to create Charter alternatives. Large non-profit making foundations are behind some of the initiatives (e.g. A. Alfred Taubman with the Leona Group in Michigan), as well as individuals who have an idealistic motivation or a business motivation.

Several initiatives have been evaluated (see Weiss 1997). It is clear that freeing up schools from bureaucracy in and of itself does not guarantee high quality learning. There are excellent as well as quite bad Charter schools (many of which go out of business quite early). There is no eevidence that the Charter schools 'produce' higher results than public schools (Weiss 1997).

In our context, it is important to note that Weiss finds that Charter schools are isolated from each other and from other schools, and that in many cases there is a need for networking and external assistance. While autonomy provides a high level of satisfaction, and gives participants many exciting opportunities, it is also isolating. Charter schools need feedback and assistance. They need a 'system' that gives them a 'home'.

FROM MANAGEMENT BY RULES TO MANAGEMENT BY OBJECTIVES

The 'new state' that Reichard (1992) has described as a wave of reform in the OECD countries during the 1980s and 1990s also has a 'new system of management' as one of its key components. We will use Norway as an example of this development, followed by a description of the practices in various countries in which this new system of management has been institutionalized.

In the national government's long-range programme (1988–89), management by objectives is defined as follows:

> By management by objectives, a superior governing authority (e.g. a govern-
> ment ministry) manages subordinate institutions by setting goals and
> priorities for each of them. Within the scope of the allotted resources, these
> institutions may themselves determine how these goals should be realized
> concretely. However, these institutions are to *report to those governing*

bodies that are above them in rank, informing them of the results of their efforts. In this context, emphasis is on developing specific result requirements. On the basis of these institutional reports, the ministries will monitor achievement of goals as well as any departure from goals, and assist in implementing any modifications that might be called for. (Parliamentary Bill No. 4, 1988–89)

There is a clear-cut hierarchical philosophy behind this 'decentralized' principle. The Center defines the overall direction and the goals; the Periphery ascertains how best to achieve them. *The ultimate responsibility* lies at the top of the hierarchy (cf Malik 1981).

It is unthinkable that any system could be guided by goals alone. Rules are a necessary management tool. Here, as in much else, it is a question of finding the right balance. The important thing about this balance is that following rules is no longer a goal in itself; rather, the goal is to achieve results (yet without violating fundamental principles).

One of the key principles of management by objectives is that roles are clarified as far as this is possible. In particular, it is important to distinguish political roles from professional ones, and to distinguish between responsibility at the central level and at the local level (cf Malik 1981).

Since the central level no longer issues directives by means of circulars and similar means, but rather concentrates on the overriding issues of goals, its ability to govern is largely determined by its knowledge of what goes on in the field. Thus the systematic follow-up of results becomes a natural consequence of management by objectives. For this to take place, an extensive evaluation must be conducted of the way in which the system works.

When it becomes clear that a summative evaluation is necessary, the goals will inevitably have to be broken down into *operational terms.* The school sector is faced with major problems here. Work with indicators and standards in a number of countries bears this out (cf, for example, OECD 1989, *Educational Researcher* 1990, *Educational Leadership* 1993).

In practice, it will be necessary to clarify what is meant by the often vague formulations one encounters in the schools' objectives. Granheim and Lundgren (1990) have sought to differentiate between:

- what constitutes fundamental principles;
- what constitutes educational objectives; and
- what constitutes objectives for knowledge.

From this they proceed to a distribution of tasks between the parliament, the national government, the municipality, and the unit of the school (see Figure 8.4).

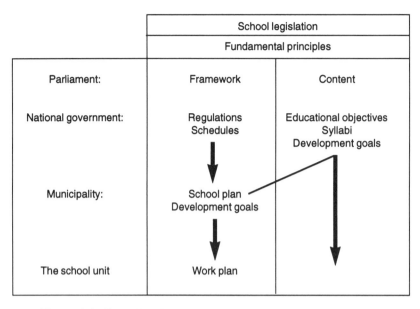

Figure 8.4 *Distribution of tasks in the management system
(from Granheim and Lundgren 1990)*

The authors point out that the arrows in the figure point in only one direction: downward, from above! They say that in a 'fully developed management and evaluation model' the arrows point in both directions, and institutions are free to provide feedback and viewpoints on overall goals and on the conduct of higher level management. We would have to say that this view of organizations is an optimistic one, to say the least! In fact, behind this construction there lurks a pronounced rationalistic organizational mindset.

As a fundamental principle of management by objectives, the authors state that political governance includes general goals and the basic legal principles for the activity in question, as well as the distribution of resources and the design and influence of professional competence through teacher training. Professional management includes each activity's concretization of national and municipal goals, as well as content and the methods employed.

Criticism of management by objectives

Management by objectives as a management principle for the educational system has met with sharp criticism in a number of countries. This criticism has taken several forms; in what follows, I will attempt to outline some of the most important objections:

1. *The rational goal–means mentality:* This is a recurring theme in the ongoing pedagogical debate. All previous attempts to distinguish between means and goals with respect to classroom teaching and learning have hardly been a rousing success (see Dalin and Rolff 1991).

2. *The significance of the goals:* Most people – and most institutions, for that matter – have not defined their goals, much less utilized them as an everyday management tool. Instead, we are experience-oriented. We learn about our goals gradually, as we become familiar with a given field of experience. The key metaphor here is 'chaos', which is 'order disguising as coincidence' (Larsen 1990). It is not *the goals* which actually steer us; rather, it is everyday *learning in practice* which gives us our bearings. It is possible that everything would go much more smoothly if all our goals were well formulated and fully internalized. However, might this not cause us to miss out on something important? What are the advantages and disadvantages of an excessive goal-orientation?

3. *School goals and product evaluation:* A number of experts have cautioned against regarding school goals as 'operable' in a strict sense. But under any circumstances, many goals will remain impossible to gauge. And there is a danger that those goals that are pursued could well prove to be merely those that can be measured, and not necessarily those that are important. This could easily lead to goal displacement and inauspicious developments in practices (see Chapter 3). As we have seen in previous discussions, we must consider the teacher more as a 'dilemma leader' who is obliged to come to grips with a range of goals, activities and processes *simultaneously* and who, in practical situations, is compelled to *make hard choices.*

4. *School culture and result evaluation:* Evaluation practice tells us that evaluation is not effective unless the school culture is open and inspires trust, and unless there is a positive relationship between the one doing the evaluating and the one being evaluated. In a national evaluation scheme, the necessary closeness is bound to be lacking, rendering the evaluation – for all practical purposes – *ineffective* as an aid to development strategy, unless the activity is specifically geared to that end.

Aalvik (1991) compares the role of the teacher with that of the meteorologist, who predicts the weather. Rationality and intuition count, even in the profession of meteorology. After all the available scientific data has been evaluated, colleagues consult among themselves; intuition and the use of one's own judgement are important factors in the determination of what sort of 'weather forecast' is sent out.

Aalvik (1991, p. 60) states:

The teacher's situation can be compared with that of the meteorologist: both work in fields characterized by complex and unpredictable interactions among a host of factors, and both professions are concerned with phenomena that appear to be commonplace and easy to grasp. Owing to the chaotic nature of the processes involved, no two clouds have ever been identical; despite this fact, it is easy for anyone to tell that what they are seeing in the sky is a cloud . . .

If results evaluation as a management tool is to be effective in the schools, it must take into account the realities of the teaching, take every teaching situation and every school seriously, and find methods and strategies of intervention that inspire trust and can contribute to the development of each school. Only then will the system obtain realistic data which can be employed in fashioning a future system.

EXTERNAL EVALUATION AS A DEVELOPMENT STRATEGY

There are many rationales for carrying out an external evaluation of a school activity. In this section we will primarily be concerned with whether or not external evaluation can contribute to *school improvement*.

What, then, does *result evaluation* mean within the tradition of management by objectives? In the Swedish study of the new management system, the following general definitions are set forth (Government proposal of 1990–91):

> A commonly accepted idea is that a result evaluation describes, analyses and assesses a given activity. It is ongoing; it should have a governing effect on the activity (at all levels); and it should be able to provide a unified, comprehensive evaluation of a complex and multifarious sphere of activity and its results. By means of an evaluation, one attempts to understand and account for what takes place and why. The aim is also to ensure that this is done in such a way as to create ownership to the process and at the same time create the mobilization that is *one of the prerequisites* for further development . . .

To the extent that this is a reasonable definition of the concept, the question is one of what aspects of result evaluation are difficult in practice, and what can be done about it so that the activity can become an effective development strategy. It has been said that:

- 'It should evaluate a specific activity.' The first thing we have to ask is what is *the unit* for a result evaluation? We recommend that it be *the individual school*.
- 'It is continuous.' If we are to avoid having the evaluation become an unwieldly bureaucracy, the external activity *must be related to the schools' internal self-appraisal*. Thus, the question of what this kind of association means becomes a key issue (who has a right to what data, etc.).
- 'It shall have a management effect' on the activity. We have seen that this requires that the information be regarded as legitimate, that there is confidence in the one doing the evaluating, and that help is available for following up the evaluation.
- 'It shall provide a unified, comprehensive evaluation.' This might mean that a wide variety of methods, quantitative and qualitative, external and internal parties and all interests are represented.
- 'One should attempt to explain and understand.' This can be interpreted to mean an expert job, with investigators poring over reams of computer printouts in an

attempt to interpret them. This might well be necessary, but it is much more important that *the user understands*; this is why experts and uses must be knit together in a learning system.

- 'A mobilization must be brought about.' I believe that this will largely succeed, provided the evaluation is made a cornerstone in a learning organization.

However, the focus on evaluation can also be directed in other ways, if developments in the United States are any indication. The Center for Policy Research and Education (CPRE) has carried out a comprehensive study on the initiative taken at the state level to create a qualitatively better school. The demand for 'higher standards' and greater control over results has been a key factor in the development (Firestone *et al.* 1989). Having carried out what is known as the five-year 'Trazer Study' in six states, CPRE discovered that all these states, through new legislation, had committed themselves to higher standards, to a more academic curriculum, to stricter teacher qualifications, and similar schemes. The variation in response from the towns and cities was extreme: from enthusiastic co-operation to sabotage.

In those states where testing of pupils was part and parcel of the reform proposals, reactions were negative. Time spent on such testing increased dramatically; so did the time teachers spent on conducting the tests – especially time spent correcting papers and interpreting and discussing the results. This was perceived as burdensome by many. But what was worse, they didn't find the information thus gained to have any real value; nor was there any mechanism by which this information could be related to a school improvement process. The evaluation became an activity in itself (Firestone *et al.* 1989, Corbett and Wilson 1990).

There is a very real danger that the evaluation will wind up becoming a set of inconsequential exercises. The testing mania in the United States is perhaps the most extreme example. However, other forms of evaluation, including the schools' self-evaluation, risk becoming bureaucratic fiats of no consequence. Precisely because pupils' test results – in and of themselves – tell us so little, and because other data are needed for applying information to school development, it is vital to find a strategy in which internal and external forms of evaluation work together.

We believe that external evaluation of schools is important. It represents a necessary corrective, an external perspective, and an alternative perspective on the school's activities – one that is both necessary and useful in a national school system. We also feel that such a system, to be effective, must 'work with people rather than shuffle paper around'.

We do not believe that increased testing leads to quality development, but that the dialogue that can be established between internal and external interests and viewpoints is useful and important for school development. Figure 8.5 illustrates what we are concerned with.

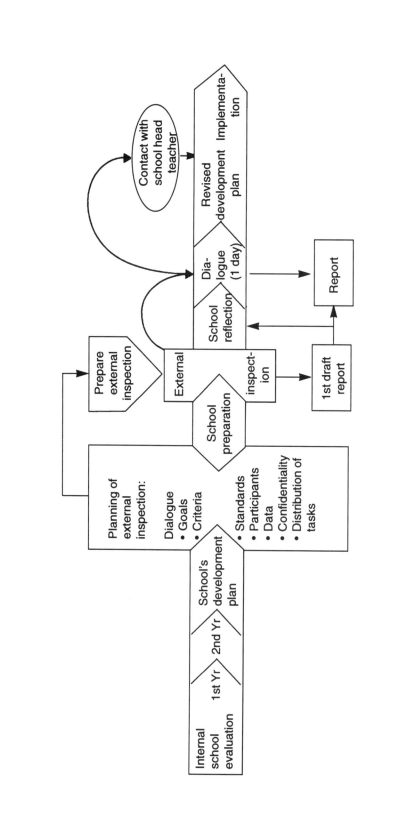

Figure 8.5 *Dialogue in school evaluation*

1. The process starts with an *internal school evaluation process*. This process is carried out routinely and is part of the school's development strategy.
2. Once every third or fourth year, the school is subject to an external inspection. Representatives from the school and the inspectorate meet for a planning and negotiation meeting, where they discuss the objectives of the external evaluation, the criteria and standards that will be applied, who will be participating (for example, colleagues, parents, representatives of business and commerce, etc.), what data the external inspection requires from the last two years of the school's operations, and what the school and the inspectorate must each do to prepare the external evaluation (collecting information, compiling data, safeguarding personnel confidentiality, reviewing reports, studying internal data, etc.).
3. The external inspection suggests an inspection scheme based on prior consultations and previously submitted material. It is determined which questions will be asked and which persons/groups will be contacted. It is important that the inspection, in every aspect of its contact with the school, is open, clear, and receptive.
4. The school lays the groundwork for the visit. The inspection consists of at least two members – although as a rule there are more than two, depending on what issues will be assessed, on the size of the school, etc. The visit extends over a period of at least two (maximum five) days. A successful inspection visit creates an open and creative dialogue between all the participants in an atmosphere of trust. The aim is to understand, and to create a foundation for further development.
5. After the inspection, a tentative report is submitted to the school for its comments within two weeks after the visit takes place. The key word here is *tentative*. The report deals with both the weak and the strong points of the school and with those areas where more work is called for. It also delineates internal and external areas of responsibility.
6. During this period of time, the school seeks to clarify what it has learned from the inspection. A *process of reflection* is set in motion relatively soon after the inspection takes place, and impressions are registered and linked to the school's own internal evaluation. What does the school itself wish to change?
7. The inspector comes to the school to make comments and engage in an exchange of views. The school's written comments are included (usually as an appendix) before the final report is written and sent to the Ministry and the school. The school then revises its development plan (if necessary).
8. The inspector contacts the head teacher within six months in order to ascertain where the school stands, and to determine whether anything can be done externally to assist in further school development (in relation to the revised development plan).

We have included this example in order to illustrate the fact that the external evaluation ought to be closely linked to the school's own work, and that it is precisely by means of an open dialogue that a propitious environment for school development can be fostered.

The new inspectorate

For many, the inspectorate conjures up associations of 'the old state', to a bureaucracy that governed according to rules and that needed to keep watch over the schools. The inspectorate was at the pinnacle of the hierarchy; it also had formal authority.

As the old bureaucracy ran up against a new order of reality, and reforms in public administration began to take effect, the inspectorate was faced with a new situation. Hopes (1992) has studied the inspectorate's position and development in the European Union. Among his findings are the following:

- In a number of countries, the Inspectorate still works with details, various administrative issues and routines. In some countries (as in a number of states in Germany) the inspectorates still monitor individual teachers' classroom teaching (by means of one-hour visits). The work of the inspectorates is not connected to central policy issues.
- There is a pronounced lack of confidence in the inspectorate as an institution on the part of teachers (which, in part, is also true of head teachers). It is thought to be irrelevant, outmoded and outlived.
- The inspectorates themselves are an isolated group. And as a group they have little real power within the Ministry (except for questions related to rules that fall under their purview) or in relation to the schools.
- The inspectorates work in an unprofessional way; they have (as a rule) no specialized training for their work; there is only a small amount of professionalization going on; and there is little time for collegial collaboration.
- The work of the inspectorates is little known to the users, and they do not lend any support to the demand for an 'open public administration'.

This situation is changing. In a number of European countries there is a development afoot whose aim is either to change the inspectorates' role and work or to do away with them altogether. This takes place as part of the following general development:

- Each school is responsible for quality development and quality assurance, which is best illustrated in the Dutch programme.
- The central authorities are responsible for the guidelines and framework conditions for quality assurance (goals, norms, procedures, who participates, etc.) and they 'quality ensure the quality assurance'.
- The schools conduct regular internal school evaluations (of different kinds).

Under these altered conditions, which have begun to take shape in a few countries and states (but do not represent a clear trend as yet), the inspectorate has begun to find a new role.

- The traditional *legal role* is weakening. This is clearly the case in Germany. In the Netherlands, the legal responsibilities have practically disappeared; the same holds true for Great Britain.
- *The individual* (the individual teacher, for example) is no longer the primary inspection focus. It is *the school as a whole* that is the object of attention – for example, with respect to its annual plans, the school's work with different groups of pupils, its curriculum, culture, management and staff development.
- *Consultancy* with respect to subject, content and processes is regarded by some inspectors as a new and important field of work; however, in some cases this is left to 'horizontal' institutions that can be chosen by the school itself.
- *Meta-evaluation* is assuming increasing importance. The inspectors work in tandem with prioritized areas which are investigated in a select number of schools; the aim is to provide relevant and tenable information for new guidelines and centralized initiatives. The Swedish national evaluation programme *(nasjonale utvärding)* is but one example.
- The *external* school evaluation, where a number of players often participate, is also becoming increasingly important. There are a number of models here.

FROM AN ADMINISTRATIVE ROLE TO A DEVELOPMENT ROLE

Up to now, the various educational systems have primarily been rule-governed. There was also a tradition in the European educational administrations that *jurists* should occupy the most important positions. The role of the heads of the educational ministries was more *administrative* than developmental. The role of the state in school development consisted primarily of appointing a commission, on the basis of which a curriculum would be developed, which was then implemented – primarily by law and a body of rules.

As developments in society made ever-increasing demands on the educational system, it became apparent that the state had a *developmental responsibility* for the system. During the reconstruction period after World War II, we experienced one centrally regulated reform after another. In Norway, the National Council for Innovation in Education *(Forsøksrådet)* became an exponent of the R, D & D work that was being done. Sweden had its *Skolöverstyrelse*, Great Britain its School Council, and the United States had their 'laboratories' and research centres. In fact, most OECD countries constructed their development policy on a model which, succinctly put, was based on a careful small-step development process, a model that analyses results, lays the groundwork for implementation in the ordinary schools, and then disseminates the results.

The so-called R, D & D model has been the object of a number of evaluations. John Goodlad was among the first to criticize the new model, which had already been allocated considerable resources and had engaged several thousand experts. He claimed that the new process was not a *development* model at all, but rather a *research model* that suited a select group of experts (Goodlad 1975). Dalin (1973) pointed to major weaknesses of the model in five countries in which the relationship (or lack thereof) between the central R & D work and local and institutional practice was documented. During the 1970s, the RAND Corporation was assigned the task of evaluating 293 federal projects in terms of their [potential] impact on individual schools. This became a groundbreaking study which showed the potential of the R & D strategy, but also its major limitations (Berman and McLaughlin 1977, McLaughlin 1990).

The R & D strategy was at the centre of an intense debate during the 1980s; the result was that most national institutions with a responsibility for development work were abolished. What remained were those institutions that could survive in a market. There are nine regional laboratories remaining in the United States, all of which depend on contracts with the federal government for their survival.

Dale Mann has the following to say about why the R & D strategy as an instrument for centrally-initiated reform was not a success:

> Two principles guided these efforts; both were wrong. First, if the national government tried to force something to happen AND if it paid for it, schools would change. Second, if better ideas were available, schools would rush to adopt them . . . (Mann 1991)

The RAND researchers came to the following conclusions: 'Implementation dominates outcomes', and 'Policy makers can't mandate what matters . . .' (Berman and McLaughlin 1977). An interesting Norwegian example is an attempt to carry out R & D work from a decentralized management perspective. Engen (1991) wrote about this; he assessed the results from six projects under the auspices of the National Advisory Council. He found (as did the RAND researchers) that these projects reveal local needs as much as they do central goals. Central control is weak and too imprecise; and yet, *the project leader* plays a role. Engen says that 'the central authorities (appear to) have had a good grip on the "discharge mechanism", but central control is gradually weakened'.

Another important aspect of developments during the 1970s and 1980s was the proliferation of 'teachers' centres' (often called 'pedagogical centres'), first in Great Britain and later in a number of other countries. As a rule, these were locally organized – by the school owners, for example – but there are also examples of centrally financed centres. Even though major reductions have been made here as well, many of these centres have nevertheless survived. Moreover, those that did are becoming increasingly market-oriented. In Chapter 6 we pointed out a number of principles that are crucial to the success of in-service training in promoting school development. To the extent that pedagogical centres can be a model for *external assistance*, Huberman and Miles conclude the following:

1. Adequate *qualified* assistance has positive short-term and long-term consequences.
2. We *cannot* expect that even adequate and qualified help during the early phase of

a complicated project will solve all our problems. Most complicated projects get off to a rocky start, *regardless* of the nature of the assistance.

3. Effective assistance is *user-oriented*, not product- or project-oriented. It lasts for the entire project period and helps ensure confidence, the development of skills, and the ability to make adjustments and continue to develop.

4. The surest way for a project to fail is a combination of a demanding project and the lack of requisite financial and professional support. Because school development takes time, qualified support at some later date is more important than the support given during the start-up phase (Huberman and Miles 1984).

This illustrates various strategies for influencing the content of the schools on the basis of an external role. What we are concerned with here is the external role in general. It can be centrally or regionally located; it can be professional or administrative in nature. What do we know about schools' motivation for participating in externally initiated reforms?

We know that conditions for growth in the municipalities (counties) are propitious for schools that show an active interest in school development. An initiative from the superintendent is often required before schools initiate a development process. There can be many motives for making a start: the need for professional development, the need for a more stimulating workplace, and an interest in having a say in influencing the development of the school. As a rule, teachers and head teachers are more interested in *how school improvement can improve the workplace* than in the strictly pedagogical and academic issues.

More opportunistic motives are also commonplace: there is little available funding. Project funds can help schools with the purchase of equipment, materials, course fees and extra teachers' costs. Projects can also be used as a springboard to a managerial career. Such motives are not necessarily at odds with school development; but if they loom too large, development work is bound to suffer.

Not many schools develop projects from within. Most attach themselves to the apron strings of some project or other that is introduced from the outside. This is why there are so few schools that undergo a problem-solving process and choose their projects on the basis of their own problems. When difficulties arise (and they are sure to arise), many schools enter a phase marked by problems and conflicts. Some choose to take the easy way out, resulting in a watered-down project that doesn't yield the expected results. But where the school owner makes demands and yet at the same time provides qualified help, the schools resolve their problems and produce good results.

Schools go through a 'mutual adjustment and development process' (see Chapter 5). The projects are modified and adjusted to the school's culture. At times – in those cases where management, both internal and external, is weak – change is brought about by interest groups; the danger here is that the weakest can wind up on the losing end of the stick. Where the schools get adequate professional help, the teachers feel better equipped to handle their classroom teaching situation; they also feel better equipped to acquire skills whose usefulness extends beyond the project itself.

Moreover, they often have a heightened sense of job satisfaction upon the completion of a development project.

Central authorities are concerned with the spread of new practices. This takes place, for example, when the school owner shows an interest in and supports the project throughout the entire project period, which leads to improved skills on the part of all parties, keener motivation and an improvement of pupil results, both cognitive, emotional and social. And if external agencies provide more than verbal support, this will bring results. But if things do not progress beyond the planning and celebrating stage, the long-term result will be frustration and a string of negative effects.

STRATEGIC CHOICES

How can school development best be stimulated *from without?* The choice of strategy is not merely a technical question. What's at stake is the choice of values, of one's perspectives on organizations and on change. What approaches are important in the choice of strategy? As we see it, there are three key questions to consider:

The distribution of responsibility. Who should be responsible for deciding whether a given school development project should or should not be implemented? In the international literature on school development, strategy issues are often problematic, because responsibility for school development is shared differently in different countries. For example, in England it used to be taken for granted that each school (and to a large extent, each teacher) would develop curricula. Nowadays, this is no foregone conclusion in England. In Norway, the allotment of responsibility with respect to school development has primarily been regarded in the light of distributional policy objectives, which is why curriculum development is also centralized (on the premise that joint teaching materials promote equality. If a project revolves around social goals in which equality issues play a key role, then the placing of decision-making authority will prove central.

The allocation of resources is closely related to the issue of the distribution of responsibility. A policy that encompasses a decentralization of responsibility for school development, along with a strong central control over resources, is a system at odds with itself. If each school is to have responsibility for its own development, it must also have control over the manner in which its budget is employed. And this is precisely the kind of development we are currently witnessing in a number of the countries we have described.

Most systems can be thought of as *negotiating systems.* Although lip-service is paid to the idea that each school should take the initiative, in reality the school owner and the state have their own vested interests. In certain cases solutions can be negotiated; in others, the entire system has to be modified.

The new management systems we have discussed so far have come up with differing solutions to the distribution of responsibility for school development. In spite of the role of the new school boards in New Zealand, this country remains the clearest example we have of centrally regulated reform, where results are expected and demanded. This is an example of management by objectives. It ought, in theory, to result in greater freedom for the local school, but we believe that in reality the schools will feel more heavily monitored. True, they will have a certain leeway, but will essentially remain tied to a relatively rigid, centrally regulated qualification framework.

The schools in the Netherlands are also 'managed by objectives'. Here, however, we have a liberal form of management which largely assumes that the local school takes the initiative – indeed, 'wins in the market' – with an educational profile that is attractive for both pupils and parents. As opposed to New Zealand, the Dutch national government has been less worried, so far, about the consequences for equality of educational opportunity.

What we are trying to illustrate is that management by objectives can manifest itself in a wide variety of ways, that the distribution of responsibility and the tasks shared by the centre and the periphery will also vary.

Intervention. In choosing ways of exerting an influence on schools from the outside, we are faced with a number of dilemmas:

- Development can be initiated by a small number of schools and then spread (cf the R, D & D model). If this model is chosen, we are again faced with a choice: should the most motivated schools (which are often the most well endowed) be chosen as pilot schools, or should those in greatest need of renewal (and which are often less amenable to assistance) be chosen first?
- Development can be initiated by encouraging a number of schools to define their own needs and start the work of development – for example, with financial and professional support – or an attempt can be made to clearly define what we feel the schools should do. In the latter case, one can even go so far as to spread 'finished packages' (e.g. thoroughly tested teaching packages) which fit those needs that the schools themselves have defined as theirs.
- The state (or the school owner) can avail itself of financial assistance; but this involves a number of dilemmas: how much funding is there a need for? Which are best: tight budgets or generous ones? Should the schools be expected to contribute something of their own resources? Should the funds be given as general support, or should they be earmarked for specific purposes?
- The state (or the school owner) can also employ professional means: should the curriculum be defined by external agencies? In that case, how much leeway should the school and the teacher be granted? Should the school owner offer professional assistance? What kind of assistance is appropriate? Is there a need for generalists or specialists? Should the assistance be concentrated on the start-up phase (giving the school more leeway later in the development process), or should it be spread throughout the life of the project? Should the school owner require that schools loyally implement a project down to the least detail, or should they be encouraged to make local adjustments? Where do we draw the line – and who is responsible for drawing it?
- Whether or not schools should be treated differently is sure to become a major

issue in Norway. We know that in some ways schools differ greatly. Equal treatment of unequal entities will only lead to continued inequality. Should the state and the school owner be able to treat schools differently? Is it a worthy goal that external intervention be adjusted to each school's culture and distinctive character and to the particular problems that each one is faced with? If the answer is yes, then what are the means at our disposal that will help us define what these differences are and how can we create an attitude of acceptance for differentiated treatment?

Monitoring the results. It is also possible for the state and the school owner to influence the development process by means of various forms of control. In the foregoing we have discussed forms of evaluation such as accreditation, validation, the inspection system, and school evaluation. These are but some of the many conceivable models for control. What approaches are important for the choice of control measures?

- Should the control be external or internal? There are clear-cut lines of distinction between those who use control as a selection criterion (should the project continue?) and those who would use it as a development resource.
- To what extent does the monitoring of results influence the development of the project? Development projects often cost more than normal operations. They are time-consuming, and it is difficult to predict the expenses involved. On the other hand, trial and effort is often a prerequisite for producing interesting results – and it is often the unintentional that commands the greater interest.

EFFECTIVE EXTERNAL STRATEGIES

In conclusion, let us return to the innovation literature and ask ourselves what it would take for centrally regulated reforms to succeed. Is there any advice we can give to the party for whom the unit of change is *the system?*

If we try to get our bearings out in the field by using the wrong map, we won't get very far. School reformers use all of their own and others' theories of change when they map out their reforms (Fullan and Miles 1992). And they often build upon theses which are patently erroneous or even detrimental, such as:

- We must always reckon with opposition to reforms.
- Schools are conservative institutions and harder to change than other organizations.
- Since we can't please everybody anyway, we might as well set the task before us and see it through to the finish.
- Everything depends on capable managers.

There are many reasons why reforms often fail in the schools. As important institutions of society, schools must make hard choices in the face of a number of complex dilemmas, none of which allow for easy answers. One of the popular fields of sport within the subject of school development is to concoct new visions and goals. But a goal without a thorough and well-thought-out plan of execution is worse than useless.

Since finding good answers to complex educational problems is such a complicated process, politicians and managers often succumb to the temptation to settle on symbolic, rather than genuine, solutions. And the solutions they do come up with are often fraught with vague objectives, unrealistic schedules, a high degree of committee work, and a deep gulf between the 'higher-ups' and the grass roots. Politicians interpret resistance negatively.

Then there are those who prefer one-sided solutions – e.g. defining goals themselves and then shoving the decision to implement them farther down the system – without providing funding at the outset. Another example is changing the structure without simultaneously making room for a change in the culture. Elmore (1996) argues that policy-makers prefer to change structures because it signals that something important is happening. Also many teachers believe that they are greatly influenced by 'structural constraints', and that structural change will lead directly to a different kind of teaching and learning. Ekmore argues that change in structure (alone) is weakly related to changes in teaching practice. As a rule, important improvements in the classroom require fundamental cultural changes in the schools.

And when the reactions come, the politician chooses to interpret resistance to the reform as something negative. After all, how could anyone who thinks constructively possibly be against something good? Well, for many reasons, in fact – one of them being that reforms in the schools have often proven to be negative. For another thing, teachers know that changes involve learning over a long period of time – a luxury they can ill afford. Furthermore, fundamental changes in the schools touch on fundamental values. Of course we need resistance! How can such centrally initiated reforms succeed?

There is no simple recipe, but as we have seen earlier in this book, both research and practice in the Western countries (and increasingly from developing countries as well) shows that there are, in fact, a number of common features.

Innovation is a learning process associated with a major degree of uncertainty. Things will often get worse before they get better; it is simply impossible to know beforehand. Although coming up with a good plan is important, it is even more important to lay the groundwork for a learning project organization which rewards the taking of chances, which gradually gives school leaders and teachers the chance to move away from trivial renewal to truly substantial renewal in the classroom.

The readiness of schools to implement and refine a reform proposal varies greatly. In fact, in many schools the daily problems loom so large that the situation more closely resembles chaos than planned rationality. Schools are seldom goal-oriented; they are action-oriented. But the practice of planning first and then acting conveys the wrong message. Negotiations take place when we see that something works. So the message we want to send is this: do something; investigate; plan – and then do some more!

Pressure and support are both necessary. The government, of course, is responsible for conceiving long-range (and bold) guidelines. It is fully within its rights to make demands on pupils, teachers and school leaders alike. But pressure without support will hardly get us anywhere. The more extensive the changes, the more (and longer) the support required.

Without support, teachers will only see problems. They automatically get shouldered with the responsibility. If problems are to be handled in a constructive manner, this calls for an open atmosphere, an acceptance of the desirability of a variety of opinions, and encouraging schools to find their own suitable, local solutions.

With support – and with ample opportunity for in-service training, in particular – for school development in the local school, for management development, and for spending time to reflect on project work, the mood will change. It is not unusual for teachers to use up to 15–20 per cent more time the first couple of years solely on the academic and methodological problems associated with reforms. International data has shown that head teachers spend as much as 30–40 per cent of their time for reform work during the first few years (cf data from New Zealand).

Success requires renewal at the local school level. If reforms are to succeed, this calls for more than merely replacing one textbook with another, or making structural changes in the curriculum or the use of time. For change to be durable, a systematic work at each school must be carried out over a period of several years. Leadership and co-operation across subject and group lines is required, involving pupils, parents and other important users.

Reforms require changes in school culture. This will take place, eventually, provided the reform is organized as a learning process. Indeed, reforms are a unique opportunity for schools to develop toward a 'learning organization'.

Reforms require system modifications. It is not just the individual school that must undergo a learning process. The same thing applies to the government and other governing bodies at various levels. It is *the relationship* between these different levels that is important if reforms are to be effective at the national level. For reforms to succeed, *we must work with all the components at the same time*. Small, individual, incremental changes are seldom successful.

The results depend on the execution. Research on reforms in the schools shows that it is not the reform concepts themselves, nor any well-laid plans which are crucial to the outcome, but rather the way the stage is set for learning and collaboration throughout the entire system.

References

Aalvik, T. (1991) 'Målstyring eller kaos?'. Oslo: Bedre skole.

Alderer, Clayton P. (1977) 'Organization development', *Annual Review of Psychology* 28.

Alexandersson, M. and Öhlund, U. (1986) *Perspektiv på personalutbildning i skolan. Att fortbildas eller att fortbilda sig.* Rapport No. 186:04. Gothenburg: Institutionen för pedagogik, Gothenburg University.

Algotsson, K. G. (1975) *Från katekestvång till religionsfrihet.*

Aliniski, S. (1971) *Rules for Radicals.* New York: Vintage.

Allport, F. H. (1962) 'A structuronomic conception of behaviour: individual and collective', *Journal of Abnormal and Social Psychology* 64.

American Association of Colleges for Teacher Education (AACTE) (1986) *Task Force on Teacher Certification.* Washington DC.

Aoki, T. T. (1977) *British Columbia Social Studies Assessment*, Vols 1–3. Victoria BC: British Columbia Ministry of Education.

Arends, J. H., Schmuck, R. A. and Arends, R. I. (1980) 'Students as organizational participants', in Milestein, M. M. (ed.) *Schools, Conflict and Change.* New York: Teachers' College Press.

Arfwedson, G. and Lundman, L. (1983) *Varför er skolar olika? En bok om skolkodor.* Stockholm: Liber Utbildningsförlaget.

Argyris, C. (1962) *Interpersonal Competence and Organizational Effectiveness.* Homewood, Illinois: Irwin.

Bacharach, S. B., Bauer, S. and Shedd, J. B. (1986) 'The work environment and school reform', *Teachers College Record* 88, pp. 241–56.

Baker, K. (1981) 'The S.I.T.E. Project', in Bolam, R. (ed.) *School-Focused In-Service Teacher Education in Action.* London: Heinemann, 1981.

Baldridge, J. V. (1971) *Power and Conflict in the University.* New York: John Wiley and Sons.

Barnard, Chester I. (1938) *The Functions of the Executive.* Cambridge, Massachusetts: Harvard University Press.

Barrows (1980) 'Findings and Implications of the Thirteen Schools Study', Paper presented at the annual meeting of the American Educational Research Association (AERA).

Bartalanffy, L. von (1968) *General Systems Theory: Foundations, Development, Applications.* New York: George Braziller.

Bassin, M. and Gross, T. (1978) *Organization Development: A Viable Method of Change for Urban Secondary Schools.* Report presented before the American Educational Research Association, Toronto.

Beeby, C. E. (1966) *The Quality of Education in Developing Countries.* Cambridge, Massachusetts: Harvard University Press.

Bennis, W. and Nanus, B. (1985) *Leaders.* New York: Harper & Row.

Berg, G. (1986) *Control Structure and Strategies for Change in Educational Research and Organization Theory II.* Uppsala University, Pedagogiska institutionen.

Berman, P. (1980a) 'Thinking about programmed and adaptive implementation: matching strategies to situations', in InFam, H. and Mann, D. (ed.) *Why Policies Succeed or Fail*. Beverly Hills, California: Sage.

Berman, P. (1980b) 'Toward an implementation paradigm'. For the Program on Research and Practice, National Institute of Education.

Berman, P. and McLaughlin, M. W. (1975a) *Federal Programs Supporting Educational Change, Volume IV: The Findings in Review*. Santa Monica, California: Rand Corporation.

Berman, P. and McLaughlin, M. W. (1977) *Federal Programs Supporting Educational Change, Volume VII: Factors Affecting Implementation and Continuation*. Santa Monica, California: Rand Corporation.

Berman, P. and McLaughlin, M. W. (1977) *Federal Programs Supporting Educational Change, Vol. VIII: Implementing and Sustaining Innovations*. Santa Monica, California: Rand Corporation.

Bik, H., Janssens, F. and Kleijne, W. (1991) *School Inspectorates in the Member States of the European Community. The Netherlands*. Frankfurt am Main: C. Hopes.

Bird, T. and Alspaugh, D. (1986) *1985 Survey of District Co-ordinators for the California Mentor Teacher Program*. San Francisco: Far West Laboratory for Educational Research and Development.

Blake, R. R. and Mouton, J. S. (1964) 'Breakthrough in organization development', *Harvard Business Review*, November/December.

Block, P. (1987) *The Empowered Manager*. San Francisco: Jossey-Bass.

Bolam, R. (1981) *In-Service Education and Training of Teachers and Educational Change*. Paris: OECD.

Bolman, L. G. and Deal, T. E. (1984) *Modern Approaches to Understanding and Managing Organizations*. San Francisco: Jossey-Bass.

Boston, J. *et al.* (eds) (1991) *Reshaping the State: New Zealand's Bureaucratic Revolution*. Auckland: OUP.

Bowers, D. (1973) 'OD techniques and their results in 23 organizations: the Michigan ICL study', *Journal of Applied Behavioral Science* 9, No. 1, pp. 21–43.

Brandt, R. (1992) 'On building learning communities: a conversation with Hank Levin', *Educational Leadership* 50, No. 1.

Bridges, S. J. (1992) *Working in Tomorrow's Schools: Effects on Primary Teachers – A Christchurch Study*. Christchurch Education Department, University of Canterbury.

Broady, D. (1978) *Utbildning och politisk ekonomie*. Report I from Forskningsgruppen för läroplansteori och kulturproduktion. Högskolan för lärarutbildning i Stockholm. Stockholm.

Broady, D. (1981) 'Critique of the political economy of education: the Prokla approach', *Economic and Industrial Democracy* 2, No. 2, May.

Broady, D. (1981) *Den dolda Läroplanen*. Stockholm: Symposion.

Brunholz, D. (1988) *Schulleitungsseminar. Evaluation der Fortbildungsmassnahme*. LSW, Soest.

Bryk, A. *et al.* (1993) *A View from the Elementary School: The State of Reform in Chicago*. Chicago: Consortium on Chicago School Research.

Bryk, A. S. and Driscoll, M. E. (1988) *An Empirical Investigation of the School as Community*. Chicago: University of Chicago, Dept of Education.

Burkard, C. and Rolff, H. G. (1994) 'Steuerleute auf neuem Kurs? Funktionen und Perspektiven der Schulaufsicht für die Schulentwicklung', in Rolff, H. G. *et al.* (eds) *Jahrbuch der Schulentwicklung*, Vol. 8. Weinheim: Juventa-Verlag.

Burns, T. and Stalker, G. M. (1961) *The Management of Innovation*. London: Tavistock.

Bushnell, D. S. and Rappaport, D. (eds) (1971) *Planned Change in Education: A Systems Approach*. New York: Harcourt, Brace, Jovanovich.

Cadwallader, M. L. (1968) 'The cybernectic analysis of change in complex social organizations', in *Modern Systems Research for the Behavioral Scientist: A Sourcebook for the Application of General Systems Theory to the Study of Human Behavior*, ed. W. Buckley. Chicago: Aldine, pp. 437–40.

Cameron, W. (1992) *Report on the Accountability of State Schools*. Wellington: Audit Office.

Carlgren, I. (1986) *Lokalt utvecklingsarbete*. Gothenburg: Acta Universitatis Gothoburgensis.

Carlson, R. (1965) 'Barriers to change in public schools', in *Change Processes in the Public Schools*, ed. Carlson, R. *et al.* Eugene, Oregon: Center for the Advanced Study of Educational Administration, University of Oregon.

Carlyle, T. (1910) *Lectures on Heroes, Hero-Worship, and the Heroic in History*. Oxford: Clarendon Press.

Carnegie Forum on Education and the Economy (1986) *A Nation Prepared: Teachers for the 21st Century*. Report of the Task Force on Teaching as a Profession. New York: Carnegie Forum on Education and the Economy.

Chapman, J. (1991) *The Effectiveness of Schooling and of Educational Resource Management*. Paris: OECD.

Chin, R. and Benne, K. D. (1969) 'General Strategies for Effecting Changes in Human Systems', in Bennis, W. G., Benne, K. D. and Chin, R. (eds) *The Planning of Change*. London: Holt, Rinehart & Winston.

Christensen, G. (1992) 'The changing role of the administrator in an accelerated school'. Paper presented at the annual meeting of the American Educational Research Association, San Francisco.

Christie, N. (1971) *Hvis skolen ikke fantes*. Oslo: Universitetsforlaget.

Clark, C. and Yinger, R. (1980) *The Hidden World of Teaching*. Alexandria, Virginia: AERA.

Clark, P. B. and Wilson, J. Q. (1961) 'Incentive systems: a theory of organizations', *Administrative Science Quarterly* 6, No. 2, pp. 129–66.

Cohen, M. D., March, J. G. and Olsen, J. P. (1972) 'A garbage can model of organisational choice', *Administrative Science Quarterly* 17.

Collins, R. A. and Hanson, M. K. (1991) *Summative Evaluation Report: School Based Management/Shared Decision-making Project 1987–88 Through 1989–90*. Miami: Dade County Public Schools.

Conley, S. C., Schmidle, T. and Shedd, J. B. (1988) 'Teacher participation in the management of school systems', *Teacher College Record* 90, pp. 259–80.

Conrad, D. and Hedin, D. (1981) *National Assessment of Experimental Education. Summary and Implications*. Center for Youth Development and Research, University of Minnesota.

Conway, J. (1978) 'Perspectives on evaluating a team intervention unit'. Foredrag ved American Education Research Association, Toronto.

Corbett, H. D. and Wilson, B. (1990) *Testing, Reform and Rebellion*. Norwood, New York: Ablex.

Cox, P. and deFrees, J. (1991) 'Work in progress: restructuring in ten Maine schools'. Prepared for the Maine Department of Education, US.

Crandall, D. *et al.* (1983) *People, Policies and Practices. Examining the Chain of School Improvement* (10 vols). Andover, MA: The Network.

Crockett, W. (1978) 'No system is forever', *OD Practitioner* 10, No. 1.

Crowson, R. and Porter-Gehrie, C. (1980) 'The school principalship: an organizational stability role'. Paper presented at the annual meeting of AERA.

Cyert, R. M. and March, J. G. (1963) *A Behavioural Theory of the Firm*. Englewood Cliffs, New Jersey: Prentice-Hall.

Dalin, Å. (1993) *Kompetanseutvikling i arbeidslivet. Veier til den laerende organisasjon*. Oslo: Cappelen.

Dalin, P. (1973) 'Case studies of educational innovation IV', *Strategies of Educational Innovation*. Paris: OECD.

Dalin, P. (1978) *Limits to Educational Change*. London: Macmillan.

Dalin, P. (1979) *Ny sykepleierutdanning en sammenliknende studie*. Oslo: IMTEC.

Dalin, P. (1982) *Skoleutvikling*. Oslo: Universitetsforlaget.

Dalin, P. (1986) *Skoleutvikling*. Oslo: Universitetsforlaget.

Dalin, P. *et al.* (1994) *How Schools Improve*. London: Cassell.

Dalin, P. and Rolff, H. G. (1991) *Organisasjonslæring i skolen*. Oslo: Universitetsforlaget.

Dalin, P. and Rolff, H. G. (1993) *Changing the School Culture*. London: Cassell.

Dalin, P. and Rust, V. (1983) *Can Schools Learn?* London: NFER-Nelson.

Dalin, P. and Rust, V. D. (1996) *Towards Schooling for the Twenty-first Century*. London: Cassell.

Dalin, P. and Skard, O. (1986) *Mot en ny sykepleierutdanning*. Oslo: Universitetsforlaget.

Dalin, P. and Skrindo, M. (1983) *Læring ved deltaking*. Oslo: Universitetsforlaget.

David, J. L. (1996) 'The who, what, and why of site-based management', in *Educational Leadership* 53, No. 4, December 1995/January 1996, pp. 4–9.

Davis, K. (1949) *Human Society*. New York: Macmillan.

Dean, J. (1994) 'Second survey of the organisation of LEA inspection and advisory services'. Upton Park, Slough: EMIE.

Dearing, R. (1993) 'The National Curriculum and its assessment: an interim report'. London: SCAA.

Department of Education and Science (1977) *Ten Good Schools: A Secondary School Enquiry*. London: HMSO.

Derr, C. B. and Demb, A. (1974) 'Entry and urban school systems: the context and culture of new markets', in Derr, C. B. (ed.) *Organizational Development in Urban School Systems*. New York: Sage, pp. 9–25.

Derr, C. B. (ed.) (1976) *Education and Urban Society* III, No. 2. Special issue: 'Schools and Organizational Development Applications and Prospects'. New York: Sage.

Derr, C. B. (1986) *Managing the New Careerists*. London: Jossey-Bass.

Dokka, H. J. (1967) *Fra allmueskole til folkeskole*. Oslo: Universitetsforlaget.

Dollar, B. (1981) 'Læring ved deltaking i USA', in Dalin, P. and Skrindo, M. *Læring ved deltaking*. Oslo: Universitetsforlaget.

Doyle, W. and Ponder, G. (1977–78) 'The practicality ethic in teacher decision-making', *Interchange*, Vol. 8, No. 3.

Drucker, P. (1985) *Innovation and Entrepreneurship*. New York: Harper and Row.

Durkheim, E. (1956) *Education and Sociology*. Glencoe, Illinois.: Free Press.

Ebeltoft, A. (1974) 'En gång til, Vad är organisationsutveckling?', in Rohlin, *ibid*.

Educational Leadership (1991) Vol. 49, No. 3, Alexandria, Virginia.

Educational Leadership (1993) 'The challenge of higher standard', Vol. 50, No. 5, February. Alexandria, Virginia.

Educational Researcher (1990) 'Educational indicators in the US: the need for analysis', Vol. 19, No. 5, June–July, Washington DC.

Education Review Office (undated) *Evaluation Towards Effective Education*. Wellington, USA.

Education Week (1993) 'From risk to renewal. Editorial projects in education'. Washington DC.

Ekholm, M. (1981) *Deltagarbedömningar av skolledarutbildningens utfall. En jamförelse mellan två enkätundersökningar*. (Report 1), Linköping.

Ekholm, M. (1992) *Lärarens fortbildning och skolutveckling. Översikt och funderingar*. NORD 1989:22.

Ekholm, M. (1993) 'Evaluation in Skandinavien', in Landesinstitut für Schule und Weiterbildung (ed.): *Schulentwicklung und Qualitätssicherung, Entwicklungen, Diskussionen, Ansätze und Verfahren aus Schweden*. Soest, pp. 115–20.

Ekholm, M., Fransson, A. and Lander, R. (1986) *Skolreformer och lokalt gensvar. Utvärdering av 35 grundskolor genom upprepade lägesbedömningar 1980–1985*. Gothenburg and Stockholm: Gothenburg University and Skolöverstyrelsen.

Ekholm, M., Stegø, E. and Olsson, K. (1982) *Skolledarutbildningens kursperioder. Reflektionsdokument från elva besök*. (Report 3), Linköping.

Elboim-Dror, R. (1970) 'Some characteristics of the education policy formation system', *Policy Sciences* 1, pp. 231–53.

Elgin, D. (1977) 'Limits to the management of large, complex systems', Part IV, Vol. II of *Assessment of Future National and International Problem Areas*. Menlo Park.

Elmore, R. F. (1988) *Contested Terrain: The Next Generation of Educational Reform*. Paper for Commission on Public School Administration and Leadership, Association of California School Administrators.

Elmore, R. F. (1992) 'Why restructuring alone won't improve teaching', *Educational Leadership* 49, No. 7, April, Alexandria, Virginia.

Elmore, R. F. (1996) 'Structural reform and educational practice', in *Educational Researcher*, Dec. 1995/Jan. 1996.

Emerson, A. E. (1954) 'Dynamic homeostasis; a unifying principle in organic, social and ethical evolution', *Scientific Monthly* 78, pp. 67–85.

Emergy, F. E. and Trist, E. L. (1965) 'The causal texture of organizational environments', *Human Relations* 18.

Engen, T. O. (1991) '"Den grimmer Ælling"; Sentralisert utviklingsarbeid i et desentralisert lys'. Grunnskolerådet, December, Oslo.

Etzioni, A. (1964) *Modern Organizations*. Englewood Cliffs, New Jersey: Prentice Hall.

Fantini, M. (1980) *Community Participation: Alternative Patterns and their Consequence on Educational Achievement*. Paper presented at the annual meeting of the American Educational Research Association.

Farrer, E. (1980) *Views from Below: Implementation Research in Education*. Cambridge, Massachusetts: Huron Institute.

Firestone, W., Fuhrman, S. and Kirst, M. (1989) *The Progress of Reform: An Appraisal of State Education Initiatives*. New Brunswick, New Jersey: Rutgers University, Center for Policy Research in Education.

Forbes, R. L. Jr (1977) 'Organization development: form or substance?', *OD Practitioner*, May.

Foster, J. A. (1991) 'The role of accountability in Kentucky's Education Reform Act of 1990', *Educational Leadership*, February, Alexandria, Virginia.

Franke-Wikberg, Sigbrit (1992) *Umeåmodellen – en motor för lokal utveckling*. KRUT: Stockholm.

Franklin, J. (1976) 'Characteristics of successful and unsuccessful organization development', *Journal of Applied Behavioral Science* 12, No. 4, pp. 471–92.

French, W. and Bell, C. (1973) *Organization Development*. Toronto: Prentice-Hall.

Frey, K. and Argegger, K. (1975) 'Ein Modell zur Integration von Theorie und Praxis in Curriculumprojekten: Das Generative Leistsystem', in Haft, H. and Hameyer, U. *Curriculumplanung, Theorie und Praxis*. Munich: Kosel.

Friedlander, F. (1978) 'O.D. reaches adolescence; an exploration of its underlying values', *Journal of Applied Behavioral Science* 12, No. 1, pp. 7–21.

Friedlander, F. and Brown, L. D. (1974) 'Organization development', *Annual Review of Psychology* 75, pp. 313–41.

Fuchs, J. (1992) 'Das Bildungswesen der Niederlanden', in *Schulmanagement* 23, pp. 38–42.

Fullan, M. (1982) *The Meaning of Educational Change*. Toronto: OISE-Press.

Fullan, M. (1988a) *What's Worth Fighting for in the Principalship*. Toronto: OPSTF.

Fullan, M. (1988b) 'Research into educational innovation', *Understanding School Management*, ed. Glatter, R. *et al.* Milton Keynes: Open University Press.

Fullan, M. (1990) 'Staff development, innovation and institutional development', in Joyce, B. (ed.) *Changing School Culture Through Staff Development*, pp. 3–25. Alexandria, Virginia: Association for Supervision and Curriculum Development.

Fullan, M. (1991) *Overcoming Barriers to Educational Change*. Report to US Dept. of Education, University of Toronto.

Fullan, M. (1993) *Change Forces. Probing the Depths of Educational Reform*. London: The Falmer Press.

Fullan, M. and Miles, M. (1992) 'Getting reform right: what works and what doesn't', *Phi Delta Kappan* 73, No. 10, pp. 744–52.

Fullan, M., Miles, M. and Taylor, G. (1980) 'Organisational development in schools: the state of the art', *Review of Educational Research* 50, pp. 121–83.

Fullan, M. G. with Stiegelbaum, S. (1991) *The New Meaning of Educational Change*. New York: Teachers College Press, Columbia University.

Gardner, H. (1991) *The Unschooled Mind*. New York: Basic Books.

Georgiou, P. (1973) 'The goal paradigm and notes toward a counter paradigm', *Administrative Science Quarterly* 18, pp. 291–310.

Getzels, J. (1973) 'Theory and research on leadership: Some comments and alternatives', in Cunningham, L. and Gephart, W. (eds) *Leadership. The Science and the Art Today*. Itasca, Illinois: F. E. Peacock.

Gomez, P. and Zimmermann, T. (1992) *Unternehmensorganisation. Profile, Dynamik, Methodik*. Frankfurt/New York: Campus Verlag.

Goodenough, W. H. (1978) 'Multiculturalism as the normal human experience', in Eddy, E. M. and Partridge, W. L. (eds) *Applied Anthropology in America*. New York: Columbia University Press.

Goodlad, J. (1976) *Facing the Future*. London: McGraw-Hill.

Goodlad, J. (1984) *A Place Called School: Prospects for the Future*. New York: McGraw-Hill.

Goodlad, J. (1990a) 'Why we need a complete redesign of teacher education', in *Educational Leadership* 49, No. 3, Alexandria, Virginia.

Goodlad, J. (1990b) *Teachers for Our Nation's Schools*. San Francisco: Jossey-Bass.

Gordon, L. (1993) *A Study of Board of Trustees in Canterbury Schools*. Christchurch: Education Policy Research Unit.

Gordon, L., Boyask, D. and Pearce, D. (1994) *Governing Schools – A Comparative Analysis*. University of Canterbury & Christchurch: Education Policy Research Unit.

Gorpe, L. (1974) 'En amerikaner ser på svensk organisationsutveckling', in Rohlin, J. (ed.) *Organisationsutveckling – organisationsteori för förändring*. Lund: Glurup.

Gorton, R. and McIntyre, K. (1975) *The Senior High School Principalship, Volume II: The Effective Principal*. Reston, Virginia: National Association of Secondary School Principals.

Granheim, M. K. and Lundgren, U. P. (1990) 'Målstyring og evaluering i norsk skole'. Final report of the EMIL project, Oslo: NORAS/LOS-i-utdanning.

Gray, H. (1993) 'OD revisited', *Educational Change and Development* 14, No. 1.

Gray, P. (1993) 'Teach your children well', *Time* (Special Issue) Autumn.

Greiner, L. (1972) 'Evolution and revolution as organisations grew', *Harvard Business Review* 50, No. 4, pp. 37–46.

Gross, N., Giaquinta, J. B. and Bernstein, M. (1971) *Implementing Organizational Innovations: A Sociological Analysis of Planned Educational Change*. New York: Basic Books.

Guskey, T. R. and Peterson, K. D. (1996) 'The road to classroom change', in *Educational Leadership* 53, No. 4, December 1995/January 1996, pp. 10–14.

Haarder, B. (1983) 'Det grundtvigske i skolen og uddannelsen', in Nissen, H. S. (ed.) *Efter Grundtvig. Hans betydning i dag*. Copenhagen.

Hagerstrand, T. (1952) *The Propagation of Innovation Waves*. Lund: Lund Studies in Geography.

Hall, G. E. (1979a) 'Levels of use and extent of implementation of new programs in teacher education institutions: what do you do?', Chicago: AACTE.

Hall, G. E. (1979b) *A National Agenda for Research and Development in Teacher Education 1979–84*. The University of Texas at Austin, Research and Development Center for Teacher Education.

Hall, G. E. (1988) 'The principal as leader of the change facilitating team', *Journal of Research and Development in Education* 22, No. 1, Autumn.

Hall, G. E., Hord, S. and Griffin, T. (1980) 'Implementation at the school building level: the development and analysis of nine mini-case studies'. Paper presented at American Educational Research Association annual meeting.

Hameyer, U. and Loucks-Horsley (1985) 'Designing school improvement strategies', in Velzen, W. G. van *et al.*, *op. cit.*

Handboek Kwaliteitszorg (1993) De ontwikkeling en invoering van systematische kwaliteitszorg in een VBR-Insteling: Nijmeegs Instituut voor Beroepssonderwijs, Nijmegen.

Hanushek, E. A. (1989) 'The impact of differential expenditures on school performance', *Educational Researcher* 18, No. 4.

Hargreaves, A. (1991) 'Cultures of teaching', in Goodson, I. and Ball, S. (eds) *Teachers' Lives*. New York: Routledge and Kegan Paul.

Hargreaves, A. and Dave, R. (1989) *Coaching as Inreflective Practice: Contrived Collegiality or Collaborative Culture*. AREA Annual Meeting.

Haugen, R. (1977) 'Skolesystemets læring', in *Fornyelse i skolen?*, NPT, No. 5/6.

Havelock, R. (1969) *Planning for Innovation*. Ann Arbor, Michigan: Center for Research on Utilization of Scientific Knowledge, Institute for Social Research.

Havelock, R. G. (1971) *Innovations in Education, Strategies and Tactics*. Working Paper, University of Michigan, Ann Arbor: Center for Research on Utilization of Scientific Knowledge.

Havelock, R. G. and Havelock, M. C., with Markowitz, E. A. (1973) *Educational Innovation in the United States. Vol I: The National Survey: the Substance and the Process*. Ann Arbor, Michigan: Center for Research on Utilization of Scientific Knowledge, University of Michigan.

Hedberg, B., Nyström, P. and Starbuck, W. (1976) 'Camping on seesaws. Prescriptions for a self-designing organisation', *Administrative Science Quarterly*, No. 21, pp. 41 f.

Henry, J. (1963) *Culture Against Man*. New York: Random House.

Hersey, P. W. (1982) 'The NASSP Assessment Center develops leadership talent', *Educational Leadership* 39, No. 5.

Hersey, P. and Blanchard, K. (1977) *Management of Organizational Behaviour: Utilizing Human Resources*. New Jersey: Prentice-Hall.

Herzberg, F., Mausner, B. and Synderman, B. (1959) *The Motivation to Work*. New York: John Wiley & Sons.

Herzog, J. D. (1967) *Viewing the Issues from the Perspective of an R & D Center*. American Educational Research Association Symposium on Educational Improvement and the Role of Educational Research. New York, February.

Hofstede, G. (1991) *Cultures and Organizations. Software of the Mind*. London: McGraw-Hill.

Holmes Group (1986) *Tomorrow's Teachers: A Report of the Holmes Group*. East Lansing, Michigan: Holmes Group.

Holmes Group (1990) *Tomorrow's Schools: Principle for Design of Professional Development Schools*. East Lansing, Michigan.

Hood, P. and Blackwell, L. (1979) *Indicators of Educational Knowledge Production, Dissemination and Utilization: An Exploratory Data Analysis*. San Francisco: Far West Laboratory for Education Research and Development.

Hopes, C. (1992) 'Inspectorates in the member states of the European Community: A perspective on current problems and consequences for central inspectorates', Opening address at the Chief Inspectors' Symposium, Brussels, 4–6 November.

Hopkins, D., Enskill, M. and West, M. (1994) *School Improvement in an Era of Change*. London: Cassell.

Hord, S. and Hall, G. E. (1987) 'Three images; what principals do in curriculum implementation', *Curriculum Inquiry* 17, pp. 55–89.

Horster, L. (1994) *Wie Schulen sich entwickeln können*, Lehrerfortbildung in Nordrhein-Westfalen, Hamm-Rhynern.

House, E. R. (1974) *The Politics of Educational Innovation*. Berkeley, California: McCutchan.

House, E. (1981) 'Three perspectives on innovation: technological, political and cultural', in Lehming, R. and Kane, M. (eds) *Improving Schools*. London: Sage.

Hoyle, E. (1986) 'The management of schools: theory and practice', in Hoyle E. (ed.) *World Yearbook of Education*. London: Kogan Page.

Huberman, M. (1983) 'Recipes for busy kitchens', *Knowledge; Creation, Diffusion, Utilization* 4, pp. 478–570.

Huberman, M. A. and Crandall, D. P. (1983) *Implications for Action. Vol. IV: People, Policies and Practices: Examining the Chain of School Improvement*. Andover, Massachusetts: The Network Inc.

Huberman, M. A. and Miles, M. B. (1984) *Innovation Up Close: How School Improvement Works*. New York: Plenum Press.

Hultman, G. (1981) *Organisationsutveckling genom ledarutbildning*. En utvärdering av skolledarutbildningens första utbildningsomgangar. Linköping: Linköping University.

Husén, T., Saha, L. J. and Noonan, R. (1978) 'Teacher training and student achievement in less developed countries', World Bank staff working paper 310.

Joyce, B. R., Hersh, R. H. and McKibbin, M. (1983) *The Structure of School Improvement*. New York: Longman.

Joyce, B. and Murphy, C. (1990) *Changing School Culture Through Staff Development*. Alexandria, Virginia.: Association for Supervision and Curriculum Development.

Joyce, B. R. and Showers, B. (1980) 'Improving in-service training: the messages of research', *Educational Leadership*, December, pp. 379–84.

Joyce, B. and Showers, B. (1988) *Student Achievement Through Staff Development*. New York: Longman.

Kahn, R. L. (1974) 'Organizational development: some problems and proposals', *Journal of Applied Behavioural Science* 10, No. 4, pp. 485–502.

Karlsen, G. E. (1991) *Desentralisert skoleutvikling*. University of Trondheim.

Katz, E. and Lazarsfeld, P. F. (1952) *Personal Influence*. New York: The Free Press of Glencoe.

Kiechel, W. (1984) 'Sniping at strategic planning (interview with himself)', *Planning Review*. May.

Lafond, A. *et al.* (1993) *School Inspectorates in the Member States of the European Community. France* (rev. edn). Frankfurt am Main: C. Hopes.

Lake, D. G. and Miles, M. B. (1975) *Communication Networks in the Designing and Starting of New Schools*. Symposium on Communication Networks in Education: Their Operation and Influence, at American Educational Research Association meeting.

Lange, D. (1988) *Tomorrow's Schools, The Reform of Education Administration in New Zealand*. Ministry of Education, Wellington.

References

Larsen, H. (1992) 'Selvstyrende kommunale institusjoner', in *På vei mot en ny institusjonsforståelse*. Birkedal, 3rd edn.

Larsen, S. (1990) 'Orden forklædt som tilfældighed', *Dansk pedagogisk tidsskrift*, No. 5.

Lauder, H. *et al.* (1994) *The Creation of Market Competition for Education in New Zealand*, The Smithfield Project, Phase One, First report to the Ministry of Education, March.

Lauglo, J. and McLean, M. (eds) (1985) *The Control of Education: International Perspectives on the Centralization-Decentralization Debate*. London: Heinemann Educational Books.

Lauvås, P. and Handal, G. (1993) *Handledning och praktisk yrkesteori*. Lund: Studentlitteratur.

Lawrence, P. and Lorsch, J. (1969) *Organisation and Environment*, Homewood, Illinois.

Leithwood, K. J. *et al.* (1978) *An Empirical Investigation of Teacher's Curriculum, Decision-Making Processes and Strategies Used by Curriculum Decision Manager to Influence Such Decision-Making*. Toronto: OISE.

Leithwood, K. and Montgomery, D. (1982) 'The role of the elementary school principal in program improvement', *Review of Educational Research* 52.

Levin, D. and Eubanks, E. (1989) *Sitebased Management: Engine for Reform or Pipedream? Problems, Pitfalls and Prerequisites for Success in Sitebased Management*.

Lewin, K. (1952) 'Group decision and social change', in Swanson, E. (ed.) *Reading in Social Psychology*. New York: Holt, Rinehart and Winston.

Lieberman, A. and Miller, L. (1990) 'Restructuring schools: what matters and what works', in *Phi Delta Kappan*, June, pp. 756–64.

Lieberman, A., Darling-Hammond, L. and Zuckerman, D. (1991) *Early Lessons in Restructuring Schools*. New York: National Center for Restructuring Education, Schools and Teaching. Teachers College, Columbia University.

Lievegoed, B. (1974) *Organisationen im Wandel*. Bern and Stuttgart.

Liket, Th. M. E. (1992a) *Vrijheid – rekenschap*. Amsterdam: Meulenhoff Educatief.

Liket, T. (1992b) 'Freiere Schule und kontrolliertere Universität in Holland. Die autonome Schule und die Rolle der Staatsaufsicht'. *Pädagogische Führung* 3 2, pp. 81–4.

Lindblad, S. (1993) 'Om lärares osynliga erfarenheter och professionella ansvar', in Cederström and Rasmussen (eds) *Lærerprofessionalisme*. Copenhagen: Unge Pedagoger.

Lindbom, A. (1993) 'Närdemokrati i Norden. Självförvaltning och skolförvaltningsreformer'. Arbetspromemoria för presentation vid den nordiska statsvetarkongressen, 19–21 August 1993.

Lipham, J. (1964) 'Leadership and administration', in *Behavioral Science and Educational Administration*. Chicago: The University of Chicago Press, p. 130.

Lippit, R., Watson, J. and Westley, B. (1958) *The Dynamics of Planned Change*. New York: Harcourt, Brace and Company.

Lister, I. (1976) *Deschooling Revisited*. Draft presented to the Writers and Readers Publishing Cooperative.

Little, J. W. (1990) 'The "mentor" phenomenon and the social organization of teaching', in Cazden, C. (ed.) *Review of Research in Education* 16, Washington DC: AERA.

Lortie, D. (1975) *School Teacher: A Sociological Study*. Chicago: University of Chicago Press.

Loucks, S. and Hall, G. (1979) 'Implementing innovations in schools; a concern-based approach', Washington DC: AERA.

Louis, K. S. and Miles, M. B. (1990) *Improving the Urban High School: What Works and Why*. New York: Teachers College Press.

Lundberg, C. G. (1976) 'It's 1986, what's OD like now?', *Changing Organization* 1, No. 1, November, pp. 1, 5–7.

McLaughlin, Milbrey W. (1990) *Enabling Professional Development: What Have We Learned?*, Report No. P90–114. Stanford, California: Stanford Center for Research on the Context of Secondary School Teaching.

McLaughlin, Milbrey W. (1990) 'The Rand Change Agent Study revisited: macro perspectives and micro realities', in *Educational Researcher*, December.

Madsèn, T. (1993) 'Skolutveckling och lärares kompetensutveckling i ett helhetsperspektiv', Manus til Torsten Madsèn (ed.) *Om lärares eget lärande*. Lund: Studentlitteratur.

Malik, F. (1981) 'Managementsysteme', *Die Orientierung*, No. 78, Berne: Schweizerische Volksbank.

Mann, D. (1991) 'School reform in the United States: a national policy review 1965–91', presented at the IMTEC congress in Sochi, Russia, 6–14 September 1991.

March, J. G. and Olsen, J. P. (1976) *Ambiguity and Choice in Organisations*. Oslo: Universitetsforlaget.

March, J. G. (1979) 'Analytic skills and the university training of educational administrators', *The Journal of Educational Administration*, 12, 1, pp. 17–44.

Marris, P. (1975) *Loss and Change*. New York: Anchor Press/Doubleday.

Mietz, J. (1994) 'Das vernachlässigte subjekt', *Pädagogik*, No. 5.

Milber, L. and Lieberman, A. (1982) 'School leadership. Between the cracks', *Educational Leadership* 39, No. 5.

Miles, M. B. (1959) *Learning to Work in Groups*. New York: Teachers College Press.

Miles, M. B. (1964) *Innovation in Education*. New York: Teachers College, Columbia University.

Miles, M. B. (1964) 'The T-group and the classroom', in Bradford, L. P., Benne, K. D. and Gibb, K. D. (eds) *T-group Theory and Laboratory Method: Innovation in Re-education*. New York: Wiley, pp. 452–76.

Miles, M. B. (1967) 'Some properties of schools as social systems', in Watson, G. (ed.) *Change in Schools Systems*. Washington DC: National Training Laboratories.

Miles, M. B. (1969) *The Development of Innovative Climates in Educational Organizations*. Research Note, Educational Policy Research Center, Stanford Research Institute.

Miles, M. B. (1971) 'Improving schools through organizational development; an overview', in Schmuck, R. A. and Miles, M. B. (eds) *Organization Development in Schools*, pp. 1–27. Palo Alto, California: National Press.

Miles, M. B. (1980) *Common Properties of Schools in Context: The Backdrop for Knowledge Utilization and School Improvement*. NIE.

Miles, M. B. (1987) *Practical Guidelines for School and Administration: How to Get There*. Paper presented at AERA annual meeting.

Miles, M. B. (1992) *40 Years of Change in Schools: Some Personal Reflections*. Lecture for AERA, San Francisco, April 23.

Miles, M. B., Ekholm, M. and Vandenberghe, R. (1987) *Lasting School Improvement: Exploring the Process of Institutionalization*. Leuven, Belgium and Amersfoort, The Netherlands: ACCO.

Miles, M. B. and Kaufman, T. (1985) 'Directory of effective schools programs', in R. Kyle (ed.) *Reaching for Excellence: an Effective Schools Sourcebook*. Washington.

Miles, M. B. and Louis, K. S. (1990) 'Mustering the will and skill for change', *Educational Leadership* 47, No. 8, May.

Miles, M. B., Saxl, E. R. and Lieberman, A. (1988) 'What skills do educational "change agents" need? An empirical view', *Curriculum Enquiry*, Vol. 18, No. 2, pp. 157–93.

Milestein, M. M. (1977) 'Adversarial relations and organization development: are they compatible?', Lecture for AERA, April.

Ministry of Education (1993a) 'Education in the 21st century – a discussion document'. Wellington: Learning Media.

Ministry of Education (1995) *New Zealand Schools 1994; A Report on the Compulsory School Sector in New Zealand*. Wellington; Ministry of Education.

Mintzberg, H. (1989) *Mintzberg on Management*. New York: The Free Press.

Mintzberg, H. (1991) 'The effective organisation: forces and forms', *Sloan Management Review* 54, Winter.

Miskel, C. and Ogawa, R. (1988) 'Work motivation, job satisfaction, and climate', in Boyan N. (ed.) *Handbook of Educational Administration*, pp. 279–304. New York: Longman.

Mitchell, D. *et al.* (1993) *Hear Our Voices. Final Report of Monitoring Today's Schools Research Project*. University of Waikato, New Zealand.

Morgan, G. (1988) *Organisasjonsbilder oversatt av Dag Gjestland*. Oslo: Universitetsforlaget.

Mortimore, P. *et al.* (1988) *School Matters: The Junior Years*. Somerset: Open Books.

Moxnes, P. (1993) *Dyproller: Helter, hekser, horer og andre mytologiske roller i organisasjonen*. Oslo: Forlaget Paul Moxnes.

Murphy, J. (1991) *Restructuring Schools: Capturing and Assessing the Phenomena*. New York: Teachers College Press.

Mutzek, W. (1988) *Von der Absicht zum Handeln. Rekonstruktion und Analyse subjektiver Teorien zum Transfer von Fortbildunginhalten in der Berufsalltag*. Weinheim.

Novotny, J. M. and Tye, K. A. (1973) *The Dynamics of Educational Leadership*, 2nd edn. Los Angeles: Educational Resource Associates, Inc.

Nuthall, G. (1993) *Education Reform Four Years On*. Christchurch Press, 23 November.

NZQA (1992) *Learning to Learn*, Wellington.

NZQA (1993a) *A Future with Standards*. Wellington.

NZQA (1993b) *Quality Management Systems for the National Qualifications Framework*. Wellington.

OECD (1981) *In-Service Education and Training of Teachers and Educational Change*, Paris.

OECD (1989) *Schools and Quality, An International Report*. Paris.

Ofsted (1994) *A Focus on Quality*. London: Office for Standards in Education.

Olsen, Johan P. (1990) *Demokrati på svenska*. Stockholm: Carlssons.

Olsson, R. G. (1980) *Ekonomisk uppföljning*. Rapport 1 från skolledarutbildningens ekonomiska arbetsgrupp, Linköping.

O'Neil, J. (1996) 'On tapping the power of school-based management: a conversation with Michael Strembitsky', in *Educational Leadership* 53, No. 4, December 1995/January 1996.

Onosko, J. J. (1992) 'Exploring the thinking of thoughtful teachers', *Educational Leadership* 49, No. 7, April.

Öquist, O. (1993) 'Nationales Bewertungsprogramm für die schwedische Pflichtschule (Klasse 9) Fruhjahr 1992'. I: Landesinstitut für Schule und Weiterbildung (Hrsg.): Schulentwicklung and Qualitätssicherung. Entwicklungen, Diskussionen, Ansätze und Verfahren aus Schweden. Soest, pp. 23–7.

Oregon Department of Education (1992) *Oregon 21st Century Schools. Task Force Report*. Oregon: Salem.

Ouchi, W. G. (1980) 'Markets, bureaucracies and clans', *Administrative Science Quarterly* 25, pp. 129–41.

Parliament Bill 37 (1990–1), Oslo.

Patterson, J., Purkey, S. and Parker, J. (1986) *Productive School Systems for a Non-rational World*. Alexandria, Virginia: ASCD.

Paulston, R. G. (1976) *Conflicting Theories of Social and Educational Change: A Typological Review*. University Center for International Studies, University of Pittsburgh.

Persons, S. (ed.) (1950) *Evolutionary Thought in America*. New Haven: Yale University Press.

Peters, T. and Waterman, R. (1982) *In Search of Excellence*. New York: Harper & Row.

Peterson, K. (1988) 'The principal's task', *Administrator's Notebook* 26, No. 8.

Pettigrew, A. M. (1982) 'School leader education in Sweden: a review with some questions'. Seminar report, Helsingør, Sweden.

Pfeffer, J. and Salanick, G. (1978) *The External Control of Organizations: A Resource Dependence Perspective*. New York: Harper & Row.

Picot, B. (1988) *Administering for Excellence: Effective Administration in Education*. Report of the Taskforce to Review Education Administration, Wellington.

Pink, W. T. (1989) *Effective Staff Development for Urban School Improvement*. Paper presented at AERA annual meeting.

Porras, J. and Berg, P. (1978) 'Evaluation methodology in organization development: An analysis and critique', *Journal of Applied Behavioural Science*, Vol. 14, No. 2.

Rae, K. (1994) *New Zealand Self-Managing Schools and Five Impacts in 1993 from the Ongoing Restructuring of Educational Administration*. NZAEA, 16–19 January 1994, Auckland.

Reichard, C. von (1992) 'Kommunales Management im Internationalen Vergleich', in *Städtetag*, 12/1.

Review of Educational Research (1993) AERA, autumn, Vol. 65, No. 3. Washington DC.

Reynolds, D. and Cuttance, P. (1992) *School Effectiveness: Research, Policy and Practice*. London: Heinemann.

Rice, A. K. (1963) *The Enterprise and Its Environment*. London: Tavistock.

Rogers, E. (1962) *The Diffusion of Innovation*. New York: The Free Press.

Rolff, H. G. (1993) *Wandel durch Selbstorganisation. Theoretische Grundlage und praktische Hinweise für eine bessere Schule*. Munich: Weinheim.

Rolff, H. G. (1994a) *Bremen: A Twofold Project in Organisational Development*. Oslo: IMTEC.

Rolff, H. G. (1994b) 'Gestaltungsautonomie verwirklichen. Lehrerinnen und Lehrer als Träger der Entwicklung', *Pädagogik*, No. 4.

Rosenholtz, S. (1989) *Teachers' Workplace: The Social Organization of Schools*. New York: Longham.

Rothchild-Whitt, J. (1979) 'The collectivist organization: an alternative to rational-bureaucratic models', *American Sociological Review* 44, pp. 509–27.

Rowan, B. (1990) *Organizational Design of Schools*. Michigan State University.

Runkel, P. J. *et al.* (1978) 'Transforming the school's capacity for problem-solving', *Eugene*. Oregon: Center for Educational Policy and Management (CEPM), University of Oregon.

Runkel, P. J. and Bell, W. (1976) 'Some conditions affecting a school's readiness to profit from O.D. training', *Education and Urban Society* 8, No. 2, February.

Runkel, P. J. and Schmuck, R. A. (1976) 'Organization development in schools: a review of research findings from Oregon', *Eugene*. Oregon: CEPM, University of Oregon.

Rutter, M. *et al.* (1979) *Fifteen Thousand Hours, Secondary Schools and their Effect on Children*. Somerset: Open Books.

Sandstrøm, B. and Ekholm, M. (1984) *Stabilitet och förändring i skolan*. Utbildningsforskning, FoU-rapport 50, Skolöverstyrelsen og Liber Forlag, Stockholm.

Sandstrøm, B. and Ekholm, M. (1986) *Innovationer i grunnskolan – metoder og resultater*, *Skolöverstyrelsen*, Stockholm.

Sarason, S. (1971) *The Culture of the School and the Problem of Change*. Boston: Allyn & Bacon.

Sarason, S. (1982) *The Culture of the School and the Problem of Change* (revised edition). Boston: Allyn & Bacon.

Sarason, S. (1990) *The Predictable Failure of Educational Reform*. San Francisco: Jossey-Bass.

Sarason, S. (1998) *Political Leadership and Educational Failure*. San Francisco: Jossey-Bass.

Sarason, S. B., Davidson, K. S. and Blatt, B. (1986) *The Preparation of Teachers: An Unstudied Problem in Education*. Cambridge, Massachusetts: Brookline Books.

Sashkin, M. and Egermeier, J. (1993) *School Change Methods and Processes. A Review and Synthesis of Research and Practice*. Washington DC: Office of Educational Research and Improvement, US Department of Education, June.

Schmuck, R. A. (1982) 'Education of school leaders in Sweden: assessment and recommendation'. Seminar report from Helsingør, Sweden, April.

Schwarz, P. (1986) 'Management in non-profit organisations', *Die Orientierung* 88, Schweizerische Volksbank, Berg.

Senge, P. M. (1990) *The Fifth Discipline, the Art and Practice of the Learning Organization*. New York: Doubleday Currency.

Shanker, A. (1990) 'Staff development and the restructured school', in Joyce, B. (ed.) *Changing School Culture Through Staff Development*, pp. 91–103. Alexandria, Virginia.: Association for Supervision and Curriculum Development.

Sheppard, D. (1960) 'Neighbourhood norms and the adoption of farm practices', *Rural Sociology* 25, pp. 336–58.

Showers, B. (1983) *Coaching: A Training Component for Facilitating Transfer and Training*. Paper presented at the annual meeting of the AERA, Montreal.

Silberman, C. E. (1971) *Crisis in the Classroom*. New York: Vintage Books.

Slavin, R. E. (1990) 'Achievement effect of ability grouping in secondary schools: a best-evidence synthesis', *Review of Educational Research* 60, pp. 471–99.

Smith, L. M. and Keith, P. M. (1971) *The Anatomy of Educational Innovations: An Organizational Analysis of an Elementary School*. New York: John Wiley.

Snyder, K. J. (1988) *Managing Productive Schools*. San Diego, California: Harcourt Brace Jovanovich.

Snyder, K. J., Acker-Hocevar, M. and Snyder, K. M. (1994) *Organisational Development in Transition: The Schooling Perspective*. Paper for AERA, New Orleans, 4–8 April.

Snyder, K. J. and Anderson, R. H. (1986) *Managing Productive Schools: Toward an Ecology*. San Diego, California: Harcourt Brace Jovanovich.

Squires, A. and Kranyik, R. D. (1996) 'The Comer Program: changing school culture', *Educational Leadership* 53, No. 4, December 1995/January 1996.

Stallings, J. A. (1989) 'School achievement effects and staff development: what are some critical factors?' Paper presented at AERA annual meeting.

Stogdill, R. M. (1974) *Handbook of Leadership*. New York: Free Press.

Tangerud, H. and Wallin, E. (1983) *Values and Contextual Factors in School Improvement*. Paris: CERI, OECD.

Tannenbaum, R. and Schmidt, W. H. (1957) 'How to choose a leadership pattern', *Harvard Business Review*, March/April, pp. 5–101.

Taylor, D. and Teddlie, C. (1992) 'Restructuring and the classroom: a view from a reform district'. Paper presented at AERA annual meeting, San Francisco.

Thomas, L. G. (1968) *Types of Schooling for Developing Nations*. International and Developmental Education Program, School of Education, University of Pittsburgh.

Toch, T. (1998) 'The new education bazaar', *US News and World Report*, April 27, Washington DC.

US Department of Education (1988) 'High school and beyond administrator teacher survey (1984)', *Datafile Users' Manual*. Washington DC: US Department of Education.

Velzen, W. G. van *et al.* (1985) *Making School Improvement Work – A Conceptual Guide to Practice*. Leuven, Belgium: ACCO.

Vormeland, O. (1982) 'Examination of the Swedish school leader education studies. Data and observations at the local level'. Seminar report from Helsingør, Sweden, April.

Wallace, M. (1991) 'Contradictory interests in policy implementation: the case of LEA development plans for schools', *Journal of Educational Policy* 6, No. 4, pp. 385–400.

Wang, M. C., Haertel, G. D. and Walberg, H. J. (1993a) 'Toward a knowledge base for school learning', *Review of Educational Research* 63, pp. 249–94.

Weber, M. (1964) *The Theory of Social and Economic Organization*, ed. Talcott Parsons, oversatt av A. M. Henderson and Talcott Parsons. New York: The Free Press, p. 339.

Weeren, J. van, Dam, P. van and Wijnstra, M. (1992) 'Zentrale Tests und Prüfungen in der Niederlanden', in Ingenkamp, K. and Jäger, R. *Test und Trends. 9. Jahrbuch der Pädagogischen Diagnostik*. Weinheim/Basle, pp. 151–75.

Wehlage, G., Smith, G. and Lipman, P. (1992) 'Restructuring urban high schools: the New Futures experience', *American Educational Research Journal* 29, No. 1, pp. 51–93.

Weick, K. E. (1976) 'Educational organizations as loosely coupled systems', *Administrative Science Quarterly* 21, pp. 1–19.

Weick, K. E. (1980) *Loosely Coupled Systems Relaxed Meanings and Thick Interpretations*. Upublished manuscript, Cornell University.

Weiler, H. N. (1990) 'Desentralisering og styring av utdanning – En øvelse i motsigelser?', in Granheim, M., Lindgren, U.P. and Tiller, T. (eds) *Utdanningskvalitet – styrbar eller ustyrlig?* Oslo: Tano, pp. 47–72.

Weindling, R. and Early, P. (1987) *Secondary Headship. The First Year*. Windsor: NFER-Nelson.

Weisbord, M. (1978) 'The wizard of OD', *OD Practitioner* 10, No. 2, pp. 1–7.

Weiss, A. R. (1997) *Going It Alone*. Boston Institute for Responsive Education, Northeastern University.

Wennås, O. (1989) *Vem skall styra vad i skolan – och hur?* Stockholm: Utbildningsförlaget.

Wilkening, E. A. and Johnsen, D. (1952) 'Goals in farm decision-making as related to practice adoption', *Wisconsin Agricultural Experiment Station Research Bulletin* 225, Madison.

Willms, D. and Echols, F. (1993) 'Alert and inert clients: the Scottish experience of parental choice in schools', *Economics of Education Review* 11, pp. 339–50.

Wilson, H. C. (1973) 'On the evolution of education', in *Learning and Culture, Proceedings of the 1972 Annual Spring Meeting of the American Ethnological Society*, ed. Kimball, S. T. and Burnett, J. H. Seattle: University of Washington Press, pp. 211–44.

Wylie, C. (1994) *Self-managing Schools in New Zealand: The Fifth Year*. Wellington: NZCER.

Wylie, C. (1996) 'Finessing site-based management with balancing acts', in *Educational Leadership* 53, No. 4, December 1995/January 1996.

Yarger, S. J., Howey, K. R. and Joyce, B. R. (1980) *In-service Teacher Education*. Palo Alto, California: Booksend Laboratory.

Name Index

Aalvik, T. 239
Alderer, Clayton P. 193
Alexandersson, M. 143
Algotsson, K. G. 11
Aliniski, S. 40, 42
Allport, F. H. 34
Alspagh, D. 170
Anderson, Robert H. 160, 162, 200
Aoki, T. T. 88
Arends, J. H. 174, 175
Arfwedson, G. 181
Argegger, K. 133
Argyris, C. 37, 55, 83

Bacharach, S. B. 15
Baker, K. 87–8
Baldridge, J. V. 40
Barnard, Chester 40, 41
Barrows 88
Bartalanffy, L. von 101
Bassin, M. 185, 191, 192
Bauer, S. 15
Beeby, C. E. 100–1
Bell, C. 185
Bell, W. 190
Benne, K. D. 98–9, 102, 105, 106, 134–5
Bennis, W. 120
Berg, Gunnar 40, 187, 198–9
Berg, P. 193
Berman, P. 88, 89, 109, 246
Bik, H. 224
Bird, T. 170
Blackwell, L. 144
Blake, R. R. 83
Blanchard, K. 83, 89
Block, P. 91–2
Blumer 43

Bolams, R. 152
Bolman, L. G. 32, 40–1, 43–4, 96, 180
Boston, J. 218
Bowers, D. 196
Brandt, Ron 200, 204
Bridges, S. J. 18
Broady, Donald 103
Brown, L. D. 187
Brunholz, D. 159
Bryk, A. S. 15, 147
Buchen, Herbert 158
Burkard, C. 235
Burns, T. 36–7, 64
Bushnell, D. S. 101–2

Cadwallader, M. L. 101
Cameron, W. 17
Carlgren, Ingrid 11–12
Carlson, R. 35
Carlyle, Thomas 83
Chapman, J. 90
Chin, R. 98–9, 102, 105, 106, 134–5
Christensen, G. 202, 204
Christie, Nils 104
Clark, C. 144
Clark, P. B. 41
Cohen, M. D. 44
Collins, R. A. 15
Conley, S. C. 15
Conrad, D. 174
Conway, J. 192
Corbett, H. D. 241
Corwin 43
Cox, P. 201
Crandall, D. P. 115, 118
Crockett, W. 187
Crowson, R. 88

House, Ernest R. 11, 96, 98, 105–12, 124, 140
Howey, K. R. 169
Hoyle, Eric 167
Huberman, M. A. 90, 115, 118, 150–1, 246–7
Hultman, G. 164
Husén, Torsten 151

Illich, Ivan 104
Isselburg, Klaus 179

Jennings, Eugene E. 83
Johnsen, D. 139
Joyce, B. R. 120, 151, 168–9, 170–1, 173

Kahn, R. L. 187
Karlsen, G. E. 13, 22
Katz, E. 139
Kaufman, T. 114
Keith, P. M. 108, 114
Kiechel, W. 50
Kranyik, Robert 17

Lafond, A. 235
Lake, D. G. 114
Lange, D. 18
Larsen, Henrik 8–9, 24
Larsen, S. 239
Lauder, High 23
Laugh, J. 22
Lauvås, P. 143
Lawrence, P. 59
Lazarsfeld, P. F. 139
Leithwood, K. J. 90, 91, 144
Levin, D. 16
Levin, Hank 184, 200, 202–3, 204
Lewin, Kurt 99, 138, 139
Lieberman, A. 16, 81, 113, 116, 117
Lievegoed, B. 62
Liket, T. 225
Lindblad, Sverker 143
Lindbom, A. 7, 9, 10
Lipham, J. 81
Lippit, R. 139
Lister, Ian 104
Little, J. W. 120, 146, 170
Lorsch, J. 59
Lortie, Dan 88, 108, 118, 141, 144, 146
Loucks, S. 148
Loucks-Horsley, S. 133, 146
Louis, K. S. 90, 115, 120, 183
Lundberg, C. G. 187

Lundgren, V. P. 231, 237–8
Lundman, L. 181

McIntyre, K. 88
McKibbin, M. 170–1
McLaughlin, M. W. 88, 89, 109, 246
Mclean, M. 22
Madsèn, T. 12, 173
Malik, F. 217, 237
Mann, Dale 246
March, J. G. 40, 41, 43, 44, 167
Marris, P. 118
Marx, Karl 40
Mayo, Elton 37–8
Mietz, J. 209
Milber, L. 81
Miles, Matthew B. 66, 90, 96, 113–17, 120, 144, 150–1, 183, 184, 185, 186, 189, 194, 196, 197, 201, 246–7, 250
Milestein, M. M. 192
Miller, L. 16
Mintzberg, Henry 32, 46–51, 53, 62, 63, 69, 76, 83, 87, 128
Miskel, C. 15
Mitchell, D. 18
Montessori, Maria 137
Montgomery, D. 90, 91
Morgan, Gareth 29
Mortimore, P. 120, 181
Mouton, J. S. 83
Moxnes, Paul 30–1, 43
Murphy, C. 169, 173
Murphy, J. 117
Mutzek, N. 159

Nanus, B. 120
Novotny, J. M. 80–1
Nuthall, G. 19

Ogawa, R. 15
Öhlund, U. 143
Olsen, Johan P. 9–10, 43, 44
Olsson, K. 163, 164
O'Neil, J. 15
Onosko, J. J. 182
Öquist, O. 228
Ouchi, W. G. 39–40

Patterson, J. 91
Paulston, Rolland G. 98, 99–100, 103–4, 105
Persons, S. 100, 101

Subject Index